YOUR NOVEL: Day by Day

A *fiction writer's companion*

Mary Anna Evans

Joyeuse Press

Other works by Mary Anna Evans:

Novels, all available as ebooks and in print:

Wounded Earth, an environmental thriller

The Faye Longchamp archaeological mysteries:

Artifacts
Relics
Effigies
Findings
Floodgates
Strangers
Plunder

Collections:

Jewel Box, a book-length collection of short stories and essays, available in e-book and print editions

Offerings, an e-book mini-collection of short stories

Individual short stories, all available as e-books:

"Low-Budget Monster Flick"
"Twin Set"
"Land of the Flowers"
"A Singularly Unsuitable Word"
"Starch"
"Mouse House"

Educational non-fiction

Mathematical Literacy in the Middle and High School Grades: A Modern Approach to Sparking Student Interest

For all those who share my love
of the art of storytelling...

Acknowledgments

I'd like to thank Rachel Broughten, Amanda Evans, and Michael Garmon for reading this volume in manuscript. There are fewer errors than there might have been without their help. Those that remain are all mine.

CHAPTER 1—FIRST STEPS: THE ONLY WAY TO START IS TO START

DAY 1—Every single day

Perhaps you were expecting a preface or a foreword or some sort of introductory text, but no. We're diving straight into our task of writing a book...your book.

I'm skipping the part where I clear my throat and talk to you about the process of writing a book. I'm skipping the part where I tell you how I will go about helping you through that process. You picked up this book because you were ready to get started. So let's do that.

Very early in my career, when I had a drawer full of unsold short stories and a single unpublished novel manuscript, I had the pleasure and good fortune to meet two people who knew the publishing industry inside and out—Joe and Gay Haldeman. Joe has had a long and illustrious writing career that has been adorned with every award that science fiction has to offer, starting with the Hugo and Nebula and going on from there. His wife Gay has been at his side the whole time, managing his career and being an integral part of his creative process.

I had no intention of telling Joe and Gay that I was a writer, despite the fact that I had spent more than a decade writing stories and watching them fly back into my mailbox, rejected. What could they possibly say to my bold and presumptuous claim of authorhood other than, "That's nice, dear..."?

The mutual friend who introduced us had no such compunctions. He announced that I had written a book and that he had read it and that it was just wonderful. Mortified, I watched as he produced the manuscript, which I guess he had hidden under his chair while we ate dinner. I snatched the manuscript out of his hand and hid it behind my back.

I was sitting beside Gay and she leaned over to speak to me, so I braced myself for the words, "That's nice, dear..."

Instead, she said, "Do you write every day?"

I'd never been asked this question, and it surprised me, but I did know the answer.

"I do. I have three children, and when they're sick or they need me somehow, I don't always get to my writing. But barring that kind of obstacle? Yes. I do write every day."

That was the extent of our discussion of this issue, but it has stuck with me for more than a decade. It was the genesis of this book.

Writing a book is a monumental task. Many, many people would like to write a book, but not so many people can scrape together the guts to begin. Far fewer people can scrape together the fortitude to finish. Yet a writer who writes a page a day generates a book in a year.

Do you write every day?

DAY 2—The first step in a marathon

It has been nearly nine years since I sold my first novel. In that time, I have written and published this book, six novels, a short story collection, and a number of short stories, essays, and articles, and I have co-authored an educational text on mathematical literacy.

Wow. Just looking at that last sentence makes me tired. But if someone told a one-year-old, just learning to walk, how many steps she would take in her lifetime, she'd probably never have the nerve to stand up and go.

Let me repeat something I told you yesterday. If you write a page a day, you'll have a book in a year. If you're the kind of person who can just sit down and do that, then you have my permission to put this book down and start typing. If you can write three pages a day, or seven, or ten, so much the better.

For heaven's sake, though, don't throw the book away. I worked too hard on it, and I think it will help you reach your goals. I believe it will still be useful to you as a resource, because it is not intended as a purely motivational text. I'm going to share with you the things that I wish someone had told me a decade ago. I'm going to talk to you about giving your characters depth and reality. I'll be discussing the difficulties of editing your own work. I'll be helping you shape your plot. And, for those of you who *aren't* sure you can generate a towering pile of pages, I'm going to talk you through the process.

Is this process going to be as simple as writing a page a day until the book is finished? No. I know people who work that way, but I'm not one of them. I need to prepare before I work, and I believe in editing thoroughly afterward, so that's how I'm going to shape this book.

You'll work at your own pace. I've structured the text as a year-long day book, simply because that is the pace at which *I* work best. Still, I know that there are marathon runners, like me, and there are also sprinters, so I've made sure the book is useful for people who prefer either writing style.

If you're a sprinter, you can read all the introductory material in the first three chapters in one sitting, then launch into your book. If you can maintain a pace of three pages a day, instead of the single page being generated by the marathon-style writers, then you'll have a draft of your book in ninety days. (And if you write nine pages a day, you can do it in a month, but I know you can do that math.) At whatever pace you write, you'll find guidance here for editing your work and for preparing it for publication.

I do encourage you to take the time to do the pre-writing exercises I will give you in the early chapters, even though I hear you saying that you want to *write*. Now.

Of course you do, and you *will* be writing—you'll be writing character sketches and developing a detailed outline and taking notes on your story's setting. Much of this text will probably find its way into your book, so writing it will in no way be a waste of your limited writing time. But if you don't know what kind of world you creating and if you don't know who is going to live in it, then how can you even begin?

With this question in mind, it's time for you to begin imagining your fictional world and how it will be shaped, which means that you need to know what kind of book you're writing. Fictional genres can be frustrating for writers who feel that calling a book a mystery or a romance is an unfair pigeonholing of a work of art. And it is. There is no reason that your finished book must fit into an existing pigeonhole. Still, readers want to know something about your book when they are considering whether to read it or not. Genres—and I consider "literary fiction" to be a type of genre—give readers a bit of information with which to start.

So...are you writing a romance? A space opera? A literary novel? Realize that a story of two lovers who are working for a radical resistance group during the War for Martian Independence could be any of these things. Your story is yours. You just need to know your goals.

What kind of book are you writing?

DAY 3—Deciding what kind of book you want to write

Your current assignment is to ruminate on a broad-brush description of the kind of book you'd like to write, thinking about its genre or lack thereof. I reject the notion that a writer must choose one genre and stay there. I have written science fiction, literary fiction, fantasy, essays, thrillers, and non-fiction. And I'm not dead yet. I fully intend to write in whatever style suits my fancy for the rest of my life.

Mystery, however, is the genre in which I can most reliably sell. It is the genre in which I have won awards and gotten good reviews and earned a reputation. The following essay was written in answer to the question, "Why do you do what you do?" Or rather, "Why do you write what you write?"

While you are musing over your own novel, consider a point I make in this essay, centered on the notion that mystery fiction could be considered the literature of justice. I've heard science fiction described as the literature of ideas. Romance is perhaps best described as the literature of romantic love. The best literary fiction examines all those things and more because, in the end, our stories and, indeed, all our art, are the tools humans use to take a clear look at our existence...to explain the unexplainable.

As you read my thoughts on why I write what I write, consider your own aims. Fiction shines a light on the important parts of human existence, but a single book cannot illuminate every corner. Do you intend to explore life's big issues in your book, or do you only aim to entertain? (Let me stress here that entertainment in itself is a worthy goal, in my mind.)

Make a list of your goals in writing this story and think of how you can build a book that will reach them.

Meditations of a Mystery Writer

Any mystery author gets the occasional question from somebody who wants to know why we write about killing people. A slightly more discerning question comes when someone wants to know if it's possible to write a mystery that doesn't involve murder. The two questions are related, I think.

To me, murder works as a starting place for a story because it is inherently dramatic. It demands that the reader care. If I wrote a mystery about a jewel theft, I would need to presume that you cared whether the victim ever got her jewels back. How can a human being not care when another human being is deprived of life?

This doesn't mean that there's only one story to be told about a murder. The murder of a desperately evil person who has spent a lifetime torturing puppies and stealing from children wouldn't be the same story as the murder of an old lady who has devoted the last fifteen years of her life to raising a child who isn't even related to her. (This second scenario is the plot of my work-in-progress, *Plunder*, in fact.) Still, though you may be glad that the evil person has died, you do care.

I think of crime fiction as the literature of justice. A crime, usually murder, sets the world askew, and the writer has about 300 pages to examine what that means. Sometimes, as a writer, I find that I'm far more interested in the repercussions for the people left behind than I am in the irredeemable piece of humanity who did the killing. Then I ask myself if anyone is ever truly irredeemable, and that question drives another plot twist or three. Sometimes being a mystery writer is philosophically interesting.

And it also gives me a chance to dream up interesting ways to kill people. (Metaphorically.) I have thrown them off cell towers, beaten them, shot them, knifed them, and I'm waiting for a chance to kill someone with candy, because I know how.

Now you're afraid to eat in my presence, aren't you? And maybe you should be...

DAY 4—My own response to this assignment

On this, your last day of meditating on the kind of book you want to write, I'd like to share with you the story of how I came to the genre of mystery. As I've said, I have written in many styles. I am an absolutely omnivorous reader. (I compulsively read the shampoo label in the shower, which was a great help to me when I took organic chemistry and I already knew the commercial uses of sodium lauryl sulfate.) Thus, I obviously read in all genres. So why did I choose to write mysteries?

The simple answer is that the story that came to me was a mystery.

I had written a thriller that got me an agent but didn't sell. This meant that I had the advice of an industry professional, my agent, as I decided what I would write next...or even whether to keep writing, after so much rejection. She urged me to write another book because we had gotten so close with the first one. As a writer with no contract and with no track record driving her to write another book like her last one, I could do any book I wanted. What did I want?

As I drove down an interstate highway, the image of a dilapidated southern plantation house came into my head—no story, just the picture of a crumbling house in the woods. I usually develop my plots by asking myself questions, which is something we'll talk about later in the chapter on plot. The question that this house brought into my mind was, "Who would live there?"

I was pretty sure it wouldn't be a debutante who had inherited the family mansion and a bunch of money. I was also pretty sure it wouldn't be a Scarlett O'Hara clone, because *Gone with the Wind* has already been done. I thought it would probably be someone who inherited the house and nothing more, which meant that she wouldn't have the money to keep it from crumbling to the ground.

This was great, because it answered my second question for me: "What is my character's problem?" The answer was simple. This person had inherited a money pit in the form of a historic home, but it was a treasured family relic and she had a deep personal need to save it.

I love the beauty and romance of plantation architecture, but it comes with moral ambiguity. This beautiful house in my head was built by slaves. A book set there could not (or, in my opinion, should not) be written for 21st century audiences without acknowledging that fact. It occurred to me that it would be exceedingly interesting if my main character descended from the slaves who built this money pit of a house. Soon enough, it occurred to me that it would be even more interesting if she also descended from the masters who lived there. Out of this collision of cultures, my series character Faye Longchamp was born, and she carries within her enough conflict and ambiguity to support seven books, so far, with more to come.

But look closely at that last paragraph. Notice that I still had not chosen a genre. I could have been plotting a romance or a historical novel. If I added some time travelers and a ray gun or two, the story could morph into science fiction. This story could be chick lit or literary or...well...anything. I needed to do some more thinking.

I asked myself what Faye would do to get the money to save her home. I realized that the only thing of value that she owned, other than the house, would be the artifacts her ancestors left behind, buried on the island where the house stands. I decided that Faye would feel perfectly ethically okay about digging up those artifacts, for which *Artifacts* was named, and selling them on the black market, because they emphatically belong to her. Then I pictured her digging for those scraps of history, day in and day out.

When I realized that the island where she was digging had been inhabited for the ten thousand years since it rose out of the water, I knew that she would, sooner or later, dig up a dead body. But even that corpse didn't make my story a mystery. She could have stumbled onto the plantation cemetery. Or maybe she has uncovered the body of a Creek warrior, killed in battle. Or maybe she has found a dead conquistador.

I pictured the moment she discovered the dead girl's skull, and in that image I saw an earring nestled nearby. Its design said that it wasn't ancient. It had probably been made when Jackie Kennedy was the nation's style icon. And that forty-year-old earring told me that Faye had found someone who had been brought to this island and buried at a time when she should have been placed in a cemetery grave. This was a body that wasn't old enough to be an archaeological find. This was a murder victim.

And it was only then that I knew I was writing a mystery.

I hope that you've been spending the past few days digging deep into the story that you're developing, making sure that you know the kind of tale that you want to write. It's the only way I know to tell a story well.

CHAPTER 2—WHO WILL LIVE IN YOUR WORLD?

DAY 5—Considering character

Okay, I've given you three days to decide what kind of book you want to write. I think that's long enough. You probably already knew the answer on Day 1, but I wanted to give you time to be sure.

What are we going to tackle next?

The big questions for a novelist preparing to start a new book are these:

Who is the story about?

What is that person's problem and how does he or she solve it?

What kind of world does that person live in?

In other words, the big questions for a novelist involve character, plot, and setting. We will begin with characterization, because nobody likes to read a book about people who feel like paper dolls. Your assignment over the next nine days, while I talk to you about characterization, is to write at least three character sketches. If your book requires more than three fully-developed characters, and most do, then write more, but the bare minimum is three: the story's primary character, his or her closest ally, and his or her antagonist.

I will not be giving you a worksheet to fill out with your characters' eye colors and food preferences. You are writing a book, not doing busywork handed out by a schoolteacher. Simply type your character's name at the top of the page, then tell yourself about him. You need not worry about format. No one will see this but you. Tell yourself who that person is inside. What drives him? What kind of experiences shaped those drives? It's okay to tell yourself what he looks like, because there is nothing more annoying than reading a book and feeling like you're blind, because the writer neglected to visually describe certain people and places. Tell yourself how that character needs to change, then decide whether he will accomplish it between the covers of the book you're planning to write.

While you're doing that, I'm going to give you a new essay on character development to read every day. My hope is that sharing my own views on the process will help you in developing a writing process of your very own.

DAY 6—Characterization: My imaginary friends

Until your characters are as real to you as your mother or your brother or your third child, it is pointless to begin writing their stories. Spend some time with your characters and with your imagination.

People...okay, women...ask me all the time whether the gorgeous and hunky Joe Wolf Mantooth is based on a real man. I don't like to dash their hopes, but the truth is that he is a total figment of my imagination.

I know writers who take a personality trait from one person and the facial features of another and the profession of a third, and they put them into some kind of mental blender. Out pops a fictional character, ready for adventure. It works for them, but if I tried it, I think I'd get something like the mythological sphinx—the head of a woman, the body of a lioness, the wings of an eagle, and a serpent-headed tail—and I think that sphinx-y character would stick out of the narrative like a sore thumb.

My characters grow out of the setting or out of their situation. As always when developing a story, I ask myself questions.

Who would live in this ramshackle old plantation house?

What would her problem be?

If she had a male best friend, where would he come from? What are his passions? Why aren't they lovers?

Or, if I'm developing a murderer, I might imagine someone who, in this particular place and this particular time, would kill out of a sense of shame.

I once had an interesting encounter while waiting to do a television interview. It was one of those shows where the other guests are usually about as famous as me—Little League coaches, Humane Society volunteers, and the like. We were all sitting in the green room watching the show, and the host said, "And today, we have Corbin Bernsen of *LA Law* fame here with us." I turned around and there he was, dressed in a rumpled white linen suit and politely begging his handlers to take him to his hotel after the interview so he could get a shower.

When the Humane Society lady and her two dogs got up out of the chair next to me, he dropped into it, looking exhausted, and asked me about my book. There followed a brief but entertaining conversation where I learned whose books he likes to read—Michael Connelly, among others. Just as he was being called back for his interview (and before I got a chance to tell him there was a helluva part for him in *Artifacts*), the conversation had turned to our respective arts. I was telling him that there is a bit of acting in what I do. I have to know who my character is and where he has been before I can know how he will react in a given situation.

In other words, there is an element of empathy in what both writers and actors do. I'm sure Corbin Bernsen has never been a cocky, hotshot lawyer, but he had to imagine he'd lived that life in order to play Arnold Becker in *LA Law*. I was never a woman of color growing up in the South in the 1970s, but I was there and I can imagine what it was like for Faye. The big difference is that Corbin had somebody to write Becker's dialogue for him, and I have to put words in Faye's mouth.

I have been writing Faye since 2001. Her stories total more than a half-million words, and I hope I get to write a half-million more. Or maybe a million. She's a deep, rich character, and I'm lucky to have her in my world. My life is so full these days that I can't see next week, but I wouldn't mind if I were still writing Faye when I'm 70 and she's 63. She can be my multiracial American non-virginal Miss Marple.

I'll write other stuff. I already do. But I love looking at American culture through the eyes of somebody who'll always be one step outside it. (And I love Joe, but you knew that.)

When I start a new book and I spend that period of weeks or months doing research and brooding over the plot, I know that it's time to start writing when I hear Joe and Faye talking to each other. (And yes, I do know that they're not real. I'm not schizophrenic. I'm a novelist...although I guess that may not speak too loudly of my stability.)

When you write your own characters, do whatever it takes to get to know them beneath the surface, or they will never be more than a laundry list of character traits. And if you know Corbin Bernsen, would you please let him know that I've got a helluva part for him?

DAY 7—Characterization: Learn from the masters

Recently, after several months of arm-twisting, I convinced my younger daughter to watch *Gone with the Wind* with me. She is generally very tolerant of Mommy's ancient movies and overwrought 1970s progressive rock, but she was balking on this one. Finally, I said, "Remember that I was right about *When Harry Met Sally?* Do Kansas and Aerosmith not rock? Sit down and look at the TV. We're watching the movie."

At some point during the second half, she posted a Facebook status that said merely, "Rhett Butler!" Styles and tastes change, but the virile appeal of Clark Gable and Rhett Butler will never fade.

As we watched, she periodically bleated, "She's so *awful!*" as Scarlett plunged through a dying civilization, trailing her swaying hoopskirts and the disapproval of every unreconstructed rebel in Atlanta. Scarlett did do some absolutely awful things, but she shouldered the responsibility of caring for her destitute friends and relatives and former slaves who didn't have her brass and determination. And she found room in that flinty heart to completely love her father and her mother and her daughter and Ashley and her Mammy and, though it took her way too long to figure it out, to love Melanie and Rhett, too. This, my cherished readers, is what one calls a memorable character. And so is her husband Rhett, the rogue who is burdened with just a little too much romanticism to be a convincing scalawag.

I've seen the movie and read the book many times, though not lately, so this was the first time I'd paid attention to the story from the perspective of a novelist. The first half of the movie is the epic war tragedy that we all remember, but not so the second half...the two hours that pass after Scarlett vows that she'll never be hungry again. I invite you to watch it through the eyes of a novelist, paying close attention to the second half. The world is changing to something unrecognizable outside the walls of Scarlett's and Rhett's mansion, but it is their domestic tragedy that rivets our attention. The second half of *Gone with the Wind* is an unflinching portrayal of the disintegration of a marriage between two people who love each other.

Watch Scarlett's face when she welcomes Rhett home from a long trip, only to be rebuffed by a man who thinks she doesn't want to see him. Watch her strike back at him with hateful words, instead of running into his arms. And listen to Mammy tell Melanie about the brutal and wounding things they say to each other in their grief over their daughter Bonnie's death.

Then read the book, so you can enjoy the character details that couldn't be crammed into the four-hour movie. Did you know that Margaret Mitchell said plainly that Scarlett O'Hara was not beautiful, but that she had the ability to make people believe she was? If you wanted to write about a character who was that strong and that dominating, how would *you* go about it?

It never hurts a writer to go back and re-read something wonderful and familiar, if only to see how its author accomplished such a feat. Now I must resume my campaign to bully my daughter into reading *Anne of Green Gables*...

DAY 8—Characterization: A master has more to teach us

I ruminated for quite some time about Scarlett O'Hara and her world yesterday, but now I'm thinking of more things I should have told you. Fortunately, I am queen of my domain here, so I'm free to sit down today and revisit a topic that has turned out to be more rich than I'd expected. This is the beauty of our art form. We novelists can spend *a whole year* exhausting a topic that interests us. (Or even *more!*) If we find out we have more to say, and if we have said it well enough that our publisher would like to hear more, then we can write another whole book on the subject. This is heaven for the long-winded.

I had no idea when I wrote *Artifacts* that I would write another book about Faye Longchamp, and now I've finished her seventh adventure. Fortunately, I find her endlessly interesting. Her family background, rooted in both slaves and their owners, gives her an inner complexity that will never go away. Her intellect and thirst for knowledge allows me to dive deep into things that fascinate me and, hopefully, my readers. And her love for...um...somebody (can't spoil the later books for those who haven't read them all) goes so deep that Faye herself is astonished sometimes.

So where do these indelible characters come from, and why am I still talking about Scarlett and Melanie and *Gone with the Wind?* Because when I set out to write a book centered on the faded glory of an old plantation house, I knew that I was treading on heavily traveled territory. I needed to find something new to say about the history of the American South.

In some ways, Faye is the anti-Scarlett. She did not grow up surrounded by wealth. She was not accepted by high society, because of the color of her skin. She and Scarlett do share the trait of intelligence. (In the book, one of the reasons Scarlett was rejected by Atlanta society was that she was better at business than the men. Particularly shocking was the fact that she could add a double-column of numbers in her head.) Faye does have Scarlett's tenacity. After Scarlett loses her wealth, she is as driven to save her ancestral home as Faye is driven to save Joyeuse. But Faye lacks Scarlett's ruthlessness. She will break the law to save her home, but she will not hurt other people. At the beginning of *Artifacts,* she has withdrawn from the society that rejected her, but she has not lashed out in revenge.

Faye's ancestor Cally, a freed slave, is like Scarlett and Faye in her drive to keep her home on Joyeuse Island, and she is like Melanie in her deep-seated need to save her baby. When Cally faces the Yankee soldiers down on the staircase of Joyeuse, her baby in her arms, she shows Melanie's quiet passion...except Cally gets to live.

My other Civil War heroine, Viola Bachelder, appears in *Findings* only in the form of love letters that passed between her and her husband Jedediah. She is yet more like Melanie, in that she poured her life into tending wounded soldiers, Yankee and Rebel and white and black, in her own home, and it cost her everything. But unlike anyone in *Gone with the Wind*, Viola used her quiet strength to convince her husband to free their slaves. Her commitment to abolition, and Cally's passion to be free, and Faye's refusal to bow down to the pressures of growing up in the South in the 1970s as a woman of color, are the things that I think set my stories and my characters apart from the tales that we've all heard before.

When I first had the idea for *Artifacts*, I could have discarded it, figuring that Margaret Mitchell had gotten there first 70-plus years ago. Instead, I asked myself, "What would be a story in this setting that would be right for 21st-century audiences?" Seven books later, I think I did the right thing.

DAY 9—Characterization: Please don't make me live with a namby-pamby weakling

I'm nearly finished ruminating on *Gone with the Wind,* but bear with me as I use it as a springboard to talk about a larger issue for writers hoping to create memorable characters.

How interesting would this story have been if Scarlett had said, "Fiddle-dee-dee. I just can't figure out how to grow enough food for my starving family. And keeping the books for my bumbling husband's business is just beyond me because math is *hard*. Ashley? Could you fix these problems for me? No? You're as big of an incompetent fool as I am? Oh, whatever shall we do? I think I'll just sit down and quit."?

How interesting would Melanie have been, if she hadn't been the kind of woman to rise from the bed where she lay, near-dead from complications of childbirth, and grab her dead brother's sword before staggering downstairs to save Scarlett from rape?

When my agent marketed my first novel, an environmental thriller called *Wounded Earth*, it got a lot of interest from some very prominent publishers and editors around New York. There were nibbles from Hollywood. I thought it was the beginning of my career as a writer, but

I had to wait three more years before *Artifacts* eventually sold. So what happened to *Wounded Earth*?

The feedback we got was that the editorial committee at an unnamed publisher loved it. They loved the story, they loved the evil villain Babykiller, and they loved the heroine, a brilliant environmental scientist named Larabeth McLeod with an Achilles' heel in the form of the daughter she has never met. Unfortunately, they thought she was too intelligent and strong and edgy for their readership. In other words, only smart people like themselves could appreciate this book.

Is it just me, or do you as a reader feel a little hurt by this?

As I began writing *Artifacts*, I asked myself if I wanted to write a meeker heroine, since that seemed to be what the marketplace wanted. Then I asked myself if I wanted to live with a wimp for 90,000 words. The answer was a resounding no, so Faye Longchamp was born. People seem to like Faye, and I do, too. What is more, I respect her.

My current publisher does not do thrillers, so Larabeth McLeod had been sitting on my shelf for ten years when I saw the opportunity for making *Wounded Earth* available to readers all by myself. I cannot tell you how happy it makes me to hear from people who love Larabeth. She has guts, and I like that in a character.

Consider classic characters like Laura Ingalls of the Little House books and Anne Shirley of Green Gables and the March girls of *Little Women*. Do you remember the passion that those little girls put into being first in their classes? If Victorian children were drawn to Anne, who certainly did not fit the prescribed standards for girls of their era, and if children ever since the Depression have been drawn to Laura, and if children ever since the Civil War have been drawn to Louisa May Alcott's little women, I think we can safely say that our readers are looking for female characters with fire in their bellies...characters like Scarlett and Melanie.

And they are looking for male characters who are their equals. Laurie Laurence stands up to his stern grandfather in defense of his friendship with Jo March and her sisters. Gilbert Blythe is a worthy adversary for Anne Shirley...until he is something more. And Rhett Butler is the only man in the world who could go toe-to-toe with Scarlett O'Hara, so I'm hoping that she went running after him as soon as the book was over, explaining that he wasn't *allowed* to leave her and that he did, in fact, give a damn. I hope she forced him to come home and be happy.

Nobody remembers the characters in those books who hewed to society's expectations, so remember that when you draft your characters. Give them a passion for something they cannot have, like my Larabeth McLeod's lifelong grief for the daughter she gave up for adoption. Give them Jo March's need to be a published author, even if it meant writing trashy stories for tabloids. Give them Anne of Green Gables' longing for a home.

And if you have ever met anyone whose favorite character in *Gone with the Wind* was the namby-pamby Ashley Wilkes, please drop me a line...although I'm not sure I'll believe you.

DAY 10—Characterization: The sidekick

You could create the greatest protagonist in the history of literature (and by this point in the process, maybe you have) but without someone by his side, he's going to spend several hundred manuscript pages talking to himself. You must expend some effort to create secondary characters who are worthy of your primary character and of your story.

Some of the great characters in literature have played a secondary role. Doctor Watson comes immediately to mind. But Sherlock Holmes is not the only character who needed an inseparable friend to help him or to cover for his deficiencies or to humanize him. Or her. Don Quixote had Sancho Panza. Batman had Robin. Lucy Ricardo had Ethel Mertz.

My series character, Faye Longchamp, has Joe Wolf Mantooth. It caught me off-guard to learn how popular Joe is. I get worried questions from readers: "Is Joe going to be in the next book???"

Well, of course he is. If I wrote a book about Faye and omitted Joe, I'd never hear the end of it. If I *killed* Joe, I do believe one of my readers might kill me. Last week, I got a note from a reader who was really enjoying *Artifacts,* until she got to a scene when she thought he was going to die. She just closed the book and almost didn't finish it.

Fortunately, curiosity got the better of her, and she did read it to the end. And she apparently enjoyed it enough to want to tell me about it

I created Joe in a fit of pique. As I've told you, my first novel, *Wounded Earth,* had gotten a lot of attention from publishers and movie folk, but never found a home. One of the publishers who came closest to buying it said their editors liked it a whole lot, but "It's a little too close to romantic suspense, and we're not doing that right now." I disagreed with that verdict and as I created the backdrop for my Faye Longchamp archaeological mysteries, I specifically plotted them so that there would be *no romance whatsoever.*

I purposely made Joe completely unsuitable as a romantic partner for Faye. He is nine years younger than she is. He's homeless. He's unemployed. He's barely literate. But he looks good and he cooks good and she has a soft heart, so when she finds him camping on her island, she lets him stay and she finds that he is the truest friend a girl could have. Imagine my astonishment to get constant demands for eight years now that I let Faye sleep with Joe. Immediately.

(This probably has something to do with the fact that he is six-foot-six, built like his Creek warrior ancestors, has sea-green eyes, and wears a ponytail halfway down his back. But I could be wrong.)

But Joe is more than a pretty face. He has a natural intelligence and deep-seated spirituality that complements Faye's clear-headed intellect. Of all my characters, he is the one most likely to do and say things that I didn't intend for him to do or say, and that is one of the times when a writer knows that she is creating art.

Faye and Joe respect each other. They depend on each other. That kind of relationship makes for a good story, and I'm all about good stories.

And, yeah, I'm all about pretty men, too. In my mind's eye, I like to look at Joe just as much as my readers do. So sue me...

DAY 11—Characterization: Villainy is endlessly entertaining

How are you doing in your quest to create an antagonist who is worthy of your book's hero? It's important for us as writers to love our villains, don't you think? I know I do.

But I'm having a tiny problem writing about the villains in my own mysteries. Think about it...If I describe the villains in my Faye Longchamp mysteries to you, then dissect each of their motives for murder, I will accomplish two things. If I do it well, I will have achieved a nice little piece of commentary on the nature of crime fiction, which is no mean feat. However, I will also have spoiled your pleasure in reading any of those books. Suffice it to say that my antagonists have motives as varied as shame and the fear of prosecution and the love of money.

I do, however, have one book that will not be spoiled by a discussion of the villain. My standalone, *Wounded Earth*, is an environmental thriller and, like most thrillers, the reader knows who the villain is from the very outset.

In the case of *Wounded Earth*, the villain is known from the first word of the first sentence:

"Babykiller was meticulous in all things."

It is very difficult to construct a three-dimensional villain who murders randomly...I guess. I've never tried it.

To me, "He's just bad," is the cheater's way out when it comes to creating a character. Now, someone who calls himself "Babykiller" is pretty darn bad. But this character has a wisp of a human side that, I hope, makes the reader want to stick with him through an entire novel. He's wrapped up in an obsessive love for the book's protagonist, Larabeth McLeod. They have a history together, albeit one that is only revealed late in the book, so he has a somewhat rational basis for that obsession. And he resents her, too, for reasons he reveals to her during one of the many conversations he uses to charm her, like a snake-charmer manipulates a cobra.

Babykiller is brilliant, resourceful, and he has a twisted sense of humor. He is a worthy adversary for my strong, successful, powerful Larabeth, and their protracted intellectual duel drives the plot. Larabeth perseveres, ultimately winning their battle, because that is who she is, but no scene is boring when Babykiller is in it.

And that, ultimately, is the secret to great villains. They can strut, they can snarl, they can be bland-faced operatives from governments not our own, but they must never, ever be boring.

May all your villains be interesting ones.

DAY 12—Characterization: Naming names

You can't get very far in writing a book without giving names to the people in it. People ask me how I name my characters, and I often answer them with an impressive and intelligent-sounding "Huh?"

Then I shift my mental gears into reverse and remember that I did go through some mental gyrations when I named my characters. It's just that I promptly forgot those gyrations once each character was duly named. If you have children, think back to the other names you considered when you were naming them. It's entirely possible that I could be the mother of three children named Daniel, Rebecca, and Susannah, but the prospect just seems...wrong. Once you hang a name on that delightful bundle of sweet baby flesh, it's over. The human mind meshes the sound of the name with the reality of the person, and any other name just feels like a masquerade.

So where did Faye Longchamp get her name? Well, I wanted something slightly uncommon, but not quirky. I had it in my mind that some of Faye's European distant ancestors hailed from France, and I wanted a French name that could be Anglicized into something that Americans could spell and pronounce. So Faye pronounces her last name like it looks (and like a Southerner): "LAWNG-champ." Her first name is just a little bit old-fashioned, and it's a name that I've encountered in several women of both European and African descent who were born in the South in the mid-20th-century. It seemed to fit my biracial and very Southern protagonist. I like its soft and feminine sound because, beneath her tough, scientific exterior, Faye is all girl.

I chose Joe's first name because it is simple and masculine. It is common enough that he needed an interesting surname. I wanted it to be somewhat Native American in sound. I remembered Randolph Mantooth from the show *Emergency!* in the 1970s, and that sounded about right. I also went to school with a girl who had that name, so I knew it wasn't incredibly rare. I felt that Joe also needed a middle name with character, and I decided on Wolf. "Joe Wolf Mantooth" suits him very well, I think.

Faye's plantation house, handed down through her family for years, needed a name as well. I remembered a book I had enjoyed called *The River Road* by Frances Parkinson Keyes that featured houses like Faye's.

A secondary character was named Joyeuse, and I thought that was a beautiful name for a house. It speaks of joy. And it makes the suffering in the house that came with slavery so poignant.

People always want to know how to pronounce Joyeuse. I tell them that Faye's as Southern as I am, so she garbles it a bit, but we pronounce it, "Zhwah-YOOSE." My French-speaking editor pronounces it more like "Zhwah-yuhz."

The most important thing about my characters, though, is that they come when I call them.

DAY 13—Characterization: Bits and pieces of myself

Many times, the primary character in a first novel is a transparent representation of the author. While there's surely nothing wrong with an engineer writing a novel about an engineer, I like to stretch myself a little. So though the protagonist of Wounded Earth, Larabeth McLeod, is an environmental consultant, which is a job I held for many years, I gave her a completely different specialty—biochemistry. I made her older than me by a number of years. Though my children have been the center of my life, I took Larabeth's one and only child away. Certainly, there are bits and pieces of me in that character, but they've been shattered and reassembled.

In the same way, I'm nothing like the villain of that book, Babykiller. (I hope.) Yet I had to imagine how I might react to the kinds of betrayal Babykiller believes he has suffered, then I had to amplify that rage a million times, until I could begin to imagine how I might take my revenge...if I were Babykiller.

There are those who still believe that Faye Longchamp is an alias for me, but I still believe they are wrong. She's younger, smarter, stronger, braver, and she carries the emotional scars of growing up biracial in the American South in the 1970s. In recent years, I've realized that she does think like me, but I still do not believe that I've created a character who is me in disguise. That just seems like cheating. I'm a novelist, darn it, and when I need a character I make one up.

I do, sometimes, wish I lived in a historic house on an island and that I got to dig up cool stuff for a living, but if I didn't want to live Faye's life, then how could I make you want to live it? Right now, I'm constructing the climactic scene of *Plunder*, and Faye is rushing into danger to save someone defenseless. There are boats involved and gorgeous scenery and sunken treasure and, just to keep Faye on her toes, vulnerable children. Who wouldn't want to be that brave?

But she's clearly not me, because I sit at a computer all day spinning stories. That makes me as happy as a hog in slop, but it would drive Faye berserk.

So much for that "my protagonist is me" theory...

DAY 14—Characterization: Use your pain

How are you doing with your character sketches? Are your characters starting to feel like real, three-dimensional people to you? Or are they still laundry lists of physical characteristics?

Does it seem like you're pushing your characters around like pawns on a chessboard, but you're not really connecting with them? Well, if they're not real to you, they won't be real to your readers. If you're just going through the motions, your readers can tell.

So where do you look for the raw material that you can hone into a story that feels completely real? In the end, the only place you can go is inside yourself. Everything else is second-hand. If it's not your emotion, how do you know whether it's true?

When I wanted my readers to feel Faye's pain at being ostracized for her race, I thought back to my years as a teenager in the 1970s South. I knew in my head what she would have experienced, but how could I bring that experience into my heart?

Well, everyone has their own memories of feeling ostracized and embarrassed and wounded during their growing-up years. (You can tell me you were Prom Queen and you never lost a boyfriend and you always wore the right clothes and you always said the right things, and you can tell me that your life was so perfect that you are not still carrying those old wounds around with you. You can tell me, but I won't believe you.)

Overlaying my own hard memories atop Faye's experiences gave me the emotional depth that I needed for her character. In a later book, she believes that she has lost Joe forever. He survives, but others in that book do not. The survivors suffer monumental losses, and Faye herself steps right up to that abyss and stares down into its depths. You have to have loved somebody and truly feared losing them to write scenes like that. If we're honest, most of us have felt that fear. If we're honest, we can write about it.

Some of us have soft spots so tender that we really can't write about them. I don't think you'll ever see me write about the suffering or death of a child. When one book's plot required a very young character to die, I could only fool myself into writing it by making the victim eighteen, so that I could pretend it was an adult who had died. Even so, I got a phone call from a horrified friend yelling, "I can't believe you killed that child!!!!"

I still don't like to read the scene where his mother learns of his death, and I wrote the damn thing.

Writing stories that ring emotionally true is not easy, but there is no better way to reach out of the pages and connect with your readers. Perhaps there is no other way at all.

CHAPTER 3—DEVELOPING A SETTING: WHERE WILL YOUR CHARACTERS LIVE?

DAY 15—Look around and tell me what your characters will see

Do you know where you want your novel to take place? More to the point, could it take place anywhere else?

This isn't a trick question. It's certainly possible to write a good story that takes place in a generic, nameless city, if the point you're trying to make is the soul-crushing sameness of a landscape dominated by faceless strangers and rock-hard surfaces. If, on the other hand, you want to write a story that truly inhabits the city of Chicago, then you had best figure out a way to make your Chicago distinguishable from New Orleans or Miami or Rome.

Your assignment for this chapter is to decide where your novel will take place. This task is as simple as writing a place name on a piece of paper, and it is as difficult as getting to know a new friend or lover. Spend the next few days giving this most important question some serious thought.

DAY 16—Reading for a living

Once you have a vague notion of where you want your story to take place, begin assembling the information you will need to make the narrative feel authentic. You'll find that plot possibilities jump out at you as you do this research.

Will your setting be a real place? If so, consider acquiring travel guides, histories, maps, and materials that will help you bring it to life. (And they will also help you avoid embarrassing yourself by having your hero walk three miles in five minutes.) The library is your friend. So are the internet and the used bookstore and maybe even your own bookshelves, if you've got the kind of eclectic library that I do.

Use this printed material to immerse yourself in the place where your characters will live. I call this part of the book-planning stage "reading for a living." If at all possible, you should try to visit your book's setting and soak up some regional flavor.

Will your setting be an imaginary place? If so, then you should write a "character sketch" of your setting, because an imaginary setting often functions as an extra character in a novel. What is the weather like? Is it an urban or suburban or rural setting? Can you close your eyes and "go" there? If not, then make a list of things that you need to know in order to be intimately familiar with this very important place.

Remember—until your book's setting feels solid and three-dimensional to you, it will be impossible for you to imagine your characters walking through it. Put in the time that it takes for you to get to know the place.

DAY 17—Try a different art form for inspiration

Time to write is always hard to come by, but when I was in my twenties, it was well-nigh impossible. I discovered my ambition to write when I was twenty-one. I was pursuing a master's degree in chemical engineering at the time. This is not an endeavor that is fraught with free time.

When I was twenty-two, as I was in my last semester of writing my thesis, I took a job teaching community college math and physics. I prepared for fifteen semester hours of lectures that first fall and defended my thesis the week I turned twenty-three. The next month, my husband and I learned that we were pregnant with our first child. Fifteen months after he was born, when I was twenty-five, his sister was born fifteen weeks prematurely, weighing one pound and ten ounces. You can imagine the medical consequences of this event.

She was in the hospital for more than three months, and it was more than a year before it was clear that she was healthy and developing normally. At about this time, when I was twenty-six, my marriage ended and I found myself the single mother of two children in diapers. Fortunately, I had those engineering degrees, so I found full-time work, but when, you might ask, did I find time to pursue my dream of writing during that endless decade?

I wrote when my children were sleeping. I wrote when I myself should have been sleeping, and I forced myself to limit the scope of my projects. I wrote many short stories during those years. There were times when I only had time to write haiku. But I wrote. And I was rewarded a bit for that dogged persistence when I saw some of those poems published. Before I sold *Artifacts* at age 40, I had never sold a single piece of my creative writing, except for those few poems written and sold in my twenties when I had no business doing anything other than feeding babies and changing their diapers.

Why am I talking about this in the chapter on your book's setting? It's because I nurture an abiding affection for the haiku as an art form. Most school children learn about haiku only in terms of its syllable count: five syllables in the first line, seven syllables in the second line, and five syllables in the third. The haiku is more than this to Japanese poets, and I'm not sure the nuances of this art form survive translation into English intact. Two more characteristics that will be useful to us in this chapter are these: a haiku traditionally depicts the natural world and it typically includes an "aha" moment wherein the narrator (and the reader) understands something in a way that he didn't before.

The mindset of the haiku writer is a good one for a novelist to use when approaching a book's setting. Your assignment for today and tomorrow is to write a haiku (or many haiku) that captures some facet of your story's world. Root your haiku in the real world by describing nature as it surrounds your character. If you give the matter some thought, you should be able to communicate an "aha!" moment for one or more of your characters. But remember...you can only use seventeen syllables, so you must select your words carefully. Provided you choose well, I believe that you will find yourself using some of the words in your haiku when it comes time to work with the setting of your novel.

DAY 18—A springboard for your haiku assignment

Tucked into my collection of writerly souvenirs are the journals where my poetry appeared in the late 1980s. They haven't seen print since then, so I thought I'd let three of them—all haiku—come out to play. Maybe they'll give you a jumping-off point for writing your own. You'll see some hallmarks of traditional haiku—the reliance on nature and the "aha!" moment of realization—along with a personification of nature that may not be quite so traditional. I also think you'll see how crafting tiny moments like these can help you create very specific feelings when you need a special moment in your fiction. Enjoy...

Earth moans beneath me
as her summer-long labor
yields newborn bounty.

ripening apples
turn rosy bellies skyward
naked to the sun

Tabby treads soft snow.
Melting, his tracks yawn wider.
Bengal tiger stalks!

DAY 19—Make every effort to visit the setting of your book

I have written and published eight novels, and I have visited the locales of each book, even the three that take place in imaginary settings. How did I manage that?

Well, in my mind, Joyeuse Island, the home of my series character Faye Longchamp and the setting of *Artifacts* and *Findings*, is located off the coast of the Florida Panhandle at the end of a long chain of barrier islands that actually exist. I took a trip to the Panhandle and drove aimlessly down the county roads on the mainland that look out over the water where Joyeuse Island should be. I chartered a fishing boat to take me out into the Gulf, so that I could look at things from a watery standpoint and so that I could pick the captain's brain. (This is how I decided what kind of boat Faye should have, and it's how I got a sense of how long it would take her to boat to shore.) And I visited one of the islands that *does* exist, so that I could better imagine my island that doesn't.

To develop the fictional river valley where *Relics* is set, I went to north Alabama and spent a weekend driving around. By the time I went home, I had seen some real river valleys and I'd gotten a good look at the towns and the trees and the farmhouses and the country roads that give that area its unique look.

I know you can't go to the moon if you're writing a fictionalization of the Apollo 11 voyage, but if it's at all within your ability, please go take a look at your characters' world. Your novel-writing experience will be the deeper for it.

DAY 20—If you can't take a trip to your characters' world, check things out somehow…

When writing *Effigies*, I talked to several employees of the Choctaw nation about elements of the culture that I was incorporating into the book, but these people were not themselves Choctaws. Despite several trips to the area, it took me a while to track down individuals willing to be interviewed. In the meantime, I needed to write a book and I had a deadline. So I used the Internet to give me some cool background info, knowing I could check it out later. And I'm so glad I did.

I had used a website of Choctaw names to give an important character his name. I chose Okshakla from this list, which was purported to mean "Deep Water." It suited him. I liked it. But when I eventually asked a Mississippi Choctaw whether it really meant Deep Water, she said, "Um. Maybe in Oklahoma...."

Oops. She told me how to say "Deep Water" in Choctaw, and a global search-and-replace gave my character the name I'd wanted him to have, but in a part of my mind, Oka Hofobi will always be Okshakla. Too bad I don't know what Okshakla means...

Here's the moral of this story: **Never bet your reputation on Wikipedia...or on any website or source that gives you any reason to doubt its accuracy or impartiality!!!** Go to the best source you can possibly find.

DAY 21—How's the weather in your book?

It was a dark and stormy night...

A frequently quoted rule of writing is that you should never start a story by talking about the weather. When it comes to scene-setting, the weather can be a convenient but prosaic way to help your reader feel like he is where your characters are. Use it judiciously. There are usually better ways to kick off a scene than by noting the raindrops falling on the roof overhead or the wind howling at the windows.

Weather was a central fact of life back in caveman days, when a day-long rainstorm meant that you either got wet while you scavenged for food, or you went hungry. These days, we look out at snowstorms from our tight, warm houses, and we use cozy cars to scavenge for our food, so there's just not much drama to be had from talking about the weather. (Okay, some people gaze at snow through their windows. I live in Florida, where a snowstorm would afford plenty of drama, since it would be a sign of climatic Armageddon. Also, it would cause stupendous traffic disaster, since none of us knows how to drive when atmospheric water freezes and drops to the ground. But I digress.)

As I guide you through your exploration of your book's setting, I'm trying to think clearly about how I use weather in my own work. My first thought is that I write about the Gulf South, so the weather isn't news. It's always the same: hot and muggy, with a chance of thunderstorms. The long 95/95 summers (95 degrees Fahrenheit, 95% relative humidity) can work to my advantage, giving the action an overheated and sweaty feeling, but I risk trying your patience if I mention the fact that Faye is sweating on every ever lovin' page. As with any telling detail, it's best to feather such descriptions into the action judiciously.

In *Relics*, I had a little fun with the weather by sending Faye to north Alabama, into the foothills of the Appalachians...in November. I did this because she spent much of *Artifacts* running for her life, but she did it on her own turf. For the follow-up book, I wanted to take her out of her comfort zone. So not only is she dealing with a region where the people don't want her and where both the hilly landscape and the very dirt are alien—not small things to an archaeologist—in *Relics*, she is *cold*. For a native Floridian, to be cold is to know that the world has been knocked off its axis. For a novelist, knocking your protagonist's world off its axis is the very foundation of a good plot.

I was nearly finished musing on how little weather figured into my storytelling style when I remembered the hurricanes. Duh. I guess when I think of the word "weather," I think of gentle rain and sun and clouds. When I think of hurricanes, I come up with the word "cataclysm." *Artifacts* ends with Faye hauling a wounded friend across her roof during the mother of all hurricanes. It even includes my personal favorite point-of-view character of any I've written (other than Faye and Joe, of course): Hurukan, the Mayan storm god. Hurukan understands that sometimes humans muck up the world so badly that it just needs to be wiped clean, and Hurukan knows that he is just the god to do it.

After the Category 5 monster in *Artifacts*, I figured I'd leave hurricanes alone as plot points, at least for a while. And I did. But four books later, I found myself setting *Floodgates* in New Orleans, post-Katrina, so hurricane-as-plot-point forced itself on me again. In my latest book, *Strangers*, there was no way to talk about the founding of St. Augustine without mentioning the hurricanes encountered by the arriving Spanish in their frail wooden boats, at least in passing. And if I follow through with my plan to set a future book in the Florida Keys, there will be no way to ignore the Labor Day Hurricane of 1935 that cut the Keys off from the mainland by wiping out the railroad, killing hundreds in the process.

Brutally hot, muggy, with occasional tempestuous disaster...these are the climatic facts of life when you live within the area influenced by the great Gulf of Mexico. These things are counterbalanced by the fact that you pretty much can't freeze to death here, and it's hard to starve when the growing season never really gets over, but heat, humidity, and hurricanes can't be ignored. Weather you like it or not...

CHAPTER 4—PLOT: FIRST, YOU HAVE TO TELL A STORY

DAY 22—I've got a character and a setting... now what?

There's always something happening. Even if you're writing a story about a character who is too depressed to get out of bed, something is happening. He is breathing.

More to the point, this character is also thinking. He is thinking that he would enjoy a beer, if he could just summon the energy to get up, walk into the kitchen, and yank open the refrigerator door. But he's also thinking that this seems like an awful lot of work. He is thinking about the work he is not doing. He is thinking about the woman he loves, but he is wondering if he'll ever be able to bring himself to ask her out. Always, he is thinking about the life that he is not living.

If you wrote this scene, there would be no action, but there would be plenty of conflict.

Conversely, if you wrote a scene featuring a woman riding her bike at breakneck speed through the streets of Peoria, you would have plenty of action, but no conflict. There is a germ of a story in the travails of our bedbound depressive, but there is no story in our bike-riding Peorian, not unless you know why she's going so fast. If she's fleeing a masked assailant, you have a story. If she's just trying to burn a few calories, you have no story...unless she's trying to drop some pounds before she attends a party with Prince Harry of England at a time when he is known to be without a girlfriend.

Begin making notes on your story's plot, and give some thought to both action and conflict. A skillful writer could write a short story wherein the protagonist never left his bed, perhaps even an entire novel, but employing judicious amounts of both conflict and action is a better strategy for most writers.

I suggest that you consider this issue on a large scale, then work it down to a smaller scale. What is the primary conflict driving your story? What do your characters want? What is standing in their way? And (this is where the action comes in) how do they go about trying to get what they want?

As you write, never lose your focus on this question: "What is happening?"

More specific to the goals of this book: "What is going to happen in your story?" Take some time today to write a few paragraphs describing the overarching conflict in your book and how you intend to resolve it.

DAY 23—Know where you're going

It's time for you to begin crafting an outline of the events in your novel. Use the paragraphs you wrote yesterday as your starting point. Over the next few days, I'll be talking about outlining and plotting, in hopes of helping you craft this outline into something that you can live with for hundreds of manuscript pages. Always remember that an outline is a living document. You can put it in any format—bulleted plot points, paragraph-based narrative, or whatever you like. (I use a paragraph-based narrative. Basically, I just sit down and tell myself a story, without worrying about format, or even about punctuation. It's for my eyes only.) The important thing is to gather your thoughts about your book into one document that you can reference at any time.

Whenever I speak at schools, somebody always asks me if I outline. I always say yes. I always get the sense that the teacher wants to give me a big sloppy kiss.

I probably disappoint those teachers when I go on to say that my outlines are for my eyes only. Therefore, they display no Roman numerals or letters or fancy formatting. Essentially, I just sit down and tell myself a story, divided up roughly into chapters. Chapter 1 may say nothing except, "Faye finds a skull," because that may be all I need to call up in my mind the windswept and lonely island where that skull waits for Faye. There is no need to say more, because I already know how I will describe the nearby island where the killer stands, looking at the light glinting on her boat and knowing that someone has found his handiwork and he now has to *do something about it*.

My outlines for other chapters may be ridiculously lengthy. If I have research notes I know I'll need, I stick 'em right in the outline, along with snippets of description and dialogue.

I have very successful author friends who tell me that they do not outline and, in fact, do not know how the book they're writing will end. They write mysteries, for goodness sake. How can they possibly lay clues when they don't know where the clues point? Yet they do it, and they do it well. I know that they are all brutal and efficient self-editors, and I do not know any published authors who are not, so they do have the option of tweaking the narrative and adding clues into the second draft. Still, this approach leaves me white-knuckled and terrified.

For *Artifacts*, I wasn't even sure I *could* write a full-length mystery. I crammed so many notes and descriptions and conversations and reminders and clues into the outline that it was 125 pages long. In retrospect, you could almost call it a very ugly first draft.

The outline for *Relics* was about 50 pages long. All the rest have been about 25 pages, and I think that's a good level of detail for me and for the books I write.

I am just barely old enough to have typed on a typewriter in high school and college, but I ditched my typewriter for a TRS-80 Model 4 in 1984, and I have never looked back. The notion of typing multiple drafts, and doing it without the capacity to correct errors, absolutely terrifies me. I won the typing award in high school, which wasn't hard to do since I've been playing piano since I was 8. My eye-finger coordination is amazing. I probably type 100+ error-riddled words per minute these days. On a computer, I can fix those errors in an instant. If I were still using a typewriter, my drafts would consider of more Liquid Paper™ than actual paper.

Also, and more to the point of this essay, a computer lets me type the final period on my outline, then scroll to the top and write my book *in the same computer file.* Oh joy!

(One of my trusted readers for this manuscript told me that he works in much the same way I do, except that he uses a different color font for the outline. I am astonished that this sanity-saving technique has not occurred to me before, but you can benefit from his wisdom.)

I often take an important sentence out of the outline, cut it, and paste it into the chapter where I'm writing. Then I have it right in front of my eyes as a beacon, telling me where to go. Remember those snippets of conversation I said I put in my outline? I paste them where they need to go, then move on.

I once sent the first hundred pages of a new novel to my agent for review, and forgot to snip out the outline from the bottom of the file. She called me and said, "What in the *hell* is this????" If I had only used a different color font for that outline, this embarrassing moment might never have taken place.

Other than that one time, I don't think anyone has ever seen one of my rough outlines, and no, I'm not pasting one here. I have too much dignity for that.

But now you know that they exist.

DAY 24—The most important plotting question: "What's happening?"

As a mystery author, I write in a plot-driven genre, and this emphasis on plot might be useful to you as you outline your novel. I will discuss plot as it relates to mystery from time to time, although I know very well that all of my readers are not mystery authors, because I think the concepts are transferrable. Just as I look to literary fiction for inspiration in matters of style, I think writers of literary fiction would do well to look to crime fiction for inspiration in matters of storytelling.

A great mystery is more than just plot, but a randomly constructed mystery will not make its readers happy. There's no rule against incorporating literary-style prose in a mystery. Evocative settings are expected. Cardboard characters will get you trashed by the critics. No writer can afford to ignore all the elements of good fiction, but I think mystery writers are especially guided by the need for tight plotting. So even if you write something completely different, I think you'll be able to tailor my observations to your project.

So to start our conversation about plot, let's take a stab at defining it. If held to one word, I'd use, "Conflict," but that's really insufficient. Two three-year-olds fighting over a pile of blocks is conflict, but it isn't interesting. (Unless one of the kids is yours.)

As I sought to refine the idea of conflict as a definition for plot, some words that came to me were "controlled" and "structured," but that begs a question. Who is doing the controlling and structuring? That would be you. Or me. The writer who is telling the story is in control. So let's craft a definition wherein we put ourselves in charge:

A story's plot centers on a conflict that is shaped by the writer.

What else does a plot need? How about an ending? Unending conflict can be both exciting and monotonous. Just check the evening news. Don't you sometimes feel that it's the same story, day in and day out?

So let's add that ending to our definition:

A story's plot centers on a conflict that is shaped by the writer, who is responsible for driving that conflict toward a coherent resolution.

Okay, so now I've made you *responsible*. How do you deal with that? Is it just too much pressure??????

DAY 25—Mary Anna's Personal Plotting Rule #1: I believe in outlines.

As I've already said, I'm a dedicated outliner. (By the way...how's yours coming?)

I find that outlines do not cramp me, artistically. On the contrary, they free me to pursue new ideas, because I have the security of knowing that my outline is a roadmap that will take me to a coherent ending. I can follow any whim that strikes me without worrying about getting lost, because I can always make my way back to that roadmap.

Despite my love of outlines, I have no use at all for rules or formulae. There are some people who say that a mystery must present a dead body within the first ten pages. Preferably on page one. And I've read books where that was done very well, but it takes power from the author. It eliminates stories that depend on the reader feeling sympathy for the victim, since that's hard to earn in a single page.

I've also heard that category romances sometimes have a required structure. (I don't know this for a fact. I'm just using the rumor to continue this discussion, so don't let this upset you, if you're a romance writer. Just find a way to make the genre your own, structure requirements or not.)

The rumored structure goes something like this:

Heroine meets hero in first chapter.

Interrupted sex scene on page 112.

Consummated sex scene on page 243.

Immediate misunderstanding that separates the new lovers.

Fifty pages of escalating complications that build to reconciliation and happiness.

Now this may be a tried-and-true structure that dates back to the Greek dramatists. If I started out to write a romance, I might ignorantly stumble on that structure. Still, call me perverse, but if somebody *told* me I had to use it, I'd balk.

Those of you who write literary fiction may feel that you have to go in a completely different direction. It's true that you can experiment with structure, and you should. But consider *To Kill A Mockingbird*, which I think is one of the great American novels. It's a courtroom drama, culminating in attempted murder. It's a coming-of-age novel, and a superb character portrait of Atticus Finch. It does not suffer in any way from the necessity of telling those structured stories clearly and coherently. Your responsibility is to fully grasp the concept of plot, then adapt it to your unique story.

DAY 26—Mary Anna's Personal Plotting Rule #2: Every scene must have a purpose

I firmly believe that every scene in your story must have a purpose. Preferably more than one purpose. Even on those occasions Herman Melville stopped the story of *Moby Dick* cold to deliver an explanation of how whale oil was produced, he had a purpose for each misleadingly unproductive scene. If you are asking your reader to spend time reading a scene, you must know why.

Yes, it's important to show the reader some scenery, but personalize it by showing it through the eyes of an important character. Even better, let that character be agonizing over a difficult decision as he gazes at the scenery. Better still, dramatize that decision in a conflict-driven conversation with an antagonist.

I could go on, but I think you get the idea.

DAY 27—Mary Anna's Personal Plotting Rule #3: Know what your big scenes are going to be, so you can work toward them

Maybe you're a third of the way into your book (or outline, since that's what you're working on right now) and you know you've got some exposition to do. You're horrified to find that even you can see that it's deadly boring even as you type it. And you're its mommy or daddy.

When you feel like the pace of your story is slumping, think ahead. If you know that an important dramatic event is coming up, you can foreshadow it, and that makes all the difference.

I picture important scenes as tent poles holding the whole structure up. As you craft your outline, try to come up with as many tent-pole scenes as you can. You'll be glad when you're slogging through an entire chapter and you feel like you're doing nothing but moving your characters around like Barbies, because nothing can happen until the victim is in that dark alley where he will die or until your heroine is on that romantic steamer ship where she will meet her one true love.

Right now, you're outlining an entire novel. If you've only got three big scenes, then stop what you're doing right now and give the problem some thought, because I think three is probably not enough. (No, I can't tell you how many you need. Figuring that out is your job. But if you've only got three, they'd better be doozies.) Do you need a new subplot? Do you need a more complex idea, or should you scale this particular plot back to short-story length and look for something bigger for your novel?

These are difficult questions, but it's far better to ask them at this stage, than it would be to ask them while writing page 81 with no notion of how you're going to fill the next 200 pages.

Even if you think you have enough tent-pole scenes planned, craft a few more. When you're muddling through your book's middle, you'll thank me.

DAY 28—Making the most of those big scenes

Many, many, many years ago, a plotting diagram came into my possession, along with a full page of expository description on how to use it. It was a thing of beauty, but I have lost it, and I have no idea where or even if it was ever published, and thus I can't even look for another copy. The diagram mimicked the traditional ski-jump shaped plotting diagram—the plot's tension ramped up and up and up, reaching a peak near the end, then dropped off quickly to the end. The difference, and this is the thing that has made me remember it all these years, is that the diagrammer had actually labeled the locations of those tent-pole scenes I was talking about in the last essay.

Now, I heartily resist the notion that a big scene must come along every 52 pages, because that is perilously close to the formulaic cliché that requires a sex scene on page 247. The thing that made this plotting diagram memorable was the author's explanation that a "push" should come after each big scene and a "turn" should come after the scene that leads directly to the climax.

My interpretation of the terms "push" and "turn" is pretty literal. After an important scene, the protagonist should feel a push toward the ultimate showdown or the dramatic climax. Don't neglect the drama inherent in your characters' reactions to major events. Take a moment to make sure they—and your reader—feel the push of destiny that says that this conflict must be resolved, no matter what.

The "turn" is another useful reaction to an important scene. When your character experiences something that triggers the response, "This changes everything!", this is a turn.

Incorporating these notions into your plot will help you milk the dramatic possibilities out of every scene. Even better, they will help you build a story so satisfying that the reader feels it couldn't end any other way.

DAY 29—The short end of the stick: Writing short stories to enhance your novel-writing skills

In just a few days, it will be time to start writing your book. This book is structured to give you nine months (What a symbolic span of time!) to do that, with the utterly doable goal of writing a page a day. This will generate a 270-page draft of a novel, which isn't the size of a Dan Brown doorstop, but it's a perfectly serviceable length. I've given the speedsters among us the option of taking a 90-day track by writing 3 pages a day. In the end, the time spent writing your book is not the issue. Finishing your book is the issue.

In the meantime, let's exercise our fiction-writing skills a bit and take a look at short stories.

I have a soft spot for short stories. I read stacks of anthologies as a young person at the bookmobile—mostly Alfred Hitchcock anthologies and science fiction collections compiled by the likes of Isaac Asimov. These days, I love to read them *and* write them. The market for them is not huge, but it isn't dead, either.

I've published five short stories in anthologies over the course of my novel-writing career, and I have others in the pipeline. But the goal of this book isn't to learn to write effective short stories. We're here to talk about writing full-length books, but short story writing is quite useful in improving your skills in writing longer fiction, as well.

This approach is a little counter-intuitive. Short fiction and novel-length fiction are, in many ways, two different art forms. Some people can write both and some just can't. Stephen King (who writes both short stories and lengthy novels very well) talks about writers being divided into two categories—putter-inners and taker-outers. It's easier for putter-inners to write long sagas, and it's easier for taker-outers to write terse, economical stories, but I find it highly instructive to work *against* a writer's natural type...to do what isn't easy.

I always dreamed of writing novels, but at the time I started writing seriously, I was in graduate school, pursuing a master's degree in chemical engineering, then I was a young mother. I had zero time for eating and sleeping, much less writing. But a writer writes and, as I've told you, I wrote poetry, especially haiku.

Nevertheless, I didn't want to write poetry. I wanted to write fiction. When I had a few extra scraps of time—in other words, when I was a divorced mother of two kids in diapers—I turned my attention to short stories. Stories aren't all that scary. Most people feel pretty sure that they could write a few thousand words, if they had to. Ten or twenty pages are nowhere near so insurmountable as a multi-hundred page novel. Yet the building blocks of a novel are in those ten or twenty pages. Characters, plot, dialogue, point-of-view, voice, setting— the elements are all there, in miniature. Which means, unfortunately, that they have to be perfect.

Sorry about that.

I was already thinking about writing something novel-length, even while I was turning out short stories. At some point in the process, I began to identify weaknesses in my work. I felt a little weak on dialogue, partially because I was most comfortable with first-person point-of-view. Then I had a flash of insight. Why not set myself a goal of writing a story in third-person? It would be a heck of a lot easier than launching into a 90,000-word novel without ever having mastered that technique.

Next, I could try a story that was mostly dialogue. And then I could write one from a male point-of-view. Whatever technique intimidated me could be isolated and attacked—sort of like isolating a single muscle and exercising it until it's firm and toned.

So I suggest that you spend the next five days writing a story, as a warm-up for writing your novel. If you want to write a one-thousand-word short-short, then you won't even have to write a page a day. If you want to charge hard and write a 20,000-word opus over that short stretch of time, be my guest.

You can use your choice of topics and genres. Your story can be starkly different from the novel you plan to write, or you can use this assignment to hone the approach you'll be using for your big project. If you want to write a story that will grow into a subplot of your novel, that's fine. I won't consider it cheating. Or you could write a story about your protagonist as a child. The whole world is open to you. Many worlds are open to you. This is the beauty of writing fiction.

DAY 30—The first day of your short story adventure

I have very little to say to you today, other than to tell you to write hard. A short story should be an itch you have to scratch...a lover that you need to get out of your system. I frequently write short stories in the first-person, which means that my characters are actually talking as I type. Oftentimes, they tell me things about themselves that I didn't know.

Let the story blast out of you at top speed, from the first page to the last. You won't have that luxury when you're crafting hundreds of words of novel, so use this experience to get in touch with your muse. Let it flow...

DAY 31—How did you do yesterday?

A few of you will have finished drafting your stories yesterday. You people carry on—edit, re-write, tear it apart and put it back together.

The rest of you shouldn't worry or hurry. You have plenty of time. Just sit down and read what you did yesterday quickly. You're not editing. You're just trying to swim out to the middle of the river, where the flow is strongest, so that you can let it carry you like it did yesterday.

Just write...

DAY 32—I'm not rushing you...

More of you finished yesterday, but plenty of you are still working. That's great. Just carry on. But for those of you who are finished, it's time to practice editing.

Read your story to see whether it hangs together from beginning to end. Even better, summarize it in a single paragraph. Is that paragraph coherent? Does the chain of events flow naturally from beginning to end?

Now consider your protagonist. What, exactly, happens to him or her in these few pages? Short fiction does not require the kind of dramatic sequence of events that a novel does; there isn't space for that. So how does a short story differ from a pleasant but pointless vignette? There are as many answers to that as there are writers, but I'm going to go with the one I've heard most often, because it feels true:

A story requires a change in the protagonist, however slight.

A child gets a dog and learns responsibility. A man realizes that his wife has never loved him. A woman notices a chip in her nail polish and, for the first time in her life, doesn't drop everything and fix it right away. These are all stories. A happy couple taking a walk is not a story.

Give the piece you just wrote a good hard look, and decide whether you have a story yet. If not, no worries. You have two days to fix it.

DAY 33—How are you going to tell this story?

By now, I think most of you have put together at least a few pages that look like a short story. It's time to decide whether you have told it in the best way possible.

Did you choose a third person point-of-view? How did that work for you? What would happen if you rewrote it in the first person?

Are you happy with your viewpoint character? What would have happened if you'd chosen another? How different might the Sherlock Holmes stories have been if Arthur Conan Doyle had chosen to write them from the obvious point-of-view, Sherlock's own, rather than from Dr. Watson's perspective?

How did time flow for you? Does the story progress chronologically, with one event happening after another? Or did you use flashbacks to adjust the flow of time to your own needs? What would happen if you reordered the scenes? Would the story stop making sense? Or would it gain depth and suspense as your readers tried to figure out what in the heck was going on?

Don't be afraid to slice up your words and shove them around on the page. This is why God gave us computers. It's just so easy to try a new structure to see whether it works. If you don't like it, hit the back arrow. Or go back to a previous version. (You didn't forget to save it, did you?)

There is nothing like a good hard edit to remind a writer that a first draft is not sacrosanct.

DAY 34—Tidying up the details

I hope I don't have to explain the importance of grammar, punctuation, and spelling. Today is your day to proof your brand-new story. Use your computer's spelling and grammar checkers, by all means, but do not rely on them.

Let me take this opportunity to urge those of you who harbor any doubts about your grammar skills to take action. Get a grammar book. Take an online class. Take a class at an actual college. Do whatever suits your personal learning style, but get the skills you need to do your work.

When you've finished polishing your story, hand it around to some trusted readers. I guarantee that they will find more errors. This is fine. It's why you asked for their help.

After they've handed the story back to you and you've reviewed their edits, put the story away. At some point this year, while you're writing your novel, you're going to hit a brick wall. You will never want to look at this book that you're writing, not ever again. Take a break from it, but don't lose your momentum. Pull this story out and read it again. Polish it some more. Then find an appropriate publication and submit it.

My guess is that this productive break will give you the "oomph" that you need to break through the brick wall that's barring progress on your novel. And maybe that story will sell...

DAY 35—Starting a book is like opening a great big box of crayons

Beginnings and endings make me think of fresh-sharpened pencils and blank sheets of notebook paper and 64-color boxes of crayons. When we were children, we had the chance to begin anew every September. Most adults have year-round lives that lack the ebb-and-flow of the academic year, and I think we all miss those annual new beginnings. Most jobs just go on and on and on, unchanging and neverending.

We writers still live in that back-to-school world, a little bit. We get the chance to actually finish something, for good. Then we get that blessed opportunity to return to the blank slate and start again, with the utter confidence that this book will be as good as the last one. Better! Maybe the best ever!

DAY 36—Get your ducks in a row

Okay, you've had a few days away from your novel-planning project. (I pried you away from it smoothly, didn't I?) Tomorrow is the day you start writing it for real.

Assemble all your notes on your characters and your settings. Open up the file holding your outline. Now read all that material in one sitting.

Your goal today is to get your arms around the project. You need to feel in control of your material. Spend today reminding yourself what it is you plan to do, then sleep on it. Any artist will tell you that your subconscious is working all the time. Give it the raw materials it needs today, then go to bed. Your subconscious will take what you've done and make it into something more. Trust it.

CHAPTER 5—YOUR NOVEL IN 270 DAYS...
OR 90 DAYS...
OR WHENEVER YOU CHOOSE...

The next 270 entries are designed to lead you through the process of drafting a book in nine months by writing a page a day. If you're in a hurry, you can read three entries a day and write three pages a day. If you live the typical American busy life, there will be some days when you don't get to read and write, so you'll need to play catch-up. The only thing that matters is setting a goal. Write down the date when you plan to finish your novel on a scrap of paper and stick it to your refrigerator. There is nothing like a fast-approaching deadline to give you focus, even if the deadline is your own.

Go ahead and put your goal date on the fridge. I'll wait...

DAY 37—Today's the day

I'll spend the next several days talking about beginning a book, but not today. Today, I want you to just sit down and write. We'll worry about the details later.

Ready. Set. Go!

DAY 38—Beginning again...and again

A novelist's work life is consumed in big chunks. When I get an email from a reader who just spent a delightful night devouring one of my books from start to finish, I'm delighted, too. And when that reader says, "I can't wait for the next one!", I'm obviously thrilled. But the undeniable fact is that the pile of paper that kept this person riveted for a night, or even a week, consumed a year of my life.

I love the rhythm of the writing life. The research, the plotting, the outlining, the excitement of actually beginning to write, the even bigger excitement of finishing a book and starting the process again... these events mark my life like the tides or the phases of the moon or the seasons mark the passage of time in the natural world. Today, while we're focused on beginnings, I thought I'd share with you the first sentences of the first chapters of each of my books. Starting a new book is like turning over an hourglass and watching the sand begin to fall again. You can think of these sentences as each book's first grain of sand:

"Faye Longchamp was digging like a pothunter, and she hated herself for it." *Artifacts*, Poisoned Pen Press, 2003.

"Faye Longchamp was born on the first floor of a Tallahassee hospital built at an elevation of fifty-five feet above sea level." *Relics*, Poisoned Pen Press, 2005.

"Faye Longchamp had work to do, but it could wait." *Effigies*, Poisoned Pen Press, 2007.

"A good day at work typically left Faye Longchamp covered in sweat, rain, dust, dirt, or mud, depending on weather conditions." *Findings*, Poisoned Pen Press, 2008.

"Faye Longchamp was surprised at herself." *Floodgates,* Poisoned Pen Press, 2009.

"Faye Longchamp was capable of lust." *Strangers*, Poisoned Pen Press, 2010.

"Babykiller was meticulous in all things." *Wounded Earth*, Joyeuse Press, 2010.

"How long have I been stealing my grandmother's stories?" *Plunder*, Poisoned Pen Press, 2012.

It's time for me to begin the next novel. Sometime soon, I'll flip the hourglass again. I can't wait to watch the sand begin to slowly fall...

DAY 39—More beginnings

I enjoyed seeing all the opening sentences of my novels all in one place. I believe I'll do the same thing with my short stories.

> "If Peter Pan had expired less flamboyantly or, better yet, if he had not expired at all, the murder of Paolo Arrezzo might have remained forever unsolved." — "Mouse House"

> "I am so old that I remember when ladies didn't swear or drive automobiles." — "A Singularly Unsuitable Word"

> "In 1954, the word "nurse" was a female one." — "Starch"

> "I am not my sister." — "Twin Set"

> "In my own defense, I'll say that the job sounded good when I took it." — "Low-Budget Monster Flick"

> "A composting toilet." — "Land of the Flowers"

DAY 40—A very pertinent beginning sentence

It occurs to me that we should take a look at *this* book's opening sentence. Maybe it sets the tone for what I intended to do with this book. Maybe it doesn't. You be the judge.

(Oh, how I hope I don't decide to change the first sentence and forget that I need to come here and change it again.)

> "Perhaps you were expecting a preface or a foreword or some sort of introductory text, but no." *Your Novel: Day by Day*

DAY 41—Speaking in your own voice

When I teach writing, I often hear questions from anxious writers, worried that they need to be working to develop a voice. I wish I could quiet their worries—not because voice isn't an important part of becoming the writer we all want to be, but because worry just isn't a constructive approach to art.

Just as worrying about writer's block is a good way to get a rollicking case of writer's block, worrying about voice is a good way to cramp your own style. I'm not saying that there's no need to analyze your work; I'm just saying that some parts of the writer's toolbox bear analysis more readily than others.

If your plot isn't working, you can outline your story. You can make a timeline. You can unravel your main plot and subplots, looking for ways they can enhance each other more.

If your dialogue doesn't feel natural, you can read it out loud. You can scan it, sentence by sentence, looking for words that feel clunky or for words that no normal human being would ever say in casual conversation.

But voice? The overarching style you use to tell your stories? I think you're better served to just keep writing more stories and let your style begin to show itself over time. If you're lucky enough to have a mentor who can provide feedback that isn't colored by his or her own opinion of the way your story should be told, then maybe you'll get where you want to go faster, but I don't think this is a necessity. Besides, mentors who are that good usually don't have time to provide this kind of feedback.

When you've put enough words on the page, you'll know when some of them are really right. You'll feel it. Your mind will file that feeling away, and you'll recognize it when you have it again. And again. You'll know that there is only one way to tell this story. And that's when you'll know for sure that this is your story to tell, and that the only voice capable of telling it is yours.

DAY 42—How's it going?

My guess is that you're still writing hard, setting down the story that's been building up in your head. This is what you're supposed to be doing.

While you're doing that, this book will be your companion, giving you a series of essays on various writing techniques. You may be so busy writing that you don't even read them now. That's okay. Save them for later, when you have one of those inevitable moments of uncertainty. When that happens, you can come back here to read what I had to say about voice and pacing and editing. I believe it will give you the inspiration—the kick in the pants, if you will—that you'll need to get your momentum back.

But even when it's hard, I still want you to write one page a day. One page. Because your pace will ebb and flow, but I don't ever want you to let it stop.

DAY 43—Prepare yourself for a marathon

I'm not all that athletic, myself. Okay, that inaccurate. I'm completely nonathletic. Right now, I'm looking down at my left shin, which is sporting an angry red scar about three inches long. There is a reddish-black scar the size of a nickel on my left knee. I achieved these badges of honor by falling off a bike.

You may be thinking, "That's not so bad. I'm sure even Lance Armstrong falls off a bike now and then." This is true, but I somehow doubt that Lance falls off his bike when it is not moving.

Bear my athletic ineptitude in mind as I discuss running marathons, because I freely admit that I have never run one. I have, however, watched the Olympics and I know some things about pushing a human body past its normal limits. I know that marathon runners worry about the weight of their shoes, down to the last gram.

Shoes don't weigh much...a few ounces, tops. An infant can pick up a few ounces. However, picking those few ounces up thousands of times will take a toll. How can it not? Taken in that light, it only makes sense to shave off an ounce by buying lighter shoes or by choosing thinner socks or by risking blisters by foregoing socks altogether.

Marathon runners prepare for their ordeal by hydrating their body as completely as possible. They train for months or years, so that their muscles and cardiovascular systems are ready. They feed their bodies the nutrients required to build those muscles and that cardiovascular system then, at the last minute, they take in the optimal amount of carbohydrates to fuel the actual race. And all the time, they know that those carbohydrates will not be enough. It is impossible for the human body to store enough fuel to run 26.2 miles. Every marathon runner is going to hit The Wall, the point where the stored fuel is gone and nothing is left but willpower and heart.

This, my friends, is what writing a novel is like. You must prepare yourself as well as you possibly can. Reading this book is one strategy, and I think it is an excellent one. (Obviously.) Reading novels written by others is another one, and so is reading background material that will help you make your story feel real. Making sure you have the right equipment—mainly, an adequate computer, an internet connection, and a quiet spot to sit—is important. Arranging to have the time to sit quietly in that spot is more of a problem for most people, but you need to do that and you know it.

Most of all, you need to mentally prepare yourself for those days when you want to write another page just about as much as a marathon runner on her nineteenth mile wants to pick her foot up one more time. You must prepare yourself for the time when you hit The Wall and you are dead-certain that you will not...you cannot...finish this book. When that happens, all you'll have is willpower and heart.

And, if you choose to think of it this way, you'll have this book and, by extension, me. Believe me when I say that I've spent time banging myself against that wall. Pick up this book and look for an essay that made you want to sit down and write something wonderful. Read it, then turn on your computer and write.

DAY 44—Check-in

It has been a week since you began drafting the first draft of your novel. (Less, if you're taking the fast train to a finished book.) We can quickly calculate that, after today, you will have written—-insert drum roll here—seven pages.

How'd you do?

DAY 45—Mary Anna's Random Writing Rule #1: Trust your instincts

It seems like a fine idea to throw random pearls of wisdom your way. As you're writing, those pearls might land in your hands at just the right time. Or they might arrive at the wrong time and bounce off your head, leaving you cranky and wondering why I'm bothering you when you're trying to get some work done. More likely, they won't arrive when you're desperately in need of that particular pearl of wisdom, but maybe you'll tuck them away for later, when you need them.

So what's today's random writing rule? Trust your instincts.

If you're like me, you sit down at the computer and scroll up a few pages, so that you can read your most recent stuff before launching into something new. As often as not, you'll hear a clunky word or an awkward phrase or (please let it not be so) a whole scene that just doesn't ring true, but you squint and rush past it. You're intent on writing something new. But you know what? Next time you read that passage, that word or phrase or scene will still sound terrible. Listen to your own writerly ear and fix it.

DAY 46—You are an artist. Write like one.

When I teach, I want my students to think of new ways to express their chosen art, fiction writing. Sometimes, I suggest that they look to other art forms to get another lens on the creative process.

Thinking about melodies and how they move people's souls will help you listen to the music in your prose. Song lyrics or poems will open your ears to your own rhythms.

A mental picture of dancing bodies will give your words motion and lightness. You want your words to leap across the page. Your readers' eyes should never plod.

A painting can be viewed as a whole in an instant, and a book can't. Even poetry can't be perceived at a glance...not even haiku. But, despite its immediacy, to truly appreciate a painting, it's necessary to stand in front of it and look at the details. The brush strokes, whether they be feathery and precise or whether they be great gobs of paint ladled on with a knife, were applied for a reason.

Spend some time in front of a painting and ask yourself where the artist spent the most time and attention. Ask yourself why he or she made that choice. Then apply the answer to your own work. What visual detail is so important to your story that you must spend precious words describing it? Because words are precious. Don't splatter them all over the page. Set them down gently, like diamonds in an antique brooch.

To me, the very definition of an art must involve the notion of communication. Artists communicate emotions that we all experience, but we're not all able to express them. That's why artists and their work have been valued since the first handprint was painted on a cave wall. Take yourself seriously as an artist, and consider how you will use the words that are your medium.

DAY 47—You're an artist. *Paint* like one.

As I read yesterday's essay about using the other arts to inform your fiction, I noticed an interesting omission that I want to remedy. I spoke with specificity about brushstrokes, likening them to the words that we writers use to paint our stories. Yet I said nothing about color.

Think about it. An artistically satisfying painting *can* be executed in black-and-white. The actual title of the famous painting *Whistler's Mother* is *Arrangement in Grey and Black: The Artist's Mother.* And yes, Whistler cheated by giving his mother natural Caucasian flesh tones, but I think his original statement stands. The subject of his painting did not require color, so he didn't use much of it.

But most paintings do require color to make their artists' points, so be aware of color in your work...color of all kinds. Physical color is important, yes—bold reds, brilliant fuchsias, soft lavenders, tender greens—but emotional color is important as well. When you write a scene that feels flat, ask yourself, "How can I give this *color?*" If you give your subconscious a chance, it might answer that question in a way that surprises you.

DAY 48—You have five senses for a reason

I love chocolate. This will be no surprise to anyone who has seen the stash of Hershey bars in my freezer. I've given Faye very few of my own traits, but she shares my love of chocolate, in general, and Hershey bars, in particular.

I've given Joe a notable knack in the kitchen and around the campfire. The man's an exceedingly fine cook, so I write occasional scenes that occur at the dining table. I try to refrain from describing every bite that goes in their mouths, because that would be boring, but I do like to use those scenes to engage my readers' sense of taste. At other times, I try to appeal to their noses. And at yet other times, I want them to hear and feel what my characters hear and feel.

It is very easy to fall into the trap of describing how a scene looks, then moving on. When I'm editing, I try to ask myself periodically, "When is the last time a viewpoint character has done anything besides *look* at the world?"

Let your readers feel the sand under their feet. Let them hear the sound a shovel makes as it shushes through that sand and makes the dead clink of bone-on-metal. Let them smell the rain as it approaches. And when your character unwraps a slab of chocolate, let your readers experience that first blast of nothing but sweetness, before the chocolate melts on their tongues, only to leave the faint gritty texture of cocoa behind.

DAY 49—Do you enjoy the process of writing?

The internet is full of sites for writers that trumpet some version of Red Smith's observation about the writing life: "All you do is sit down at a typewriter and open a vein."

When I see these people talking about the agony of living this life that I love, I have to wonder why they keep doing it. Passing few of us make a great deal of money. I, for one, am certain-sure that I could make far more money if I went out and got a real job using the Professional Engineer's license that I worked so hard to earn. Heck. I could probably make more money writing continuing education courses for people who want to keep those licenses. I like engineering work, but I love to write. I choose to do what I do.

I do understand the rationale behind comparing writing to opening a vein and bleeding all over the page. My characters' feelings can only come from inside me. In a way, I feel everything that happens in my books. The grief for a dead child. The fear that a murderer lurks behind a closed door. The knowledge that time is passing and age is creeping up behind me. The surge of joy at hearing words of love. I don't often re-read my books, but when I do, there are passages that make me cry, every time.

I find it rewarding to translate my own feelings into stories that generate those same feelings in my readers. If I found it too painful, I would go back to environmental consulting, which was rewarding in a different way. More to the point of this post, I enjoy the process of sitting down and spinning tales, all day and every day. If you don't, I advise you to get up and walk away. Even if your life's dream is to write a book, if you don't enjoy the doing of it, my advice is to find a new dream. Or, if that's too stark, scale your dream back and write short stories or poetry.

Life is too short to do things you don't enjoy.

DAY 50—If you're still reading after yesterday's observations...

...then I'm going to assume that you love this writing life as much as I do. Take a moment to be grateful that you have a chance to live it, then write today's page.

DAY 51—Check-in

Do you remember memorizing your multiplication tables, way back in third grade?

Please don't tell me that you grew up in the post-calculator years, and that you weren't required to learn your times tables. If so, take a break from you writing and repeat after me:

Seven times one is seven.

Seven times two is fourteen.

Seven times three is twenty-one.

Seven times four is twenty-eight.

Seven times five is thirty-five.

And so on, all the way up to this one:

Seven times thirty-nine is two hundred seventy-three. And our goal is two hundred seventy pages, which takes nine months at a page-a-day rate.

In less than thirty-nine weeks you'll have a book in your hand. No. Less than thirty-seven weeks, because you've already finished two weeks. That's about the length of an average pregnancy, so think of your book as your baby. (Which means that the 90-day sprinters among us must be very efficient at baby...I mean, book...production.)

Now...get back to work.

DAY 52—Give some thought to these first pages

Eventually, you're going to be able to look back at the opening pages of your book and gauge whether they launch the story in the direction you want it to go. In some ways, you can't be expected to know whether these first pages are the best they can be. Still, it wouldn't hurt to look at them with a critical eye.

Did you waste page 1 with a static description of the main character and his world? Does anything *happen* on page 1? What about Chapter 1? Does the story really begin pages later?

It's never too early to think about pacing. The goal of the opening pages is simply to make the reader keep the book open. After you write today's page, read what you've written so far and assess whether you've accomplished this goal.

DAY 53—More on pacing

My main purpose in outlining a book is to identify key scenes that will form the shape of the main plot. My outline also contains the key scenes that will support any subplots, but they must never take the focus away from the main narrative thread.

In most cases, a book will begin with one of those key scenes, so I assume that you have written that scene by now. Once it's finished, you need to look ahead and see the next scene coming. Will you reach it soon, or will you need to write several chapters before you can drop the next bombshell on your readers?

If the next big scene is going to take its sweet time in arriving, then you must guard against letting the pace sag in the meantime. This is why we have subplots. Consider introducing an important subplot now to perk up your readers' interest. If all goes well, you can place some of the subplot's big scenes into this dangerously slow passage.

Many writers, myself included, use the metaphor of braiding a strand of hair when we discuss the interweaving nature of a book's main plot and subplots. When deftly written, these storylines twist around one another, taking turns being front and center. When *very* deftly written, those storylines lead the reader through all those twists effortlessly, as if there could have been no other way for them to go.

DAY 54—Do you have one or more subplots so compelling that it will not annoy your reader when you divert their attention from the main storyline?

As I discussed yesterday, early in the novel-writing process, it is important to give serious thought to any subplots your story needs. This is one advantage to outlining. It is so much easier to see the shape of your story. You'll have a feel for where exciting scenes are needed to ramp up the tension, and you'll know where to put quieter scenes that develop character and make the dramatic scenes even more riveting by contrast. A subplot, designed so that its ebb and flow is roughly opposite to the pace of the main plot, can serve this purpose.

This is not to say that you should come up with a secondary plot that is completely separate from your main storyline. You don't want your reader to wonder what in the heck is going on. (Probably. Maybe that *is* your goal. Just make sure you're confusing your reader on purpose.)

A good subplot might flesh out an important secondary character. In a mystery, it might serve as a red herring, misdirecting a reader's attention away from the real killer. In a romance, it might narrate the relationship of the main character with a man who is completely wrong for her and who will not be her eventual One True Love. In a literary novel, it might be a flashback to an earlier incident in the main character's life, one that shaped the person she is today.

Take the opportunity to explore possible subplots now, early in the first draft. It's so much easier to make them an organic part of the book now than it will be later

DAY 55—I bet you're tired

Writing is probably the most sedentary profession there is. Why does sitting with a computer in my lap make me so darn tired?

I suggest that you get up and run around the block before you write today's page. Or, if you're like me, you can walk around the block. Getting some blood flow to your brain will help you concentrate when you get back. Really.

DAY 56—Mary Anna's Random Writing Rule #2: Choose your trusted readers wisely

All writers need someone to put an unbiased eye on our work. *All* of us. I'm serious about this. Nobody has the emotional distance necessary to be completely unbiased. Nobody.

Some people are lucky enough to have a spouse with good taste and fabulous grammatical skills and a rabid reader's eye for a spellbinding story. Some of us have friends like this. (I have children like this. Lucky me.) Some people skip this step and send unvetted manuscripts to their editors. (Now that's a scary thought.)

Some people swear by their writers' groups, saying that they would never have gotten published without the critique of their respected peers. In a well-run writers' group, that critique is delivered with the sensitivity and respect that an artist's soul requires. I can't stress enough how important this is. One mean-spirited member is all it takes to tear down the confidence of a vulnerable artist. Even a member with the best intentions is no help if that person's suggestions don't ring true to *you.*

The perfect critique partner could be at your workplace or online or at church. She could be your mother.

It may take you some time, but the search for the right trusted reader is worth it.

DAY 57—A caveat to that last recommendation

Writers' groups can be a lifeline, both professionally and socially. I've heard David Morell, author of many fine books including the one that launched Rambo on the world, say that television writers are virtually the only writers who do not write alone. I think he's correct. Even the people I know who collaborate work separately, passing the manuscript back and forth.

Writers' groups can fill that social hole. When they function well, they can also give the participants valuable feedback from their peers. Be aware, however, that there are many ways that they can function poorly.

A writer who has reached a higher skill level than the other members of a writers' group will give more than he receives, not because the other members don't wish to help him, but because they just can't. A writer who is too jealous or bitter to give constructive criticism can render the entire group nonfunctional. A writer who is not yet secure in his abilities will not be able to take well-intentioned criticism. Be aware of the interpersonal atmosphere of any group that you might consider joining.

Remain aware of your time commitment to any group you do join. If you are working through this book, one essay at a time, then you have made a commitment to yourself to write a page a day. Make sure that your obligation to critique the work of your fellow group members doesn't make this impossible. If it does, then consider joining a group after you've completed your first draft. A functional writers' group can be a godsend during the editing process.

Most of all, be true to your own vision. Constructive criticism can give you fresh insight into your work. Seek it out. Criticism that isn't helpful, however, can be safely discarded.

DAY 58—Check-in

You should be twenty-one pages along.

How are you doing?

DAY 59—Want to get this book published when you finally finish it? Get a cat.

A few weeks ago, I told you about my brief conversation with Corbin Bernsen, and I mentioned that on the day he and I were on the same television show (!), three of the other guests were representatives from the humane society: a human and two dogs. Or, come to think of it, maybe it was two cats, because the humane society was promoting their month-long two-for-one cat promotion special.

I think I saved a few kitty lives that evening when I spoke to the local Sisters in Crime chapter about how to start a career as a mystery writer. I told them that I had pursued publication for many years. (Many, many, many years. So many years that I'm pretty sure my sanity should be in question.)

Mystery readers and writers, I reminded them, are notorious for loving cats, yet I had always been a dog person. (Do you know how to distinguish a woman who loves her cats from a crazy cat lady? Crazy cat ladies kiss their cats on the mouth. Or so I'm told...I limit myself to nuzzling my kitty on the top of his adorable head and behind his sweet little ears.)

When my daughter turned seven, I caved in to her badgering for a pet. We went to the pet rescue place and brought home a gray tabby cat who had been born on the street and who now, many years later, still retains some of that bad-boy, streetwise attitude.

One month later—just one short month after I acquired the mystery writer's archetypal companion—I sold *Artifacts* to the wonderful folks at Poisoned Pen Press.

Coincidence? I think not. I told the lovely folks at the Sisters in Crime meeting who were hoping to sell their books to run, not walk, to the Humane Society and get a cat. Or even to get two, because the second one was free! I hope there are kitties living in lovely homes even now as a result.

My kitty loves it when we start a nice writing day. I feed him, stopping to pet him frequently because he's more interested in the petting than in the food and water. Then I get in the recliner where I always work, put my computer in my lap, then wait for the 14-pound cat that I *know* will launch himself into my lap and stand there, purring and blocking my access to the keyboard. I pet him for awhile, then he remembers that he's a cat and he's supposed to be aloof, so he jumps onto the floor and stalks away to do whatever it is cats do. (Right now, he's sleeping.) This is not a bad way for a writer to begin her day.

So let me take this opportunity to save a few more kitty lives. If you want to get published, go adopt a cat. Preferably two.

DAY 60—Things I've Already Said That Bear Repeating #1: Every scene must have a purpose

Every scene must have a reason for taking up space and wasting ink and consuming a reader's time. Let me say it yet again. Every scene must have a purpose.

It's even better when a scene has more than one purpose.

Your goal is to write a book so tight that no scene could possibly be removed. I read a book back in 1980s about a woman who ran away from her cheating husband. She ran away to a fabulous beach house, which I think is a very good place for a wounded wife to go. As I recall, a man from her past showed up there. I have no recollection why, but his arrival got the story rolling.

Unfortunately, every seventy-five pages or so, the author sent her main character out on the beach to look at the water. Each time, she made the woman—and thus, the reader—look at the water *for an entire page*. There was no purpose for these scenes, other than perhaps to illustrate that the poor woman was suffering and perhaps to demonstrate the author's powers of description. I learned to recognize these scenes and skip them.

As you write, presume I shall one day purchase and read your book. Please do not write any boring scenes that I'll be compelled to skip.

DAY 61—You saw this one coming, didn't you?

Print out the 25 pages you've already written. Read every scene and decide why it needs to be in the book. Take a red pen and write that reason (or those reasons) in the margin. Delete any pointless scenes, or rewrite them until they have a reason for being.

Now, place your marked-up manuscript next to your computer, so that it can remind you to keep those scenes useful and pertinent. And don't forget to write today's page. There will be times during the 270 days that you are writing your book that I tell you to print something out or to read back through a few chapters. Even if I don't say so, you still have your daily assignment of one page to do. There are a few days when I'll tell you to "Take a day off!", but you'll still need to make that page up sometime, if you're going to stick to the 270-pages-in-270-days schedule.

You can probably do that math yourself, but I thought I'd spell it out for you, just in case.

DAY 62—Now look at those scenes again

All I asked you to do yesterday was to print out your manuscript and decide whether every single scene needed to be there. Do you notice what I *didn't* ask you to do? I didn't ask you whether you were *missing* any scenes.

Do your best to wipe the storyline, as you know it to be, from your mind. Read those opening scenes as if you were coming to them for the first time. Are you left with questions like, "Who is this person and why is she in this story?" or "How did those people get from here to there?"

Be careful with how you choose to plug these plot holes. You may not need to create an entire scene giving the backstory for a character who is more mysterious than she needs to be. Maybe you do, or maybe just a sentence or two tucked into the scenes you've already written will tell your readers what they need to know. Similarly, you may not *need* to specify how your characters got from here to there. If you were to follow your protagonist's every step, from getting up to going to bed, your readers would be snoring before your character ever crawled beneath the covers. When you find an omission like this, just determine what it is that you neglected to communicate, then look for the most efficient and effective way to fix the problem.

DAY 63—You went to the trouble to print them out. Let's look at those scenes one more time.

Okay, yesterday and the day before, you looked at the scenes you've already written. You asked yourself whether they all needed to be there and whether they provided all the information that your reader needed to make sense of the narrative.

Today, I want you to play with them a little. Shuffle them around to make sure they're in the right order. One of the most common mistakes I see in early manuscripts is the inclusion of too much detail. The first scene is not necessarily the place to tell us about your protagonist's childhood trauma, although this worked brilliantly in the opening scene of Stieg Larsson's *The Girl Who Played with Fire*. It is not necessarily the place to tell us what he or she looks like, and it is almost certainly not the place to describe the interior of his or her home. If you find that the beginning of your book drags, consider whether you've weighted it down with too much information. Maybe those information-heavy scenes will work better if they occur later.

Conversely, did you save anything important or exciting for later, when you really should have used it to punch up the opening? Consider moving those scenes forward, so that you can grab your reader attention immediately.

DAY 64—Mary Anna's Random Writing Rule #3: Let your subconscious work

Maybe you're still having trouble getting some momentum going with this book. You're not sure what it's really about or you just can't get that first chapter the way you want it. Lay your fear down and walk away.

Am I telling you to stop writing? No. You need to make a routine appointment with your subconscious and you need to keep it. You need to condition yourself to feel the stories flow when you sit down at your computer. You need to hear your characters' voices in your ear when your hands rest on the keyboard. This will not happen if you are in front of the TV, nursing a beer and worrying over the book you're not writing. Even if you feel like you're typing drivel, I truly believe it will help your artistic process if you sit down and at least try to write, every single day. Hence, this book.

In the meantime, know that your subconscious does not wait for those daily appointments. It chews on your knotty plot problems and it spits out the answers while you are washing dishes or planting a garden or driving to work. I've said it before and I'll say it again: Trust the process.

Feed your subconscious the information it needs by reading about your story's setting or researching important plot points. Give your creative mind a chance to talk to you by sitting at the keyboard and typing something...anything...every day. Then be quiet and listen.

DAY 65—Check-in

You should be on or around page twenty-eight today. That's a chapter
by almost anyone's definition. If you're Dan Brown, it's a whole lotta
chapters.

My chapters tend to run in the vicinity of ten pages. I find that, on
the scale of a book-length manuscript, this gives me the rhythm that I
want. I am not so obsessive as to determine ahead of time which events
will occur in which chapters. I tend to write along until I finish a
particularly dramatic scene and think, "Hey! That would make a good
chapter break. I wonder if it's time."

Then I check back and see how long the current chapter is. If I'm in
the vicinity of ten pages, I break the chapter. If I'm still blathering on
after twenty pages, I'll go back to see if I need to find another dramatic
chapter break. If I'm only on the fifth page, then I'll usually keep going.
Truthfully, in an ideal world, every single scene would have an ending
that is dramatic in its perfection, so I'm okay with leaving that great
scene ending in the middle of a chapter.

On that rare occasion when I really feel strongly that *this* scene is so
key to the plot that it must end a chapter, then I go back and twiddle
with all the chapter breaks to make them come out right. Or I just
break the chapter after five pages and I don't worry about it. It's my
book. The chapters can be as long or short as I damn well please. But I
do make it a point to construct my chapters consciously, rather than
just starting a new one because I feel like it.

Bottom line—you can construct your chapters however you like,
and now you know all my secrets on this subject. Just make sure your
chapters are shaped the way you want them.

DAY 66—Work with discipline

By this point in the process, you will have noticed that a book is a huge,
monumental project. It is daunting. There's no way around it.
Discipline and consistency are the only way to tackle any large project,
be it a making a quilt or painting a house. You have to block out the
time required for the task, then you have to use it well.

There is a common theme in virtually all the things in my life that make me proud. The accomplishments that bring the most pride are the big ones, the ones that make me look back and say, "How in the world did I do that?"

Raising children.

Buying a house.

Learning to play a musical instrument.

Earning a college degree.

Writing a book.

Writing ten books.

The only way to do these things is to set short-term goals and summon the discipline to meet them. You have to say, "Today, I'm going to put 10% of my paycheck in a savings account." Or "Today, I'm going to practice piano for an hour." Or "Today, I'm going to start that term paper that is due next Tuesday."

Or, for you, "Today, I'm going to write at least one page of my book. Because Mary Anna told me to."

For me, right now, I can look at this book I'm writing as three-hundred-and-sixty-flippin'-five separate essays. What idiot would voluntarily take on such a project?

Um...that idiot would be me.

Every morning, I say to myself, "Today, I will write essays until I run out of ideas." (Because I don't want to take a year to write this thing, and also because this is my job and I have all day to do it.)

Now. Go write your page.

DAY 67—Things I've Already Said That Bear Repeating #2: Very, very few people are all bad

Several years ago, a friend told me that her editor had told her to write a serial killer book. She was three or four books into her mystery series, the editor thought it was time to do something a little different.

Serial killer books were hot and it would be easy to find a way for her series character, a private detective, to get crossways with a demented homicidal maniac.

My friend told me this with a sigh, and I wasn't sure why this was *such* terrible news. As we talked, my thoughts crystallized and I understood her pain.

If a writer is operating on the presumption that a serial killer kills because he (or she) is crazy, then what is there to write? There is no conflict. The book quickly devolves into fear, stalking, killing, and horror, over and over again, and it's all the same. There are obligatory flashbacks to terrible events in the killer's childhood that might explain the madness. The killings get more grisly, because there's no other way to ramp up tension, but honestly. The reader has been here before. Many times.

This question is not limited to mysteries. In any genre, it's so much better to craft an antagonist who is *not* crazy, then watch that person squirm under the pressure of justifying the unjustifiable. Give the reader a motive for wrongdoing that is at least a little understandable. Let that reader wonder whether he or she could be swayed by money or love or guilt.

Give your bad guy a good reason to be bad.

DAY 68—What's your excuse?

If you have not spent time every day for the past month working on your book, then you'd better have a good reason. And if I sound like your mother, good.

Nag over.

DAY 69—Write what you know?

Purveyors of popular wisdom have always told writers to "write what you know." It only makes sense. I would be hard-pressed to put myself in the shoes of a Japanese woman living under the American occupation after World War II, particularly if I were a novice writing my first book. For me, such a book would take a ton of research. It would be so much easier for me to write about a middle-aged woman watching her children grow up and start families of their own, because that's who I am. I could just skip all the research and launch right into telling my own story.

But I'm not writing my first book. I did that long ago. Did I write what I knew then?

When I began *Wounded Earth*, I was a 33-year-old mother of three, working as an environmental consultant. I took the write-what-you-know advice seriously and made my protagonist Larabeth McLeod an environmental consultant. This did not free me from research. In fact, writing about a scientist requires a degree of accuracy that many other occupations do not. I feel somewhat confident that, after a little research and after talking to a few people, I could fake a story about a teacher or a minister or a nurse or a cashier because I've spent a great deal of time watching them work and because much of their work involves interacting with people, which is a fairly transferable skill. Microbiology, on the other hand, is pretty incomprehensible to those of us who never studied it.

What was I thinking when I made Larabeth a microbiologist?

Larabeth differed from me in other, even more important ways. She was older by about ten years. She'd served in Vietnam. She'd given up a child for adoption. She was never-married. She'd founded a successful company. I could research the science behind her work as a microbiologist and environmental scientist, but I was going to have to look inside myself to write about living through a war and loneliness and the loss of a child.

Writing about such personal things is an act of empathy, and you can't research it, not unless you're writing an autobiography. I asked myself what it would feel like to know your daughter was walking around the world without you. I asked myself how a person could ever recover from serving in a bloody war. When I felt sure that I'd imagined those answers, I was ready to write Larabeth.

DAY 70—Write what you know, redux

Here is a question for the people who think we should only write about our own experience and knowledge: Am I allowed to write about men? Or people older than I am? Or people of other cultures or races?

I myself am monotonously Caucasian, as far as I know, so my books will lack diversity if I am not allowed to write about other races and cultures. I do not think that being female makes me monotonous, but if I am only allowed to write about people who have shared my experiences, my books are going to lack men, and that could turn monotonous. And, though I am no longer 25, I ain't 75, either. Sometimes, my stories require 75-year-old characters, or even 95-year-old characters. I think I have sufficient life experience to draw plausible conclusions about the life of an older person, and I'm perfectly willing to do book research and interviews. I think I would rephrase "Write what you know," to say, "Make sure you know something about what you write."

DAY 71—Write what you know, yet again

To date, I have written seven books about my series character Faye Longchamp, for a total of more than 650,000 words. She is an archaeologist, and the plots of all seven books are steeped in archaeology. Am I an archaeologist? Oh, heck no, but I love to read about what they do. I am not shy about dropping an email to an expert when I can't answer my questions through book research. I am serious about making my books as true-to-life as possible, while still making sure that they're entertaining. (I am well-aware that it is highly unlikely that Faye would find such significant artifacts so often and so quickly after beginning a job...but it is not impossible. This, dear reader, is why they call it fiction.)

A more sensitive issue on the "write what you know" scale is this: Faye is biracial, and I wear the whitest shade of makeup that Mary Kay manufactures. I realize that this leaves me open to the criticism that I could not possibly portray her life and her feelings accurately. Maybe that criticism would be deserved, and maybe not. I did not grow up in the South in the 1970s as a person of color, but I was there. I can imagine how difficult Faye's life must have been, and I think I have sufficient empathy to describe the pain she felt and to make her present-day actions appropriate, considering her personal history. Like any fiction writer, there are times when I am forced to use my imagination. And so should you be.

DAY 72—Check-in

You are on page thirty-five by now.

If you're not, type something. Even if it's wrong.

DAY 73—Why are you doing this?

You are at an interesting point in the writing of your book. You're starting to see the pages pile up—figuratively, since they're probably in your computer—but you're also starting to comprehend just how far away the finish line is.

Why are you doing this?

People who are successful in sticking with the writing life are people who love to spin stories, but there is more to it than that. I know many people who can *tell* fascinating tales, but they are so extraverted that nothing could compel them to choose to spend enough time alone to write a book. Successful novelists have a compulsion to see their words in print, both because they are lifelong booklovers who revere the object we call "book" and because they know that a written book will spread their stories to far more people than they could reach by sitting by campfires and telling tall tales.

Some people feel a need to get their stories written down, whether anyone ever reads them or not. These are the people who kept journals as teenagers and who wrote elaborate tales that they never let anyone see. If I am to be absolutely honest, I must tell you that I am not one of those people. If no one else is to read one of my stories, then I'd just as soon keep it in my head.

I can't tell you why I feel this way. I am a serious amateur classical pianist. I practice most days, and I'm always working on a piece that's probably too hard for me. It does not matter to me that few will ever hear one of those pieces outside my family members in my own living room. I play for the joy of being part of a work of art.

Why don't I approach my other art—fiction—in the same way? It isn't because I think my books are only worthwhile when someone wants to buy them.

Here's the only answer I have that makes any sense: I need a sense of communication with my readers. As I write, I need to think, "Wait until they get to *this* part! They'll never see it coming."

Even though this book isn't fiction, I've approached the writing of it in the same way, the only way I know. I imagine myself in conversation with you, my readers, and I do my best to share things that will be entertaining and valuable to you. Perhaps that's the answer to the question of "Why do I do this?"

I write because I want to connect with other people.

DAY 74—The most useful sense is common sense

Whether you are writing in the first person or the third person, or whether you're the unusual soul who is attempting to write an entire novel in the second person, you still must assume the personality and mentality of one or more characters in order to write fiction. (Notice that I used the word "characters" instead of "people." This is to prevent "gotcha" emails from people who are writing from the point-of-view of a great white shark or the West Wind. Please do not forget with whom you are dealing. I have a published book that includes a scene written from the point-of-view of the Mayan storm god Hurukan. Hurukan does not fit into the category of people, but if I had not found a way to assume his personality and mentality, then that scene would not have worked. Instead, Hurukan's cameo appearance routinely gets fan mail.)

When you are in the head of a person or a great white shark or a storm god, you must feel what that character feels, see what he sees, hear what he hears, taste what he tastes, smell what he smells and—

this is important—you must know what he knows. If you fail to understand what is in your character's mind, then his actions will be random and inconsistent.

If you want your character to do something unforgiveable, yet still remain a sympathetic character, then your reader must understand her reasons for that unforgivable act. If you need your very intelligent character to place himself in danger, then you can't accomplish this by having him do something very stupid. You have to make your reader understand the reasons for this fateful act. Maybe the character doesn't have sufficient information, so he blindly walks into danger. Maybe he knows full-well what he's doing, but he has no choice because his girlfriend has been kidnapped and there is no other way to save her.

People make mistakes all the time, but your reader will find it hard to retain sympathy for your character without a clear understanding of the reasons why. For God's sake, either give your characters some common sense, or establish from the outset that they ain't got any.

DAY 75—The past is never dead...it's not even past

I'll open with a special thanks to William Faulkner for the famous quote in today's essay title. Nobody understood the impact of the past on the present better than Mr. Faulkner.

Do you write historical fiction? Do you write stories that require you to write long flashbacks set in another time period? Do you write about people who have a past? Of course you do.

How do you incorporate a rich sense of history or of your characters' pasts into your story without stopping the plot cold? And where do you find those historical details?

The central problem to writing about the past is obvious: You weren't there. Do you try to duplicate the way people really spoke and acted? Or do you mimic modern readers' false impressions of the past?

A related problem is respect. If you use real people, how do you treat them respectfully? And I'm not just talking about individuals like, say, Grover Cleveland. When I used Choctaw history and folk tales in

Effigies, I had to be very conscious of how I would and would not be willing to muck about in their history and culture.

The behavior of women is of special note, because many of us use female protagonists. The vast majority of women in the past just didn't lead lives conducive to an interesting story. They were confined to rigid, limiting roles. The women who behaved differently paid a price. We almost have to take creative license in this area, but how much?

How do I apply this to our work as novelists?

My Faye Longchamp archaeological mysteries are set in the current-day, but they all feature plotlines that take place in the past. I accomplish this through flashbacks and by using the kind of written materials that archaeologists use for research—journals, letters, oral histories, folk tales, memoirs, maps, photos, books. This has proven to be a very rich and detailed way to bring the past alive, because when I quote from a journal or letter, I can let someone alive in 1798 speak in the first person, as if I've gone back into their time and shaken the dust off all those old things in their lives.

I have found it useful to look for real journals and letters and such, written during the time period of interest. There's a wonderful book called *Letters of a Nation* by Andrew Carroll that compiles letters from Americans of all walks of life for the entire life of our country. For a historical novelist working in the United States, it is an amazing resource.

The internet is a boon to writers like me. When I wanted to create a fictional priest for my sixth novel, *Strangers*, tending his flock in the vicinity of St. Augustine, Florida, in the late 16th century, a simple web search gave me a translation of the diary of the priest who actually traveled with the Spaniards who founded that city in 1565. The fact that I was able to read it instantaneously and for free, in the comfort of my home, still astonishes me.

Sometimes you do have to leave the house. Experts are notoriously thrilled to talk about the work they love so well. While writing *Strangers*, I spent a happy afternoon with St. Augustine's City Archaeologist, learning things about the city that I could never have gotten from a book.

To tell the story in *Floodgates* of the flood control system that failed so disastrously after Katrina, I read documents that were written to get that system on the National Historic Register and I read the study done by an independent panel of scientists and engineers to pinpoint what went so terribly wrong. I called experts. And I traveled to New Orleans to see the situation for myself. I do these things because it's important to me to get things right, and because I love doing it.

You're just setting your book up now. Give some thought to the history that brought your characters to this point. If you need to do some research, now's the time.

DAY 76—Never forget your protagonist's job

A protagonist is a hero, and a hero does what must be done. Never forget that.

DAY 77—Never forget what makes a villain a villain

A villain wants what he (or she) wants. A villain will stomp on other people to get it. A hero will not. Fortunately, in most books, the hero finds a way to win, despite this disadvantage.

DAY 78—Never forget why the protagonist and the antagonist are in the same book

Have you ever read a book and, as you were reading, you felt that the action didn't make sense? The bad guy kept doing terrible things to the good guy for no discernible reason. The good guy kept taking all that punishment, without rising up and taking a stand. Then, eventually, the good guy was triumphant and the bad guy was vanquished, but you just didn't really care all that much.

Where did that author go wrong? More importantly, where did the book go wrong?

The book went wrong when the author failed to establish a connection between the good guy and the bad guy. In those books, the hero is just the person who is unlucky enough to be standing within reach when the villain reaches for another victim.

Now, this format can certainly work. One need look no further for proof than *The Man Who Knew Too Much*, Hitchcock's classic film about a man whose only mistake was being in the wrong place at exactly the wrong time. Still, I think that personal conflict raises the stakes. Hannibal Lecter may be insane, but there are few sounds more personal and gut-freezing than Anthony Hopkins' portrayal of his greeting to the young FBI Agent Starling: "Good evening, Clarice."

Your villain need not be a cannibal for your reader to feel personal conflict at the core of your novel. The snobbish denizens of high society who stand between Elizabeth and Jane Bennet and true love in *Pride and Prejudice* hold a grudge against those two remarkable young women because they have the effrontery to want a happy life, despite their lower social position. That, ladies and gentlemen, is a personal conflict. Feel free to adapt it to your own opus, because jockeying for social position is a human pastime that will never end. I'm sure Miss Austen won't mind. Even in 1813, she knew how to craft a fictional conflict that has made readers care for two centuries and counting.

DAY 79—Check-in

How's it going? Do you have forty-two pages yet?

I think it's time for you to print them out and admire that big stack of paper. Then read those pages. I can almost guarantee that they'll read differently on paper than on your computer screen.

Don't do a full edit. Just read them quickly and see whether the pacing is brisk and whether you see any obvious plot holes. At this point, you should feel a story taking place, and that always feels good.

DAY 80—Things I've Already Said That Bear Repeating #3: Use all five senses.

Imagine that you're a small woman alone in a dark alley. You have already been spooked by a wadded-up piece of trash blowing past your feet. You hyperventilated when an emaciated cat scampered across your path. How would you react if someone walked up behind you and whispered in your ear?

You would probably jump out of your designer shoes, even if the voice was as familiar as your best friend's.

What if you could feel the warmth of the invisible speaker's breath on your cheek? What if you could smell his spearmint gum? What if his face brushed past your hair as he leaned in to whisper in your ear, and you could feel it stir?

The sense of sight is useful to a writer, but it is the least tactile and palpable and immediate. Remember to use all of a reader's senses to make your story come alive.

DAY 81—Nit-picky character naming issues

Upon opening a book, a reader is dumped into an unfamiliar world full of unfamiliar people. It behooves a writer to make this experience as easy as possible. A quick-but-memorable description of the setting is important. So are quick-but-memorable descriptions of characters who have distinguishable names. I know you've read books where this wasn't done well. You know...the kind of books where you're on page 72, but you're still trying to figure out who's talking.

I had a writing teacher who kept a list of every character in her book, no matter how minor, and she refused to give any of them names that started with the same letter. I have not adopted this rule, since it seems to me that once you have more than, say, ten characters or so, you could find yourself painted into a corner with some unattractive options. I don't want to be forced to name a character Opal or Zelda or Xerxes because all the good letters are already taken.

Still, I do pay attention to her rule, even when I break it. In a couple of books I have both a Joe and a Jodi. I satisfied myself that they were clearly distinguishable people, then I let them keep the names they needed to have. Nevertheless, in my series of mysteries about a woman named Faye, I doubt I will ever have a character named Farrah or Faith.

There are other situations that can create character confusion, and one of them is cultural. A character in *Relics* has the surname of

Martinez. I would likely not include another character named Hernandez in that book. They are very different names, but I would worry that they might look a little too similar to English-speakers, and I have many other names of Spanish derivation at my disposal that do not end in "ez."

When you introduce a character, you have a lot of work ahead of you to make that character feel real. Don't make your job even harder by choosing a name that doesn't stand out in the crowd.

DAY 82—Does your book have a name yet?

I know people who can write an entire book without giving it a name. They do this routinely.

I, on the other hand, must name it before I start writing. I *must*. A book is an amorphous thing, a mere idea, until I make it real with a title. Therefore, my pre-book conversations with the editor for my Faye Longchamp mysteries follow a typical pattern. We discuss where Faye will be taking her archaeological skills next. This brings us to a cursory discussion of the history of the area, as it pertains to Faye's work. If there is no archaeology to be done in...say...Peoria, then I can't send Faye there to excavate. Fortunately, there's history everywhere and there is archaeology everywhere. If I can find a way to incorporate the history and archaeology of Peoria into an engrossing mystery, then I can set a book there.

After settling on a location, my editor and I talk about what will be going on in Faye's personal life. I decided early on that I would age her in real time. She was an unmarried 34-year-old college dropout in *Artifacts*. Over the course of the series, she has gone back to school, earned three college degrees, dated some losers, dated a nice man who wasn't right for her, married a man who *was* right for her, started a business, and become a mother. I think the fact that I have given Faye a life other than stumbling over dead bodies is the reason people relate to her.

Once we have established these things, I'm ready to give the book a name. My Faye books have one-word titles, which means that I must come up with a single perfect word. I can use longer titles for my other work, and I do, but I still gravitate toward short, pithy, and memorable. "A Singularly Unsuitable Word" is the exception that proves my story-naming rule.

I make a list of candidates, then I comb the internet for references to other books with the same title. Nobody can copyright a title, but it would be silly to name my next book *Anna Karenina* and think that I might be fooling someone.

When the right title crosses my mind, I know it. It "feels" like the book I have in mind. I've never had a publisher force me to rename a book, which is a good thing. I can only imagine that it would be like someone telling you that you had to stop calling your 1-year-old child Rachel and start calling her Rebecca.

DAY 83—A book-naming secret

Two of my books were named before I even knew what they were about. Can you guess which ones they were? I'll tell you tomorrow.

DAY 84—The book-naming answer, Part 1

Effigies and *Findings* are the books I named, sight-unseen. I'll tell you the story behind *Effigies'* title today. Tomorrow, you'll get my rationale behind naming a book *Findings*.

Effigies came about because my agent suggested that I peruse an archaeological dictionary for possible future book titles. Then she asked me to put together a couple paragraphs of synopsis for five or six future books, in case she needed them to prove to an editor that I was no flash-in-the-pan. (That was easy for *her* to say. I'd like to see *her* try to come up with ideas for five or six books, all at once and on command.)

One of the titles that emerged from the archaeological dictionary exercise was *Effigies*. I like my titles to relate to my stories in multiple ways. One definition of "effigy" might be "a physical model or representation of a person or animal." Other definitions might refer to the representation as "crude." Sometimes the word is used in the sense of "hanging someone in effigy" or "burning someone in effigy," which would mean that a crude model of a person had been hung or burned in a public display of contempt.

With those images in my mind, I wrote a book about archaeologists who are excavating at a mound built by ancient Americans. There is some possibility that it might be an effigy of a bird, which would be academically noteworthy and pretty darn cool, but they're not sure. Later, they find tiny beads, carved as effigies of eagles.

In another subplot, an elderly man has come home to Mississippi, after a long and successful life elsewhere, because he needs to seek justice for a near-lynching decades before. Although he escaped that fate, I would say that a lynching victim, hanging dead from a tree, is the tragic and real-life manifestation of the mob mentality involved in hanging someone in effigy. It's a subtle reference, and not something that I expect all readers to get from the story, but it was an important image in my mind as I wrote.

The word "effigies" reminded me as I wrote that not all mobs stop with building a straw man and hanging it. Sometimes they destroy real people. I think that keeping that subliminal image in my head, every time I thought of the book as *Effigies*, made it a better book.

DAY 85—The book-naming answer, Part 2

While I was writing *Effigies*, my friend Julie told me that she thought that *Findings* would be a cool name for one of my books. Archaeologists find things. We don't ordinarily use the word in this way, but one name for the artifacts and bones and historically significant debris found by archaeologists could be "findings." And, as she pointed out, "findings" is also the name for a very specific part of some pieces of jewelry.

A finding is the small device, usually wire, that attaches one part of a piece of jewelry to another. It might, for instance, attach a gemstone to a chain, thus making a necklace with a pendant. Those of you who have read *Findings* will know that I took this definition and ran with it. Faye finds a finding that will lead to murder, and it also leads her to the fate of one of our country's more famous missing hoards of treasure. The big honkin' emerald that was originally associated with that finding occupies a prominent place on the cover of *Findings*, and it belongs there.

Every time I do a web search for this book, I am reminded of yet another definition for "findings." Scientists write reports describing their findings all the time, so searching for "findings" and "Evans" gives me the results of every piece of research ever done by someone with my very common surname. Since the plot of *Findings* involves the theft of Faye's field notes, this gives yet another satisfying reason for me to feel that I chose the right name for that book. If my publisher had asked me to change it to...um...*Emeralds*, I would have been confused forever.

DAY 86—Check-in

You should have 49 pages by now. In other words, you're knocking on the door of the half-century mark. How cool is that?

DAY 87—By the time you get to page 50, you should have...

...introduced all your major characters, unless you have a fabulous reason for holding someone in reserve. (Few reasons are as fabulous as you think.)

...generated some serious conflict or drama. (In other words, something must have happened.)

...communicated to the reader where and when the action is taking place.

...foreshadowed the journey that your protagonist must take.

...initiated at least one subplot to provide depth and variety to the narrative.

DAY 88—My mind keeps wandering back to titles

A couple of days ago, I told you about the two books that I named before I'd even decided what they were going to be about. That's unusual for me. For me, the sequence of naming a book or story usually goes like this: Decide what it's going to be about, name it, then write it.

Artifacts got its name very early. I was inspired by a James Michener book I loved as a teenager called *The Source*. It features a group of archaeologists and tells their modern-day story, then it flashes back in time to tell the stories behind the artifacts they dug up. I've never quite used that exact structure. The backstories in the Faye books tend to focus on the documents she uncovers in her research—journals, letters, oral histories, and such. Still, the artifacts are central enough to the plot that the title just seemed to be a natural fit, and I like the fact that "artifacts" means made by human hands.

Relics seemed to be a natural follow-up to *Artifacts*, in terms of titles. It also works very well with the plot, which features a relic population of multiracial people tucked away in a remote valley in Alabama.

Coming up with a title to *Floodgates* took some serious thinking on my part, followed up by some serious discussions with my editor. The disaster following Hurricane Katrina forms the backdrop of the story, so it seemed worthwhile to acknowledge the storm in the title. I rejected *Deluges* as hard to say. I considered *Maelstrom*, but realized that I'd be spelling it and defining it for people from now on, forever. (I have that problem with *Effigies*, to an extent.) I knew that the engineers who designed the levees and canals and dikes and pumps that made New Orleans possible would play a large role in the story, and one day the word *Floodgates* just came to me, and I knew it was right.

My editor Barbara, who did not have the advantage of knowing what I was planning to do with the story, did not like the title. We discussed it for a while, then Barbara told me to go write a hundred pages and send it to her. She said we'd talk again after that. After Barbara saw those hundred pages, she said, "I see where you're going with this. I like the title now. Carry on." So I did.

Strangers wasn't easy to title, either, until I read a history of St. Augustine, where the book is set. St. Augustine has been a tourist town for a long, long time, before the word "tourist" was used as commonly as it is now. The locals used the word "stranger" for these people who came to town to *see* the town, rather than for reasonable reasons like to visit kinfolk or to do business. A significant subplot of the book deals with the arrival of Spaniards in the Americas. When it occurred to me that, in the sixteenth century, Europeans in the New World were the ultimate strangers, I knew that my book had a name.

My most recent book, *Plunder*, is set in south Louisiana, during the time between the moment the Deepwater Horizon exploded and the moment all that oil started washing ashore. I thought of how many profiteering corporations and individuals had made money at the expense of the environment and the people in that part of the world, then I thought about the word "profiteer" and remembered that pirates had plied these waters long before BP and all the other oil companies arrived. I knew immediately that pirates would inhabit this book, and I knew that there could be no other title but *Plunder*.

DAY 89—What about your title?

Does your book has a title that speaks to you? Does it capture the essence of what you're trying to say? When it is splashed across the cover of a book, will it sell copies? Do you need to rethink your title?

DAY 90—Three nags for you. Take your pick.

If you're writing every day, you can skip this. If not, these nags are for you. They begin with a nudge so gentle that it could come from your elderly grandmother, and they end with the kick in your pants that could only come from your best friend. Or from me. Choose the one that works for you. You're welcome.

"You look tired, dear. You should leave the dishes in the sink and work on your book instead."

"How are you doing on your book? What? You're falling behind the pace? Well, nobody's going to set your priorities but you. Turn on your computer and write until you catch up on your pages."

"You lazy bum! What's more important...your book or the fate of the tone-deaf contestants on *American Idol*? You know how to operate a remote. Turn off the TV and get to work before I send Simon Cowell over there to insult you properly."

DAY 91—Things I've Already Said That Bear Repeating #4: What does your story need?

Much ink has been spilled—or perhaps I should acknowledge current technology by saying, "Much ink has been jetted"—in attempts to define a story. Well, a story is many things working together. Character, setting, plot, and style all work together in service of storytelling. But I didn't ask "What is a story?" up there in the title line. I asked, "What does your story need?"

Well, it needs a lot of things. One of them, which I laid out for you back on Day 32, is important enough that I'm going to repeat it, now that you're well into the development of your own story:

A story requires a change in the protagonist, however slight.

You're more than fifty pages into your story now, so it's time to revisit that rule. Do you know how the events of this story are going to change your protagonist? If not, now's the time to figure it out.

DAY 92—How will your protagonist change?

Yesterday, I reminded you of my belief that a story requires a change in the protagonist, however slight. Did you check your own story arc? Are you satisfied with your plan for the course of your protagonist's development? If not, here are some thoughts. Your character could...

...find love or lose love.

...achieve professional success on a grand scale or find success through making a single small but important sale.

...learn something wonderful or horrible about himself or herself.

...learn what it means to be an adult. (Yes, it's hackneyed, but excruciatingly well-regarded literary novels are still being written with this theme, and they always will be.)

...commit a huge sacrifice because it is the right thing to do, or fail to do so.

...finally, after a lifetime of struggling, achieve a tiny sliver of wisdom.

...find the One Ring to Rule Them All or perhaps simply find a lost puppy shivering in the night.

It does not really matter how your character changes. Your job is to convince your readers to care about it.

DAY 93—Check-in

I won't mince words. What page are you on? Fifty-six? Write hard today, because tomorrow we're talking about dirty words. Soon thereafter, we'll talk about sex. You don't want to miss that, do you?

DAY 94—Dirty words happen

Have you given conscious thought as to how you will deal—or not deal—with adult language in your novel? Does your subject matter answer that question for you? In that respect, people who write for young people are lucky. So are people who write about the underbelly of prison culture. The rest of us live somewhere in between, and we have to make the decision of just how many dirty words we're willing to type without donning rubber gloves.

How do you feel when you're reading a mystery and a character lets a really foul word fly? Does it upset you? Or do you sigh in relief, certain that you're reading a book with the appropriate level of literary maturity?

For the record, I'll say that I think the language in my books is remarkably mild, but every word isn't squeaky clean. People who are in danger for their lives tend to express themselves strongly. On the other hand, I don't write about desperate citizens on the mean streets who use the saltiest of language before they eat breakfast. I write about academics and scientists. Many of my characters are churchgoing rural Southerners. I'd certainly never claim that these types of people don't curse, but their speech patterns are quite different from your average pimp. (Well, I've never actually met a pimp, but I do have an imagination.)

Yet I still catch flak from some readers who are upset when one of my characters takes God's name in vain. Or from teachers pleading with me to keep the content appropriate for their students. Or from people who think my work can't possibly be serious if it doesn't use words so foul that they'd make your grandmother's eyes bleed.

Probably the vilest word I've ever used in print was not a profanity nor an obscenity, but a racial slur. Because I believe in the power of words, I will not repeat it here, but it carried a powerful message in the context that it was used. In this scene, a man informed another man that he would be blackmailing him for the rest of his life, and that he would get away with it because he was white and the other man was black. A scene like that should leave an indelible image. When I ended the conversation by having him call the man by a very old and derogatory term, the intent was to seal the reader's image of the speaker's character. I think it worked. I have never once been called to account for the use of that word.

On a less serious note, I had a little fun with the issue of dirty words in a short story called "A Singularly Unsuitable Word," which I wrote for an anthology called *A Kudzu Christmas*. (And which is now available in ebook form as a standalone story, or as part of my collection *Jewel Box*.)

The premise of the story was that a little girl had witnessed a murder committed by a leading citizen of her small town. No one is willing to convict the man based on her word...until she gives her account of the crime, which includes a terrible word that no one of her age could possibly know. (Sadly, I had to set the story in the 1930s to make this part plausible.) Because the story is told from the point-of-view of the protagonist in old age, we learn that she has flatly refused to say the word ever since...which means that she can't say it while narrating the story, but the astute reader should be able to put two and two together. (It rhymes with "love your truck" and it is a major violation of the commandment against honoring your mother.)

In the end, I think the use of strong language in literature is a creative decision best left to the writer. I don't, however, think that the lack of such language automatically points to a lack of sophistication on the part of the writer or of the readers who enjoy the work. The most important thing is to tell the story you must tell, using the best words possible for the job.

DAY 95—Tomorrow...

...we talk about sex. Write hard today, so you won't be too stressed to enjoy it.

DAY 96—We think about it. We do it. We don't talk about it much. Should we write about it?

Yesterday, I brought up the delicate subject of foul language in mysteries. Emboldened, I thought I'd move on to an even more delicate subject...human sexual activity. Oh, boy...

Not that such activity is new. On the contrary, along with eating and drinking and sleeping and breathing, it is one of the oldest human habits. And not that such activity is new in fiction. If my memory serves, in *The Maltese Falcon*, Sam Spade is established at the outset to be sleeping with his partner's wife, and he beds Bridget at the earliest opportunity. The modern approach simply delivers more details.

As I see it, there's room for great variation on this topic. (Oh, stop. I know what you're thinking. I'm talking about literary variation here.) There are stories with breathless, heart-stopping plots that simply do not allow time for the principal parties to stop running for their lives in order to get up close and personal. This does not mean that the story is not written for adults. It simply means that adults cram a lot of activity into their lives and all of that activity can't be sexual.

My books, so far, have fallen into this category. Faye meets men. She dates. But by the time she might be thinking about a little intimacy, she's generally in mortal peril. The next book may be different. I don't know yet. But I'm not planning to stick in a sex scene that doesn't fit, just to prove I know how certain anatomical parts work.

Some books, on the other hand, just scream out for an R rating. If your heroine is a hooker, well, she just might find time in her busy schedule for a little money-making activity. If you're writing a serious exploration of the consequences of rape, or a light-hearted caper starring a studly young jewel thief...well, I won't write your book for you, but I can think of some incredibly effective ways to use sex to construct stories like those.

An interesting offshoot of any discussion about sex in books is the issue of reader expectations. There is no ratings system for books. Parents wring their hands when their children who read at an advanced level venture out of the YA section, but what's to be done about that?

Some clues to a book's content can be inferred from the cover art and the dustjacket text, but if you haven't read a book, you really don't know what your child might encounter between its covers. A good bookseller or librarian will have many suggestions for precocious readers, but we're not all lucky enough to have those in our lives.

And ideas about what is appropriate for young readers change. A few years ago, I saw *Stranger in a Strange Land* on my high schooler's summer reading list. Let's see. That book is about free love and cannibalism. If I recall correctly, there is group sex involved. I read it when I was in my twenties and married, and I wasn't sure I was even old enough then. But it was a great book that left me with substantive ideas to think about. I'm glad nobody censored it, and I'm glad it's available for people to read and discuss. How do we decide whether *Stranger in a Strange Land*, or any other book, is appropriate for young readers? Heck if I know, but I do think we should keep asking such questions.

Think back to books you've read that did sex particularly well or particularly poorly. Why did those stories work or not work for you?

Did the sex scenes enhance the book? Did they slow down the story? Did there seem to be a reason, beyond the prurient, for them to be there? And do you find books with no sex in them boring or childish?

The next time I have a free moment, I have my eye on a mystery I'd like to read. I have absolutely no idea whether there are any sex scenes in it. The anticipation is killing me.

DAY 97—Mary Anna's Random Writing Rule #4: People need to eat

People eat several times a day. If your frenetic plot doesn't leave time for eating, at least make sure your characters notice...and that they complain. You would.

DAY 98—Mary Anna's Random Writing Rule #5: People do other things

I don't insist that you tell me whenever your characters go to the bathroom, but if you trap them in a confined space for days, be prepared to address the problem somehow.

DAY 99—The Page 69 Test

I'm told that some discriminating readers employ a terrifying strategy for choosing which book on a bookstore's groaning shelves to buy. They open a book, read page 69 totally out of context, then decide whether the writer and her work is worth their time. A couple of years ago, I was asked by Marshal Zeringue, who runs several literature-related blogs, including *Campaign for the American Reader*, whether I'd be willing to contribute to a blog called *The Page 69 Test* by writing an essay about page 69 of my new book, *Floodgates.* I said yes without checking page 69, then I regretted it. What if page 69 turned out to be inane?

You will reach page 69 in *your* book in just a few days. In honor of that accomplishment, I'll publish the essays I wrote for Marshal about page 69 of *Floodgates* and *Strangers*, right after our weekly check-in. I hope your own page 69 is splendorous.

DAY 100—Check-in

Nine times seven is sixty-three. That means you'll reach page 69 sometime this week, and someday somebody standing in a bookstore will judge your entire book on its basis. Try not to let this bother you.

DAY 101—*Floodgates*: The Page 69 Test

Any writer aware of The Page 69 Test who will not confess to feeling a chilly hand on the nape of the neck while scanning that page is a bald-faced liar or an egomaniac.

Listen to my thoughts while flipping open *Floodgates*: "What if I indulged myself in two full manuscript pages of aimless musing? What if my characters are eating breakfast and I spent the entirety of page 69 documenting the crispness of the bacon?"

Imagine my relief at finding that page 69 opens with my protagonists, Faye and Joe, talking with the detective who has hired them as archaeological consultants to an unusual murder case. Joe has just made an excellent point.

True to form, quick-witted Faye has interrupted him in mid-thought. But at least she's self-aware enough to realize that, "...once again, Joe was thinking of people and she was thinking of reasons. She then reflected that if Joe intended to talk at any time, for the rest of his life, then his wife-to-be would be smart to buy herself a muzzle—before he bought one and strapped it on her."

More conversation follows, then all three characters bend over some important evidence, two photographs found folded in the pocket of the victim, Shelly. They are aerial photos of Shelly's New Orleans neighborhood, one taken sometime before Katrina struck and one taken immediately after.

Joe's response to a scene that I describe as "a dark and tragic stain" is the only appropriate one, just a hushed whisper that says, "Look at all that water."

In stark contrast, the older photo shows "regular, everyday, dry city streets full of cars, signifying that day-to-day life was proceeding as usual. There were no tarps on roofs nor any swaths of empty land, where the houses that should have been there had been washed away."

After a moment of staring at the enormity of what happened to New Orleans in 2005, Joe brings the conversation back to the murder but, as Joe always will, he does it in human terms. He wants to know why Shelly was carrying before-and-after photos of Lakeview, when her body was found miles away, in the Lower Ninth Ward.

To tell you more of the story, I'd have to turn to page 70, and that's not what this essay is about. Nevertheless, page 69 holds key fragments of the story I set out to tell in *Floodgates*. It's the story of real people who love each other and laugh and work hard, but who are completely unable to grasp the full scope of a drowned city ... an American city, a city full of people just like the rest of us.

In *Floodgates*, I try to show you that immense tragedy but, in the end, it's far easier to feel real, personal grief for a single person. So I've given you Faye and Joe and Jodi and their search for justice for Shelly, a woman who died trying to save people she loved and people she never even met. And all the while, Shelly was carrying a photo of her drowned home in the pocket of her wet blue jeans.

DAY 102—*Strangers:* The Page 69 Test

Ahhhh...the Page 69 Test. It's terrifying. What if every word on the page is insipid? What if you've devoted half the page to ruminating on your character's bedtime snack? Um...well...that's what I did. But I had a good reason. Let's look at Faye and that bedtime snack.

> [Faye] was curled up in bed in front of the TV, her head on Joe's shoulder and a chunk of blueberry coffeecake on a plate in her lap. More accurately, the plate was sort of balanced on her belly, because she couldn't actually see her lap any more. Even

more accurately, the blueberry coffeecake was crowned with a dollop of ice cream, thanks to Suzanne's amply stocked kitchen.

The coffeecake was so good that she wanted to grab it with both hands and shove it into her mouth all at once.

So why would I risk enticing my readers to put down the book and go get some blueberry coffeecake? (And if you're doing that right now, don't forget the ice cream.) Because Faye has had a harrowing day that included the kidnapping of a young woman named Glynis, who is in one of life's most vulnerable conditions—pregnancy. And because Faye is in that condition herself.

So go get some ice cream and we'll continue this Page 69 essay tomorrow.

DAY 103—Page 69 of *Strangers:* Why is she eating coffeecake?

Constant intensity doesn't work for me, plot-wise. It leaves me numb. It diminishes the drama of things that are to come, and this is only page 69. I felt that the story needed a quiet moment to punctuate the action. Before Faye finishes her page 69 coffeecake, she and her husband are going to argue over her willingness to work too hard and to put herself at risk while she herself is pregnant. By the time she's ready for another before-bed snack, she will have looked into the face of a man whose throat was slashed before he was dumped into the Matanzas River.

It is no accident that I showed you Faye balancing that plate on her big belly. Any woman who has ever been eight months pregnant will read that scene and remember how it feels to be bloated and heavy and ravenous and exhausted. By the end of the book, even my male readers will know how it feels, too, if I've done my job right. And anyone with a heart will be deeply concerned for Faye and Glynis, as they struggle to protect their unborn children and themselves.

But the blueberry coffeecake incident only occupies the second half of page 69. What else did I do with that page? Well...an ancient and probably homeless old man named Victor gives Faye a dime. Why? Well, I had my reasons.

She glanced down at the coin on her palm. It was a dime, but the gleam of the sun on its worn surface was all wrong.

Looking more closely, she saw why the light reflected strangely from the dime. It was silver.

Minted in 1941, Faye's gift coin was a Mercury dime, adorned with the head of Liberty wearing a winged cap. Looking over Joe's shoulder, she saw that he'd gotten a modern Roosevelt dime, while Levon held an older Roosevelt dime, also with the unmistakable sheen of silver.

"He does that...gives away dimes, I mean," Suzanne said. "The cook grew up here, and she says he's done that for as long as she remembers."

So what was I doing here? Well, Victor and his dimes serve the story in some important ways. Victor is old and mysterious and child-like, but his inappropriate outbursts carry important information. It's just too bad that the highly competent and far younger people who hear those outbursts don't understand what he's telling them. There's a reason Victor gives away dimes, and there's a reason the dates on his dimes span the twentieth century. There's a reason he hangs around the mansion where Faye is excavating, Dunkirk Manor, telling tales about the glittering people who lived there. Victor has seen a lot in his 90-plus years, and he's trying to find someone who will listen to an old and destitute man who's apparently unbalanced. When Faye finally figures out what Victor is saying, she'll learn a lot about the people who lived and died at Dunkirk Manor. Until then, she'll have to content herself with admiring the play of sunlight on her dime's burnished face, loving its worn beauty as only an archaeologist can.

I could tell you the things that Victor knows, but then I'd have to kill you. Far better for you to follow along with Faye as she unravels his hints and clues and ravings, looking for the truth about a haunted beauty and a murdered silent movie starlet and the man who loved them both.

DAY 104—Try not to think about…

…what you're going to say on your own page 69.

DAY 105—Have I nagged you lately?

You know you've got a weekly check-in coming up in two days. Are you behind the pace? What are you going to do about it?

Tell your children to go eat a carrot and a cheese stick, and you'll get them their supper in an hour. They will survive for that long. My children have all survived to a healthy adulthood.

Tell your cat that his litter box can wait until you finish this page, but don't make him wait any longer than that. Cats have claws.

Remind your spouse of that "in sickness and in health" clause, and make the case that the need to write a book is a form of mental illness. Then achieve today's goal quickly and go snuggle with him/her, because I do not want any divorces on my conscience.

A page a day…three pages a day…it's not that hard. Go do it.

DAY 106—What did I say yesterday?

Yesterday, my daily essay ended with "A page a day…three pages a day…it's not that hard. Go do it."

Perhaps you read that and thought grumpily, "Easy for her to say. She's forgotten how hard this is."

Well, maybe I haven't. And maybe today I want to eat those words.

(Mmmm…printer ink is so tasty! And pixel photons are even better!)

Maybe I do have eight novels under my belt, but I haven't written a single how-to-write book before now. Last year, I co-wrote a book on mathematical literacy. Had I ever written non-fiction for an educational audience? Nope.

Right now, I'm splitting my time between writing this book and editing a collection of my short stories. (It's called *Jewel Box*. It's a lot closer to finished than this opus, so if you're reading this, then I presume *Jewel Box* is done, too. Yay!) Have I ever done either of these things before? Nope.

Writing this book, in particular, is a very interesting experience, because the writing process I'm suggesting to you is the one I'm using right now. I'm writing a book constructed in 365 bite-sized chunks. Every day, I write one or three (or seven, because this is my full-time job and I want to finish this thing) essays.

There are days when I think, "Three-hundred-and-sixty-flippin'-five essays? What was I thinking? I will *never* finish this. Never. Besides, I don't have that much to say."

But I do. Being a novelist means that I never get finished talking. Being long-winded is an important part of how I'm made. Every day, I wake up and find that I have something else to say, so I come to this computer and I write it down.

It's not so different from what you're doing. As I see it, we're all in this together.

DAY 107—Check-in

Seventy pages. Did you get there?

If not, you know what to do.

If so, take a deep breath and enjoy the moment, because I'm going to spend all of next week on something so nit-picky and precise that it may try your patience. Tomorrow, we begin Punctuation Week.

So polish off your commas and make sure you know how to use them, and put most of your exclamation points in the bank, because I'm not going to let you use very many of them.

Punctuation Week...I'm so excited. Now you know exactly how much of a grammar nerd that I really am.

DAY 108—Punctuation Week: Because the devil is in the details

If you have the slightest lack of confidence in your punctuation skills, get yourself a grammar book and do what you need to do. Don't give an agent or editor or reader a chance to reject your work based on something that has nothing to do with the entertainment level of your story.

You should also have a style manual to help you decide what to do with text that is in that gray area where something can be technically correct, yet still look and sound terrible. I believe publishers of fiction generally use some adaptation of *The Chicago Manual of Style*. Even if they do not, if you adhere to this manual, you will not look ignorant. Your editor will gently say, "This is the way we do things here," and then you'll adapt.

DAY 109—Punctuation Week: Leave your semicolons at home

I like semicolons. I use them in nonfiction, because there are times when I have two ideas that I want to shoehorn into one sentence to serve my point. When it weakens that point to separate those ideas with a conjunction, I use a semi-colon, because that is why God gave them to us.

I do not use semicolons when they are not warranted in order to make myself look smart. (You've seen people do that. Don't tell me you haven't. If you've ever been guilty of this, keep it to yourself and, please, don't ever do it again.)

Despite my affection for semicolons, I do not believe they belong in fiction. There is always a semicolon-less way to say the same thing, and I think they distract from the narrative. In fiction, semicolons call attention to themselves, and you don't want that. You want your punctuation to be invisible, acting only in service of your story. Readers notice fancy punctuation, just as they notice incorrect punctuation. Neither of these things has any impact whatsoever in the imaginative quality of your story, but they can make a reader stop reading and think, "A semicolon. Is that right?"

Stick to invisible punctuation.

DAY 110—Punctuation Week: Leave your exclamation points at home, too

I will pull no punches here. There are passing few valid reasons for using exclamation points in fiction.

There are occasional lines of dialogue that might benefit from an exclamation point. It might be a valid choice to write something like this:

"The house is on fire! Go get the baby!"

Tell the truth, though. Is that the best you can do? Try this instead:

Anne woke to the fire alarm's insistent shriek. The air on her face delivered heat and pain, and her throat burned. Tom's voice rasped in her ear as he squeezed a few quiet words past his own seared vocal cords.

"I'll get the twins. You get the baby. If you're not out in five minutes, I'm coming back in for you."

As for putting exclamation points in narrative passages...just don't. You'll sound like a teenaged girl writing in her diary. I'm not sure I can even imagine a good enough reason to do that, so I'm not even going to try, but here's an example to bear in mind if you're ever tempted to slip one in.

My flatiron spazzed out again and it rained yesterday and my hair is so frizzy that I want to fall in a deep hole! On top of that, I think I grew three inches this week, because my jeans are so much too short, and I know what Angelique and the popular kids are going to say about that! And now I'm standing in chem lab, wishing for death (or at least a coma) because the most beautiful man ever born is sitting at my lab station!

DAY 111—Punctuation Week: Standing firm for the serial comma

In a list of three or more items, you're going to have to use at least one comma. You always need to use a comma to separate items that are not separated by a conjunction. There is a difference in opinion as to whether a comma is also needed before the conjunction. This comma is called "the serial comma," or sometimes "the Oxford comma" or "the Harvard comma."

"I had soup, salad, and quiche for lunch."

or

"I had soup, salad and quiche for lunch."

Both of these versions are considered correct in most circles. Journalists tend to leave out the serial comma. Everyone agrees that there are times when that comma is necessary.

"I'd like to discuss my parents, Mother Teresa, and God."

"I'd like to discuss my parents, Mother Teresa and God."

In other words, if there's a chance of confusion, use a serial comma. Since a serial comma is never wrong and since there certainly exists a possibility that I will fail to recognize confusing constructions, I use it always. I suggest you do, too.

DAY 112—Punctuation Week: "I'll take two quotation marks, please."

Which is correct?

Mary Anna says, "If you're writing in American English, punctuation marks go *inside* quotation marks."

Mary Anna says, "If you're writing in American English, punctuation marks go *inside* quotation marks".

In American English, which is my personal dialect, the first sentence is the correct one.

DAY 113—Punctuation Week: Use quotation marks. Really.

In recent years, there have been occasional rebellions against traditionally punctuated dialogue. And how is dialogue traditionally punctuated?

Direct quotes are placed within quotation marks. The speaker is denoted with an attribution like, "he said" or "said Johnny." A new paragraph is used whenever a different person speaks. That's about it. I would say that it's easy, but it's really not. Writing dialogue that flows easily to the ear and eye is an art that takes years to develop.

I'm not really against nontraditional punctuation of dialogue. I think there are many skilled writers who have done it very well. (William Faulkner comes to mind.) Still, there is a risk involved when you elect to omit all punctuation marks and attributions and paragraph breaks. *If* you're good enough to pull it off artistically and *if* you can still tell an intelligible story, then take all the risks you like. But since you're just getting started in writing fiction, I'd suggest you save those experiments for later. You have time. Right now, concentrate on telling a story.

DAY 114—Check-in

If seven is a lucky number, then seventy-seven has to be extra-lucky. Did you get there?

DAY 115—Things I've Already Said that Bear Repeating #5: You are the responsible party

Way back on Day 24, we established a definition for "plot" that I rather like. As I write, this book is obviously not published yet, but I've already taught two classes based on this one sentence, because it's just so useful.

A story's plot centers on a conflict that is shaped by the writer, who is responsible for driving that conflict toward a coherent resolution.

Conflict is good. (In a story. Not in real life.) It keeps the reader's attention and it gives you a chance to show what your characters are like when they're under duress, but remember that you must control the conflict. Even when your characters feel like they have no control over their destinies, you do, and your readers can sense that. Unfortunately, they can also sense when you're *not* in control of the action.

Never fear. Just maintain your focus on the last two words in our definition: "coherent resolution." If you outlined, you wrote down your notion of how your plot will coherently resolve. If you're winging it, then I hope you have an idea of how you're going to pull that off tucked into your cerebrum. Either way, focusing on the outcome will help you shape your story into something that makes the reader feel that it can only end one way...*your* way.

DAY 116—Practicing resolution

In my last essay, I discussed conflict and resolution on a book-length scale, but think about what it would like to read a book that consisted of 250 pages of conflict, followed by 20 pages of resolution. Doesn't that sound monotonous? It puts me in mind of a movie that is one big chase scene. After watching that for two hours, I really wouldn't care if the chaser ever caught up with the chase-ee.

Your plot and subplot should have an ebb and flow. Your protagonist should solve one small problem, only to have a larger one arise. Your star-crossed lovers should come oh-so-near to declaring their feelings, only to be interrupted by a tragic misunderstanding or by the threat of an asteroid strike destroying the earth. Your weary traveler should have a moment at an oasis to bandage her feet and sip some cool water before being forced back onto a road through the Sahara.

Look back through your manuscript and make some notes on how you are handling conflict and resolution. Does the excitement ramp only up, up, up? Or do you loosen the tension now and then, so that your readers will be lulled into a moment of calm that makes the surprise of a plot twist even more startling? Make a list of the scenes and page numbers where your reader will feel a sense of resolution. Do any of those resolutions occur at the end of a chapter? Are there any places where you think that unremitting tension goes on for too long? What can you do to change that?

DAY 117—I know you're busy, but...

It happened again today. I was having a nice conversation with someone, and he mentioned that he had an idea for a book he was going to write someday.

Now there's nothing wrong with having a good idea and sitting on it for awhile, until both the idea and you are ready. There's also nothing wrong with having a cool idea for a book that you know you're never really going to write. The potential heartbreak in this situation is embodied in the word "someday."

By working through this book with me, you are doing more, by far, to support your dream of writing a book than most aspiring writers.

Maybe you're at that point in your project where you despair of every finishing it. Ignore those feelings. If you truly hope and plan to write a book or a story or your memoirs or a poem, you must decide to do it, then you must make it so. If this book-in-a-year project has shown you that you're truly too busy now, then look ahead and make a plan. Say, "When school starts and the kids are on a regular schedule, I will get up an hour early and work on my book before I start my day." Or maybe you do have time now, if you tell yourself that you will have dinner with your family, but that they can then watch TV without you for a day or three per week.

Notice that these plans do not involve the word "someday." "Someday" is the enemy of dreams.

DAY 118—Five Senses Week: Make the most of all five senses, even sight

I realize that we've already talked about using our senses to make our fiction feel real, but I find that I have more to say...so much more to say that I'm giving the five senses their own week. Really, what do we have at our disposal as novelists, but the five senses? So let's return to them, beginning with the big obvious one, vision.

It's very easy to get in a rut while writing, describing the way things *look* in your characters' world, but forgetting to acknowledge the fact that most or all of them have five senses at their disposal. Even so, it's also easy to underestimate the impact of a highly visual scene. In particular, the unexpectedness that goes along with visual contrast can be a highly useful tool.

A person who has discovered a blood spatter might suddenly feel as if the rest of the world is black-and-white in comparison with that splash of red.

The girl who wears simple black silk to a high school prom that is otherwise attended by girls who have chosen the brightest and most spangle-covered dresses in the mall will stand out. (And the other girls will hate her for it.)

The soft glow of a strand of pearls can't be ignored, even when those pearls are surrounded with a rainbow of flashing gems.

For all its softness, a rainbow can't be ignored, either.

Go beyond a simple narrative describing what everything looks like. Think of ways to use prose to call your readers' attention to the things you want them to notice.

DAY 119—Five Senses Week: Do you hear what I hear?

There are two layers to the sound of your fiction. The obvious layer is the sounds that you describe in your fictional world—the people talking, the traffic noise, the background music, the barking dogs, the babbling brooks. You cannot dump your readers into a silent world and expect them to be happy there. (Unless you are writing about a deaf person and or an astronaut orbiting the earth alone, and you want readers to feel the silence in their very bones.)

The second, underlying layer of sound can be perceived as the sound of your authorial voice. What is the rhythm of your prose? If you listened to it being read aloud, would you sense a melody in the rising and falling pitches a speaker would naturally give the words?

Do you need to add clatters and booms and hums and buzzes to your narrative?

DAY 120—Five Senses Week: Use the sense of smell sparingly, but don't forget about it

People often ignore the sense of smell in real life, so it would feel strange to have scents and odors wafting through your book on every page. However, science has shown that the sense of smell is primal, having the capacity to trigger memories in a way that no other sense can. The scent of sweet peas can take you straight to your grandmother's garden. A particular brand of hair spray can make you think, for the first time in decades, of a girl you dated in college. The scent of death, once smelled, is with us forever.

Use this sense a few times in your book, but remember the punch it carries.

DAY 121—Check-in

I'm interrupting Five Senses Week to tell you that should have written eighty-four pages by now. I'm feeling terse today—verbally economical, as it were—so I'll just ask, "Did you get there?"

That's all I have to say.

DAY 122—Five Senses Week: How does your story taste?

The senses of taste and smell are so inextricably wedded that I almost put them in the same essay, but this is Five Senses Week. I can't cheat you of a day.

In a thriller with a particularly breakneck pace, your characters can find that they have no time to eat. Ordinarily, though, sharing a quiet meal is one thing that can give two major characters a chance to bond, just as it is in real life. In either case, the need to eat is such an innate human drive that a strong flavor will rivet your readers' attention.

If you're writing a thriller and there will come a time when your characters will be forced to forage the woods for acorns and berries, then you might want to taste a few acorns and non-supermarket berries so that you can describe them well. (Do this at your own risk and make sure you know what you're eating. I'm unhappy when my readers expire from eating death cap mushrooms.)

It may be that your protagonist will taste blood or tears before your story is done. Be ready to make those flavors real.

DAY 123—Five Senses Week: Touch your readers

At the moment of birth, I'm sure that we feel our mothers' bodies surrounding us before we see the bright blast of first light. And at the moment of death, I'm not sure whether our last sensations will be the sight of a tunnel of white light or the ebbing of the sensation of air on skin. In your fictional world, you can decide how you think these experiences happen and you can describe them accordingly.

Except for extraordinary cases like anesthesia or rare neurological conditions, every conscious moment of our lives is accompanied by the sense of touch. We live in a tactile world. Use it.

Let your character feel the wind cool her skin. Let him crawl into a car on a summer day and feel his hand recoil when it touches the hot steering wheel. If you choose to write about sex, give serious thought to the different ways to touch another human being. (Feel free to enjoy your research.)

As a writer, I find that the feel of my fingertips on the keyboard can trigger a story and all the emotions that come with it. Pay attention to that feeling as you write your page today.

DAY 124—Nag, nag, naggety-nag

Are you keeping up the pace that you set for yourself?

If not, take a good hard look at your situation. If you've got three preschoolers at home or if you're working two jobs to make ends meet, then maybe you set the bar too high for yourself. There's nothing wrong with that. I'm not telling you to give up your dream. I'm telling you to reassess the schedule on which you hope to achieve it. If you set yourself a goal that you cannot possibly make, then you risk discouragement and eventual failure. If, instead, you reassess your goal and set a new and more reasonable one, then you will eventually succeed.

On the other hand, if you have not achieved your goal because you were playing Mario Kart Wii...well, you know what to do.

DAY 125—Where do you like to write?

I wrote my first two books on a desktop computer which was located (obviously) on a desk. While writing my third book, I acquired a notebook computer but, being a creature of habit, I put it on the same desk and sat there to write. However, while writing that book, I suffered increasingly intractable neck and jaw pain, until I was forced to sit in a recliner to write, computer in my lap.

While writing my fourth book, I had surgery to repair my neck and jaws and, as the pain receded, I could have chosen at any point in time to return to my desk. I found that I was spoiled. There is something decadent about kicking back in my recliner, spinning stories and calling it work.

I've worked in a recliner ever since. I think the neck and back and leg support make sitting in a slightly reclined chair far easier on my body than sitting upright all day. I've read lately that sitting for long periods of time is terrible for your cardiovascular health, even if you exercise for the recommended amount of time every day. (Some days I do, some days I don't...) I'm trying to remember to take regular breaks to get up and move around, but I don't always think of it when the writing is flowing well, so this is an ongoing thing for me.

How do you work?

DAY 126—Mary Anna's Random Writing Rule #6: A chapter should end with a bang

You've finished a few chapters by now. I hope you gave some thought to how you shaped their endings, and I really hope you didn't just chop off the narrative because you thought it was time to start a new chapter. With all due respect to T.S. Eliot, a chapter should end with a bang, not a whimper.

Dan Brown knows this. Why do you think people chewed up *The Da Vinci Code* like it was candy? Because Brown knows how to end a chapter (or a scene or a paragraph) with a hook that makes you want to keep reading, even when you know you should turn out the light and get some sleep...even when you know you've got to get up before dawn and go to work. Dan Brown doesn't care that you need your beauty sleep.

When my son was eleven-ish, he went on a Hardy boys kick. His dad went to a garage sale and scored a huge box of Frank and Joe Hardy's most exciting adventures. Michael chewed them up like they were candy. After he'd read a few dozen, he came to me and said, "Mom, I've noticed something about the Hardy Boys books."

I was afraid I was going to have to tell him that Franklin W. Dixon was a figment of "his" publisher's imagination, in a category with Santa and the Tooth Fairy, but it wasn't a question of the books' authorship that had put the pensive look on his little face. No, he's a novelist's son, so he was deconstructing "Dixon's" plots.

"I noticed that the chapters all end the same. Either a bomb flies in the window, or Frank gets amnesia and tries to kill Joe."

When I finished laughing, I agreed that the action-adventure and thriller genres did tend to use that story structure a great deal, but that was probably because it worked. The ghostwriters of those Hardy Boys books, masquerading as Franklin W. Dixon, knew how to make eleven-year-old boys want to turn the page and keep reading.

Give some thought to how you can stir the same desire in your readers.

DAY 127—Your book should end when it ends

It's kinda early for me to be telling you how to end your book. Never fear. I feel sure I'll revisit the subject when the time comes, but I just finished talking about how to end a chapter and that gives me the urge to talk about ending a book.

One very satisfying way to close a book is immediately after the climax. The hero and heroine embrace and kiss. The detective unmasks the killer and he is carted off to jail immediately. The protagonist has a moment of epiphany that shows her that her entire life was meaningless. And the curtain falls.

Sometimes, this abrupt ending isn't practical. Sometimes, the main plot resolves itself, but there are subplots to unsnarl. Sometimes, that great love story *is* the subplot, and the hero and heroine cannot fall into each other's arms until the other obstacles fall away. Resolve those subplots, yes...you *must* resolve those subplots...but when the loose ends are tied up, say good-bye, even if it hurts. Don't leave your readers wanting less.

DAY 128—Check–in

Are you on page 91? Or are you behind the pace? Well, it's still early in the game, so it isn't too late to catch up.

If you're ahead, good for you, but don't rest on your laurels. You could get the flu or you could get sent on a business trip to Kalamazoo.

(This has happened to me. Seriously. Kalamazoo, Michigan. It's a very nice city that doesn't deserve to be a synonym for "the ends of the earth." I have also been sent on a business trip to Smackover, Arkansas, which is also a very nice place, albeit much smaller than Kalamazoo.)

Whatever vicissitudes come your way, keep marching toward your goal. You'll get there.

DAY 129—What's your goal today?

I know what you're thinking. "That's a stupid question. My goal, today and every day, is to write one page. One measly page. It's not easy, but I can do it."

You're right. That's the goal you assumed when you started working through this book with me. But what are your goals as you write that page?

I'd argue for clarity first. There is a time and place for artistic obscurity but, on the whole, you want your readers to understand what you're saying. It's not hard to read over the page you just wrote and make sure it says what you intended. So make that a habit.

Next, I'd argue for artistry. There are many ways to describe the feel of the ocean. It can be a warm and nurturing trip back into the womb. It can be a wet and iron-cold coffin closing over a drowning woman's head. It can be a dappled mirror, reflecting all the colors of the sunset. It can be a great big pool of H_2O. You can look back over a single page and know whether you have used the English language to communicate your world to your readers in the best possible way to further your story.

Progress toward some of your other goals is harder to assess in a single page. Let's leave the bigger picture until tomorrow. Today, look over your page and see whether you said exactly what you wanted to say and whether you said it well.

DAY 130—What's your goal this week?

This can be no surprise to you, but this week's primary goal is to write at least seven pages. Even if they're horrible. (But they won't be.)

What else can you achieve this week? If you follow yesterday's advice and check each day's page for clarity and artistry, then you can focus on something else when you're looking at the time scale of a week. A week's worth of writing, seven pages, can be several scenes or a short chapter. I have constructed this book to give you a weekly check-in, if you're on a page-a-day pace. Why don't you use the check-in as a reminder to go back and look at how those pages fit together?

Is each scene a coherent whole? Does each scene have a reason for being? Is there a logical flow from one scene to another, even if the time, location, and point-of-view changes? If there is a chapter ending in your seven-page chunk, does it fall in a logical place? Even better, does it fall in a place that will compel the reader to turn the page and start the next chapter?

A novel is a huge undertaking. I like to approach it one bite at a time, and a week is a reasonable bite.

DAY 131—What's your goal this month?

Let's say a month has 30 days, for convenience. If you're writing at least a page a day, you'll probably generate whole chapters in that amount of time. My chapter length is wildly variable, but it runs ten pages on average. What can you do in three chapters?

If you're following your main character for all three chapters, without much deviation to check out what other characters are doing with their subplots, then you have probably written at least one major dramatic scene this month. If you haven't, then check those 30 pages closely to make sure that they don't drag. At the least, there should have been considerable development of the main plot this month.

If you're flitting between the main plot and one or more subplots, you may have been able to get away with several scenes that are riveting but not central to the plot. If you've chosen that storytelling technique, please be sure that there has been forward motion in all the parallel plots or that you plan to get back to all of them soon. You don't want readers wondering "What happened to Sally Jo?"

It isn't a bad idea to flip back now and then and read several chapters back-to-back, and a monthly schedule might work for you. On the first of the month, read a goodly chunk of recently written text and ask yourself whether it feels structurally sound. More importantly, ask yourself whether it's interesting.

When you get to the last page and realize that it's time to edit this monster, you'll be glad you did a monthly check.

DAY 132—Approaching the century mark

You should be approaching page 100 by now, a fact of which I plan to remind you several times. Why? Because it is just so flippin' awesome.

On page 50, I told you that you should have accomplished the following things:

...introduced all your major characters, unless you had a fabulous reason for holding someone in reserve. (Few reasons are as fabulous as you think.)

...generated some serious conflict or drama. (In other words, something must have happened.)

...communicated to the reader where and when the action is taking place.

...foreshadowed the journey that your protagonist must take.

...initiated at least one subplot to provide depth and variety to the narrative.

All these recommendations still hold true on page 100, so give them another lookover. Tomorrow, we'll talk about what you should have accomplished in the 50 pages you've written since I gave you this advice.

DAY 133—In the first hundred pages, you should have...

...revealed new qualities in your main character that will give him or her emotional depth.

...revealed the ways that the conflict at the center of the story affects your main character. (It is okay to hold some information in reserve here. Perhaps you have revealed that your protagonist has had a long and cordial relationship with the person who has been kidnapped. It's okay to wait awhile before you jolt the reader with the knowledge that the endangered person is the protagonist's long-lost son.)

...showed your protagonist's decision to act. It is not enough to tell your readers about your protagonist's problems. You must show them that he intends to do something about them. (Unless you're writing Hamlet, in which case you can feel free to let your character twiddle his thumbs while he agonizes for another hundred or hundred-and-fifty pages. Hey. It worked for Shakespeare.)

...set your subplots into play. I'm not going to tell you how many subplots you have to write, but I do think you need more than one.

...begun pushing the action toward a climax that is inevitable because you wrote the entire book with that climax in mind.

DAY 134—Mary Anna's Random Writing Rule #7: Throw away your thesaurus

Cramming your manuscript full of flowery descriptive passages is a rookie mistake. Don't do it. And be aware that the urge to comb your thesaurus for a word wonderful enough to describe your book's drop-dead scenery is a big red flag.

I suspect you have a vocabulary big enough to write a good book. If your thesaurus teaches you a great word that you didn't know before, the odds are good that you'll use it inappropriately. Or, even worse, that you'll twist a sentence into an unnatural shape to accommodate this fabulous word you just learned.

Modern readers appreciate spare prose. Verbs are preferred to nouns are preferred to adjectives are preferred to adverbs. Would you prefer a character who sniffs derisively or one who snorts?

Yes, I know that William Faulkner was the king...no, the emperor... of flowery and convoluted language, but he was William Faulkner. He chose every last polysyllabic word for its literal meaning and for its connotation and for the way it sounded in the reader's mind's ear and for the way it looked on the page and for the way it tasted in the mouth. I could be wrong, but I do not believe he found those words in a thesaurus.

What makes me think that? I'm convinced by the fact that he used those big words so well. They flow organically, as if he reached into his head for the perfect word, not into a book of conveniently arranged synonyms.

Reach into your own head and see what comes out.

DAY 135—Check-in

By my count, you should be at the 98-page mark. In other words, you're on the verge of hitting triple digits. Doesn't it feel like one of those landmark birthdays when you were a kid? At age ten, you hit double-digits. At age thirteen, you were a teenager. At age sixteen, you could drive. At age twenty-one (or eighteen, if you're a baby boomer, or seventeen if you're a baby boomer from New Orleans), you could drink. At twenty-five, you could rent a car.

After that. the birthdays grow steadily less exciting, but this doesn't happen when you're writing a book. Twenty-one is good. One hundred is better. Two-hundred-twenty-seven is sheer ecstasy.

Today, enjoy being ninety-eight.

DAY 136—Let's take a good hard look at your book's opening

As I've already said, you should be somewhere close to a hundred pages into your book, which I've arbitrarily decided will be about 270 pages long. (Feel free to write something longer or shorter. It's your book.)

A hundred pages is a good chunk of text. You've had time to introduce your characters, describe the environment where they live, and present their problems. Your goal thus far has been to set the wheels in motion for a plot that will carry you through the middle of the book, where you will develop all three of those plot elements. This will give you the momentum that will propel the story's climax and ending.

After you write today's daily page, take some time to read those hundred pages. As you write the middle of your book, we're going to spend some time considering whether your book's opening achieves its goal, so make some notes as you read. For today, though, your primary goal is to read like a reader, for pleasure. Soon enough, we'll start being analytical.

DAY 137—Happy unbirthday

I'm writing this on my birthday. It's one of those significant birthdays with lots of round numbers in it. In other words, it's one of those days that makes a person think.

I'm putting 365 essays in this book—365??? What was I thinking??? —but I haven't given them dates that tell you to read this one on March 15 and that one on September 3. Therefore, I can't put my birthday post *on* my birthday, but that's okay, because there's no way on God's green earth that I could put it on yours, not unless there's only one of you reading this. Let's just all enjoy a metaphorical birthday today, together.

What do you want for your birthday? A finished book, ensconced at the top of the bestseller list? Well, I can't give you that. Nobody can give you that but you. But if you stick with me through the rest of this book, maybe I can help you give yourself a finished book with the *potential* for scaling the bestseller list.

What else would you like? Are you afraid you don't have the confidence or drive or ability to finish this book that you've started? Well, you had the initiative to buy this book and to stick with it for 137 essays and to write a hundred pages or fifty pages or two hundred twenty-two pages or whatever it is you've managed to do. Just sit down, day by day, and put your book on the page, word by word. That's all you have to do. It's all you *can* do. Nobody who ever wrote a book was able to do it any other way.

So what do you want for your unbirthday?

Here's my suggestion. A birthday serves to mark the time that has passed. Why don't you look to the future and give yourself the gift of time. Give yourself the time to write the best book you can. Give yourself permission to take longer to write it than you'd planned, if that's what it will take to do your best work. Give yourself time at the keyboard (or if you're a total Luddite, with pen in hand), because it takes time to learn anything. In my opinion, it takes more than a little time to learn to write a novel. It takes a lifetime, because every book is fresh and new. Nobody can discover that in an afternoon.

Happy unbirthday!

DAY 138—Put an unyielding and unsympathetic eyeball on your first two chapters

We're talking about editing today, and I have a juicy tip that I've never seen anywhere else, but it'll take a few paragraphs for me to get there. Bear with me. I shall get there, eventually.

A friend of mine told me yesterday that she's heard a Pulitzer Prize-winner speak about his blog. He says that he always deletes the first two paragraphs before he hits "Publish." He says those two paragraphs were "just throat-clearing."

When I heard that the Pulitzer dude said he always cut the first two paragraphs, I thought it was glib advice. Sometimes those early paragraphs are *good*. And sometimes you need to cut five. Better advice, in my opinion, would be to scrutinize the first paragraphs extra hard, because they *are* often weak in early drafts.

But don't stop with the first two paragraphs. (Here's the secret I promised you up top—the writing tip I've never seen elsewhere.) Look at your novel's first *chapter*. Many times, it's backstory that turns out to be unnecessary. If you spend a chapter telling the reader your character's life history, however, then you should probably eventually refer to that information. But please, please, please do it later, as part of the real action, then cut out the repetitive info in Chapter One.

With my first two books, I found that I'd written first chapters that dragged, but I'd progressed enough in my craft by that time to see that they weren't completely extraneous. It was simply that Chapter 2 was better, in both cases. After scrutinizing the situation for a moment, I realized that these chapters worked better *in reverse*. The material in Chapter 2 made a slam-bang beginning. Then, after the dust from all that action settled, the material in the original Chapter 1 made a nice quiet flashback to other things the reader needed to know.

I haven't used this technique since, but both those books were greatly improved when I reversed the first two chapters. Because of this, I always look Chapter 1 over hard. If you do that, you may find that a chapter switcheroo will wake up your story and grab the attention of an editor from Word One.

DAY 139—While editing, keep an eye out for your personal tics

Tics. We've all got 'em. Sometimes I get a word stuck in my head, like maybe "overt." If I use the word "who" a hundred times in my book, you won't notice. If I say "overt" more than twice, you will. As you edit, look for words that you love too much.

DAY 140—What are you forgetting?

Another thing to watch for as you edit—oversights. A mystery writer once said, "I keep forgetting to bury my dead." She'd kill a character, which happens routinely in mysteries, but there was never a funeral, nor any mention of one. The person just died and disappeared. Give some thought as you read to things that are happening in the background, like funerals. If they bear mentioning, do so.

DAY 141—Don't give your reader too much of any good thing

I'm going to give you one more piece of editing advice as you read your first hundred pages, then I'll leave you alone until it's time to do another critical read-through:

> **Be sure you don't fall in love with one storytelling technique, to the exclusion of others.**

Sometimes, you can just look at a page and see when you're making this mistake. If it's all dialogue, with no narrative whatsoever, then something is askew. Conversely, if you see pages and pages of description with no dialogue, you may have a problem. (Long, long paragraphs, with nothing but ornate and flowery description...are you getting sleepy yet?) Consider whether you can insert some characters into those pages, so that they can do some talking or maybe even just move around a little. At the very least, think about whether you can vary the length of those descriptive paragraphs, or even the length of those flowery sentences.

You're trying to write a fascinating story. Don't let a monotonous style obscure just how fascinating it really is.

DAY 142—Check-in

You should be at page 105 today, so even if you're slightly off your goal pace, there's still a good chance that you've passed the hundred-page mark. Perhaps you have other novels under your belt, or perhaps you've had some lengthy false starts in the past, or perhaps you've written something like a dissertation. More likely, though, you've never written a hundred-plus page document of any kind before.

Kinda cool, isn't it?

DAY 143—Do you have a career goal?

Do you have just one book in you that you must write or die trying? Do you aspire to a career as a writer, generating one book after another until you retire or, if you're like most writers, until you expire? Do you want to write a lot of different things for pleasure—books, short stories, essays, memoirs—more than you want a career that might confine you to a single genre? Are you enjoying this exercise in fiction, or do you think you might want to try something else with your next writing project?

You don't need to decide this now, but it's worth thinking about. When you finish the book, we're going to talk about editing it and sending it out into the world, but we're also going to talk about what you want from this writing life. And we'll talk about how you might work toward getting what you want.

For now, just try to decide what that is.

DAY 144—Mary Anna's Random Writing Rule #8: Use the vicissitudes of life to your benefit

The beauty and curse of the writing life is that we are always working. While washing dishes, my mind turns to plot twists. When meeting a new person, I think, "Oh, that's a cool name. I should use it for a murder victim sometime." When reading for pleasure, I think, "Why did you do that??!? If you'd ended the chapter two pages back, this thing would have been *so* much tighter!" Sometimes, I wish I could turn off the incessant chatter between my ears, but I'm rarely lonely and I'm never bored.

For those of us who don't live alone, surrounded by piles of money, the need to find time to write is a constant struggle. We have to go to work when our characters are whispering stories in our ears. A child who needs a diaper change is not going to wait quietly until we solve a knotty plot problem. It can be frustrating, but frustration will only block your creative flow. I suggest that you try to let the frustration wash over you and just be in the moment with your interruption.

Especially when the interruption is a charming infant who needs a diaper change.

Remember what I said: The beauty and curse of the writing life is that we are always working. The odds are excellent that you will someday write about a character who needs his job because he needs money, but who wishes for freedom from the daily grind. Pay attention to your feelings as you drive to work, and you might someday capture the moment as well as Sting did when he wrote "Synchronicity 2":

> packed like lemmings into shiny metal boxes
> contestants in a suicidal race
> Daddy grips the wheel
> and stares alone into the distance

Or, just as likely, perhaps you'll need to write about parental love. (I profoundly hope, however, that you never need to write about changing diapers in excruciating sensory detail.) In my upcoming book *Plunder*, Faye is talking to a friend about a woman whose son was murdered just the day before. This is how I described that moment.

> "I can't imagine losing a son." Faye's mouth went dry as she said it. She pulled Michael's shirt down over his round belly.

That paragraph could have ended after Faye's mouth went dry, but I thought she needed an intimate moment with her own child, who is sitting on her lap. Having spent many such moments with my own children, I know the meaningless but caring gestures that mark the mother-child relationship, so I pulled one out of my vast repertoire and gave it to Faye. I think the scene is better for it.

So live your life and write when you can. If you pay attention to your life as you're living it, your writing will be better and maybe your life will too.

DAY 145—What did I say yesterday?

I said, "Live your life and write when you can."

Today, I want you to go outside and play.

DAY 146—What do I want you to do today?

Today, I want you to stay inside and read for pleasure. The lack of time for reading is a constant issue for me. My books soak it all up, and they soak up all my creative energy, too. For me, reading fiction has a creative aspect, because I am participating in the creation of the author's fictional world. When I finish writing, it's often easier to read something factual that catches my interest easily, rather than trying to find my way into someone else's universe.

If you have the same problem, I want you to fight back. Read something frivolous today. You'll have to catch up the two pages you missed yesterday and today, but sometimes I think it's important to let your brain rest. Often, those are times when my brain gets into the most mischief, and that's a good thing for a novelist.

DAY 147—Things I've Already Said That Bear Repeating #6: Give your character some passion

A memorable character reaches out and grabs the reader, demanding that he or she understand his feelings. Even better, a memorable character can make a reader feel those feelings.

A novel-length plot gives you time to work with your characters' desires. Make them chase their dreams. Give your characters some passion for the things that they cannot have, then watch them find a way to get those things.

DAY 148—How do you depict passion on the printed page?

The words, "I love you," presented bare of description or accompanying action, really don't say much, not when you consider the emotional freight that they carry. When they are accompanied by a gaze deep into your eyes, an embrace by arms that tremble, and the feel of your loved ones hands stroking your hair, those three words convey passion. Even without the three words, those actions say "passion" to me.

Margaret Mitchell did not just tell us that Scarlett O'Hara had a passion to hold onto her ancestral home, Tara. She showed us a woman willing to work until her hands bled and cracked. She showed us a woman willing to marry men she did not love. She showed us a woman willing to sell herself to a man who would not marry her, if only he would give her the money to save Tara. These actions are not attractive and they are not easy to watch, but they convey a woman who wants something. They show us a woman who is alive.

Harry Potter's mother, Lily, was dead long before the first book begins, yet her passion to save the child who was more important to her than her own life drives the plot of seven gripping books. When you can make your readers love a dead woman whom they have never met, then you will have accomplished something.

DAY 149—Check-in

How are you doing? Sixteen times seven is a hundred-and-twelve pages, and that's quite a lot. Are you starting to get a little frayed around the edges?

Sometimes I find that it helps to get as far away from my computer as possible.

Why don't you get your writing quota done early in the day and take the family out for pizza tonight? Or take your sweetie someplace elegant-ish?

Your computer will look less nasty and forbidding when you get home. Really.

DAY 150—When all else fails, ask yourself questions

When I am first starting a book, I find that I ask myself a lot of questions:

Who is my main character?

Where does she live?

What is her problem?

How does she try to solve that problem?

What obstacles will she encounter?

Well, you're no longer at that beginning stage. You're several chapters into your book, but that doesn't mean that you've got every last detail in your book worked out. Oh, maybe you do. Maybe you've got a flow chart on the wall, color-coded to match your scene-by-scene flow chart, and maybe all those colors tell you exactly where your book is going to go. But I really doubt it.

There will be those times when you feel like you're flying by the seat of your pants. Sometimes that feels like a good thing and sometimes it doesn't. When the uncertainty gets to be too much, ask yourself some more questions. Maybe they'll be the same questions you asked at the beginning of the book, but I doubt it

DAY 151—What questions should you be asking yourself now?

I just listed some questions that I recommend asking as you start a book. Well, you're not just starting a book now. You've got 100-plus pages behind you. You're developing the midsection of a book, and that's a different thing. Your questions are going to be more specific, so much so that I can't write them for you. They will reflect your increasing grasp of your characters and their problems. Here are some plot development questions I've asked myself:

If I had grown up biracial in the South in the 1970s, how would I respond if a wealthy and powerful white man asked me out to dinner?

If I saw a gun pointed at the love of my life, would I be able to throw myself in front of the bullet?

Could I ever feel sympathy for a killer?

What are some plot development questions that you could ask yourself right now?

DAY 152—A nag only a mother could write

Maybe you have the kind of mother who dreams of being able to tell people about your literary successes. Maybe not. Most of us keep our book-writing aspirations to ourselves out of fear our loved ones will dismiss them or, worse, that they will laugh.

Let me step in with a loving maternal nag. I'm very good at this, having brought three children into the world who are perfect in every way, yet who somehow still need me to tell them what to do, now and then. I'm sure they're glad that I'm nagging you and not them.

> "How's the book coming along? I bet it's exciting. When can I read it? I can help you with it. I'm very good at spelling and punctuation, really. What? You don't want to show it to me. Oh. That's okay. I'm just your mother, not somebody with feelings. I just want to know one thing. When are you going to finish that thing? My mahjong ladies are all atwitter to read it. You spend too much time on Friendbook or Faceblog or...you say it's called Facebook? Fine. Facebook. Everwhat it is, turn it off, because I want you to finish that book before I die!"

DAY 153—Have you revisited your outline lately?

I've told you that I paste my outline into my working manuscript file, keeping it at my fingertips for easy reference. Did you do that? Or maybe you printed it out and taped it to the wall over your desk. The old-school way is sometimes the best.

I'm guessing, though, that there are some among you who haven't looked at the outline since you wrote it. If your book is going well and the writing is progressing smoothly, then this approach is working for you. Still, it wouldn't hurt you to look back at the outline, if only to laugh at the ways you've strayed from it.

My guess is that even the most inveterate outline-haters will be reminded of some plot twists in the outline that they still want to take. They might also find that following their nose has taken them to a place from which the ending they'd planned cannot be reached. Maybe this is good and maybe it's bad, but better for them to find out before they've spent two hundred pages painting themselves into their own personal corners.

I asked you to write an outline for a reason. Now's a good time to take a look at it.

DAY 154—How are your characters developing?

Today's a good day to look back at your character sketches. I don't expect this to be as big a shock for most people as looking back at a neglected outline can be. Character sketches are written before the writer has had a chance to get to know the people. On re-reading, they don't often feel wrong, but they can feel thin.

You've put more than a hundred pages into developing your characters. Now's a good time to assess whether they've turned out to be the people you thought they were. If they've changed significantly, now's a good time to make sure you're okay with that. Good characters, like real people, are hard to pin down and they're hard to synopsize in a one-page description. That's okay. Just make sure they haven't developed into people who can't plausibly be expected to do the things you need them to do, if they are to advance the plot.

DAY 155—No education is ever wasted

This was one of my father's favorite sayings, and I think of it often. Nothing that you have ever seen, heard, tasted, felt, or smelled has been a waste, because you can use it in your writing. When you have a day when the words are coming slowly, or not at all, get out a piece of paper (or go find your journal or open a new word processing file or use the "Notes" app on your smartphone...you know how you like to work...) and make a list of things you know a lot about. Make a list of classes you've taken and loves you've lost. Remember the best trips you've ever taken and the best books you've ever read.

Buried in all that experience and education are all the stories you need to tell. Spend some time sifting through it, and I'm betting that you'll find a fresh approach to the manuscript that's plaguing you.

DAY 156—Check-in

You should be past the hundredth page and making progress on the triple-digits. (And since I think passing few of you are pecking away on thousand-page tomes, you're going to stay in triple-digits.)

Your plot should be well underway. You've set up the forces that will drive the plot. You've already written some scenes that show how your characters are responding to those forces. You've got some more big scenes in mind that will unfold soon enough.

Good job! Carry on...

DAY 157—Oh, how I long for the good old days

I just read this wonderful quote from Mark Twain. In a lifetime of reading and writing, I cannot believe I've never seen it before:

> "Substitute 'damn' every time you're inclined to write 'very;' your editor will delete it and the writing will be just as it should be." - Mark Twain

Unfortunately, in the current century, our editors allow us to curse, so we cannot rely on Twain's method. All those "damns" would find their way into print. But I still like the quote.

DAY 158—But maybe the good new days have their merit, too

After reading yesterday's quote, I started digging around for more gems and I found this one:

> "Under certain circumstances, profanity provides a relief denied even to prayer." - Mark Twain

Mark Twain understood the English language, as practiced by Americans, as few ever have. Today's loosening of standards allows us to show our characters letting a curse fly when the need arises. I have been criticized for the very mild profanity in my books, but I stand by it. If I were fleeing from a homicidal madman, I imagine I might use language that's a little saltier than my usual ladylike vocabulary.

Nowadays, you have the freedom to use almost any language that you and your editor see fit. Use your freedom of speech wisely, and don't forget to be grateful for it.

DAY 159—You've been working hard

How are you feeling? Burned out yet?

I'm feeling soft and generous and kind. I think my heart has turned into a marshmallow. Why don't you take the day off, with my blessings?

Tomorrow, you'll feel rested and able to write doubly fast, so you'll have no trouble catching up to our usual unrelenting pace. What? You thought I was going to let you slack off without eventually paying the piper? I said my *heart* was a marshmallow. I didn't say I'd turned into a marshmallow through and through.

Enjoy your day off.

DAY 160—Did you enjoy your day off? Time to get back to work.

What is your personal work ethic? Do you get up early and churn out enough pages to meet your goal at breakfast? Do you squeeze in your writing time at work, during work? Do you sit in the family room with your kids, laptop on lap, and write while they're watching TV? Do you cram it in at bedtime? Where is the time for this project coming from—sleep, leisure, family activities?

There's no right answer. I'm just curious. Now that I write full-time, I approach it like a job. I take my daughter to school and I'm in front of the computer as soon as I get home. When I had a day job or when I was a stay-at-home mom, my writing time came late at night or when the kids were sleeping.

Whatever you've done to find the time, I applaud you for it.

DAY 161—Mary Anna's Random Writing Rule #9: Don't leave your head empty

I have been an omnivorous reader since I was four years old. If my hand falls on it, I will read it.

Most of what I read is lodged in my brain, waiting for me to need it. My choice of career means that I frequently *do* need the random information crammed between my ears and behind my eyes. If I need a random interesting tidbit about...um...monumental architecture during the Mississippian period, I generally know just enough about the subject to be able to construct a successful web search.

This disorganized filing cabinet in my head came in handy when I was preparing to write *Artifacts*, only I didn't know it was going to be *Artifacts*. My agent and I had been talking about my next book, and I hadn't even picked a genre yet. While driving down the highway, I suddenly had a mental picture of an abandoned and dilapidated plantation house. By the time I'd figured out who might live there and what her problem would be and how she would try to solve it, I had plotted out the book that would launch my career and win me some awards and kind reviews that I treasure very much.

Why did I have that mental picture? Because I've had a lifelong fascination with pre-Civil War domestic architecture in the South. It was a pointless fascination, but that didn't keep me from accumulating books and touring houses and doing internet research on the subject. When I needed that knowledge, I had it.

It's okay for an artist to pursue varied interests. It's probably necessary. If you thought about nothing but your book, you'd have nothing to write about but your book. If I ever thought of a recipe for 350 manuscript pages of boredom, that would be it.

DAY 162—Let us define boredom, so that we may avoid it

Think of the most boring books you've ever read. My guess is that these gruesome books were forced on you in school, because most people don't read books they hate. What made these books boring? Remember that I'm asking about boring books, not book that you disliked for other reasons like excessive violence or a world view that contradicted yours.

One reason that a book might bore you would be that its subject matter just didn't interest you. I personally think that this book contains deathless prose, but I imagine that it would be snore-inducing for people with no ambition to write a novel.

A worse sin on the part of the writer would be the production of a book that bored people who were actually interested in its subject matter. I have little interest in professional sports, so you might not use my response to a book about life and love in the pro hockey world as a gauge, but if you wrote a novel featuring antique roses or classical piano music, you might want to reconsider your approach if I told you that I didn't find it fascinating.

What kind of sin might you have to commit to bore me with a book on antique rose? Since we're talking about novels, let's presume that it's a novel about antique rose enthusiasts, but that the storyline gives you some scope to discuss some facts about old roses. I think the way to make that storyline boring would be to use an inappropriate level of detail for your audience. If your book mentioned a couple of the most common varieties, most of which I'd grown myself, without giving me any history or any special tips on how to grown them better, then the lives of the characters had better be interesting or I'm going to be disappointed. Conversely, if your book abandoned the storyline to provide botanical detail at a cellular level that's useful to a research scientist but not to an amateur gardening enthusiast, then you'd probably lose me with that narrative strategy, as well.

Know your audience. Learn what they care about and what they don't. You can certainly put whatever you like in your book, but if it's something your audience doesn't already care about, it would behoove you to figure out how to make them do so.

DAY 163—Check-in

By my count, you should be about 126 pages along. How does it feel? Is the story flowing out of you, or do you feel like you're dragging it out of your psyche?

Either way is fine, and I'd be astonished if you didn't experience both feelings many times during the course of writing a full-length book. If you're slogging along right now, just relax and slog. My experience tells me that this difficult experience won't last forever. Keep going...

DAY 164—Merry unChristmas!

I'm staring Christmas in the eyeballs, and neither of us is going to back down. The big day is going to arrive very soon, regardless of whether or not I've figured out what to buy my sister. 'Tis the season of baking and wrapping and tree-trimming and, though I surely enjoy all those things tremendously, most of them are done largely for others and not necessarily for me. In a perfect world, somebody else would be doing Christmas-y things for a group of "others" that includes me, and my world is fairly perfect, so I expect this to be a season during which I both give and get.

However...

There's something inherently unhealthy about a mindset that always considers others but never allows one to consider oneself.

So what are *you* getting next Christmas?

Next time Christmas rolls around, I suggest that you give yourself some time before Christmas to relax and look around. How can you write about a world that you're too busy to observe? Reach out with all five senses, so that you can describe what you sense when you sit down to write. Watch the people around you and go beyond your five senses as you try to understand them. Why do they behave the way they do? How are they feeling *right this minute*? Where have they been on their way to this place and time? You have to make an effort to understand people who aren't you, unless you plan for all your characters to be little pieces of you.

Take some time at Christmas to feed the part of your soul that describes your world.

DAY 165—Merry unHanukkah and unRamadan and unKwanzaa and...

I wholeheartedly hope that my readership is not confined to Christmas-celebrating Christians and I wholeheartedly hope that no one felt left out by my desire to write that last essay about the holiday that I celebrate. I have been known to prepare a seder for my Jewish friends, because I think Passover is so cool in terms of faith and history and culture, and I am always fascinated to learn about the traditions of others. The similarities are so life-affirming, and the differences are so interesting and eye-opening. I write about Christmas because it is the tradition that I know best, but I believe that the feeling of meditative anticipation that leads up to Christmas and the celebratory nature of the actual day and the return to workaday life that must follow are universal human feelings that are found in celebrations wherever there are people.

So if that last essay didn't do much for you personally because... well...Christmas doesn't do much for you personally, consider how your own cultural traditions inform your writing. Are there aspects of your own culture that put you in the right frame of mind to consider the world deeply, looking for new ways to describe it to your readers? What parts of your life make you a better writer?

Everyone in the world has stories to tell, and we would be so much poorer if any one of us chose to keep our stories to ourselves.

DAY 166—Merry unChristmas, part 2

In my last unChristmas essay, I suggested that you invest in some meditative time during the days leading up to Christmas. Now I'm going to tell you what to do on Christmas and afterward.

I can be so bossy, sometimes.

If your family is the type to encourage your dreams—and if they are, consider yourself lucky—then you may have gotten gifts on Christmas Day that recognize your efforts. Perhaps you received books like this one or t-shirts with captions like "Careful...I might put you in my novel." If you have big-spending loved ones, maybe you got a new computer or maybe someone registered you for an important writing conference. Cherish the encouragement inherent in these gifts, but remember that the only thing anyone can give you that will directly help you finish your book is time. Here's my Christmas Day suggestion: Ask for that time now, when they are in the spirit of giving.

Give your family your single-minded attention on Christmas Day, but look ahead. Most people have a bit of extra time off work during the holidays on New Year's Eve and New Year's Day. Ask your family for a little bit of that time. Tell them that you're getting up early on New Year's Eve, so that you can put in three hours on your book before you gather with them to watch the big game or to head out for an evening of parties. Try to indulge wisely at those parties, so that you can get up on New Year's Day and do it again.

When you make your Christmas list, don't forget to ask for the gift of time.

DAY 167—Things I've Already Said That Bear Repeating #7: Let your readers feel the push of destiny

Don't forget to milk the drama inherent in your story. Your characters must feel the push of destiny toward the story's resolution, or your readers won't. From the very first word on the very first page, you must know where you're going, so that you can lead your readers down a path that feels inevitable. And if you find that you didn't know where you were going after all and you need to change your story's thrust, that's okay. This is why we edit. Just make sure that the finished draft leans toward the ending on every single page, and your tale will never feel random or aimless.

DAY 168—Despair is temporary

You should be approaching the middle of your book about now. If you're like me, you are also approaching an attitude of despair. This is the point in the process when I'm pretty sure that everything I've written is completely awful. I'm also pretty sure that I'll never write another word worth reading again. If you are actually feeling good about your project, kindly skip this entry, because I don't want to jinx you. If you later feel despair coming on, you can always come back and read it then.

When I was writing my fifth book, *Floodgates*, I had a particularly hard time writing the chapters in the middle. I've done a ton of research, so I had some fascinating stuff for the New Orleans setting. (It's hard to lose with a setting like that, huh?) I knew who the murder victim was. I knew why she must (sniff!) die. I had a pretty good idea of what the red herrings were going to be. I knew who the killer was. I knew who most of the supporting cast would be. I had established a troubling personal issue for Faye to tackle. And I had an idea of some larger societal issues I want to address, because I just like to make things harder for myself.

So why was I feeling bogged down? Well, first of all, there were three other people in the house with me, and one of them was 2 months old. And let's not forget that there's always a cat living here. Still, feeling a little crowded wasn't the real issue.

I always feel like this when a manuscript is just getting underway. I have no trouble writing an exciting opening sequence—50 or 100 pages of fun—and I have no trouble with the slam-bang action ending and the final tying-up of loose ends. It's always the middle part of a book that's hard for me to slog through. And if I feel like I'm slogging, then my readers will, too.

I got to this point with *Findings* along about the time the final Harry Potter book came out. My son called and told me he was reading it, then he asked how my writing was going. I said, "I'm wandering in the wilderness." He laughed and said, "So's J.K. Rowling."

When I read the book, I saw what he meant. Harry and friends spend most of the middle of that book wandering from hiding place to hiding place, quarreling and trying to figure out what they're supposed to be doing. Why...that sounds like me! Sometimes, I wish somebody would tell me what the heck I'm supposed to be doing.

It was comforting to read that book, because I really did have the feeling that this plot device was her (successful) response to the writer's eternal problem of knowing where her story was going to start and where it was going to end, but having no earthly idea how to connect the beginning to the dramatic conclusion.

After I read J.K. Rowling's tale of the wilderness, I developed a plan. I drove four whole miles down the road to my mother's house. I hid in her office for maybe five hours, and I came home to my houseful of people with a feeling of accomplishment. I'd mapped out some important scenes that took me from the beginning of the book—the setup, if you will—into the part of the book where I needed to develop my themes to their fullest. I did it again the next day and completed a revised outline for the first half of the book.

Was it all downhill from there?

Well, no, but at least I had a road map leading me out of my own personal wilderness.

DAY 169—Is mid-book despair getting to you?

Go get a cookie. Then hit your writing goal. You'll feel better.

DAY 170—Check-in

One hundred and thirty-three pages.
> One. Hundred. And. Thirty. Three. Pages.
> Did you get that far yet? Can you believe it?

DAY 171—Know your audience

While re-reading something I wrote a few days ago, I noticed the phrase "know your audience," and I wondered how I could possibly have gotten so far into this book without using it. I was so convinced that I must have already discussed this truism that I asked Microsoft Word to search the entire document for it. Nope. This leaves me wondering what other important information I have neglected to give you. Fortunately, I've got maybe 40,000 words left to write, so I still have a chance to impart plenty of wisdom.

So let's think about your audience. Are you writing for adults? Young adults? Children? Your target audience will determine the level of reading difficulty you'll use, obviously. It will also determine how much profanity you'll use, if any, and whether you'll be explicitly describing sex or violence. Please remember that writing for adults doesn't *require* you to incorporate sex or violence into your storyline. It merely gives you the option.

Are you writing in a particular genre, like mystery or science fiction or romance, or are you writing fiction for a general audience? You cannot really understand your audience unless you read many books written for the same audience, in my opinion, so if you feel under-read in your chosen field, I recommend that you take a break from writing and do some research. Read the books on your genre's bestseller lists, then find a list of the classics in your field and read a pile of them, too.

Sometimes I give you advice because I don't want you to make the mistakes I made. While I am a lifelong mystery reader, I am not exclusively a mystery reader. I simply did not have the depth of knowledge in the field that I would have had if I had *only* read mysteries for my entire reading life. I had noticed that many mystery authors wrote series, but I did not realize the extent to which series books dominated the marketplace. I had an idea for the book that became *Artifacts*. I wrote that book, a mystery, and its main character was an archaeologist named Faye Longchamp. I did not also plan to write a series of books about Faye, because I didn't understand that mystery readers expect and enjoy series that return again and again to beloved characters and settings.

How fortunate I was that Faye was a character with enough depth to support a series that has stretched to seven books and counting.

Genre books can encompass great variations in style and plot, but there are storytelling conventions that readers expect writers to follow. You can flout them at will—and I have—but you must know what they are. I will always remember what the press's editor-in-chief Barbara Peters said to my editor for *Artifacts*, Ellen Larson, as we began the editing process. "We are going to take a good book that is nominally a mystery and make it a very good book that *is* a mystery."

I believe we succeeded and the response to *Artifacts*—great reviews, two significant awards, and many years of good sales—is evidence to support my opinion. Nevertheless, you will save yourself some trouble if you give some thought to your audience as you begin writing your book, instead of while you're editing it.

DAY 172—Know your audience: Agents and editors

I have purposely left matters of marketing and sales for later, after you finish writing your book, but I'm going to make an exception now. In many ways, you cannot second-guess the marketplace while you are writing, because it takes most people many months to write and edit a book. Books about cute boy vampires who sparkle may be hot when you start writing, but they may be colder than a vampire's heart when you finish. In the end, you have to write what's in your heart.

However.

There's no need to make your life harder than it needs to be. If you have two book ideas of equal importance to you torturing you to be set free, but one of them is a rip-roaring thriller and the other is a grim and gritty tale about people who are totally unlikeable and who enjoy violence that would make a serial killer blanch, take some time to consider. I'm not telling you to abandon that book in favor of a sequel to *Rebecca of Sunnybrook Farm*. I'm just telling you that the darker story might be a tougher sell, and that you are making a certain commitment when you choose it over the other story, which might catch the eye of more agents and editors. One of the many things you might consider as you decide which book to write is the possibility of writing the pricklier book after you've written the crowd-pleaser and after you've developed a relationship with an editor that might make it easier for her to decide to publish the riskier book.

Or maybe you should ignore everything I just said. (Darn, this is hard.) I'm all about artistic freedom, and I have, in fact, ignored the advice I just gave you. When my first book, a thriller, was rejected (warmly and with compliments) by the big houses, my agent said, "If you got that close the first time, you should write another book."

After muttering under my breath, "That's easy for *you* to say. You're talking about a year of my life," I started thinking about another book...the book that became *Artifacts*. In a sense, I did consider the marketplace when I wrote *Artifacts*, because I asked my agent what she thought about a historical novel and she said she couldn't possibly sell that. But in another sense, anyone who has read *Artifacts* knows that I wrote a historical novel anyway, cleverly buried within a mystery that my agent thought she could probably sell.

And in the most important sense, I ignored all popular wisdom when I wrote *Artifacts*, because I consciously rejected all thoughts of dumbing down the vocabulary and sentence structure for the masses, though some might have advised me to do that. (And that attitude is pretty condescending toward the masses, isn't it?) It is a book full of social commentary and ideas, and I pulled no punches when it came to serpentine sentences and polysyllabic words. Because I realized that no one might ever read it but me, I wrote the book I wanted to write and it changed my life.

Read this essay and understand that you must consider an audience that includes agents and editors and marketing people. Then write the book that is yours to write.

DAY 173—Know your audience: Reviewers

Now we're looking waaa-aaaa-aayy into the future. One day, people will read your book, develop a good or bad opinion, then tell it to the entire world. This is a terrifying event. My seventh Faye Longchamp novel, *Plunder*, is in the hands of reviewers right now and I'm as terrified as I was the first time.

Writing with reviewers in mind is a fool's game. Writing the best book you can possibly write, and trying really hard not to write a book that is indistinguishable from everything else on the market, is the best way to prepare yourself to be reviewed. Be strong. If they love it, good. If they don't...well, it can't be helped. And what do they know, anyway?

DAY 174—This is not a nag

If you're still reading this, then I have a feeling that you're still working on your book. It's entirely possible that you have fallen behind the pace, but I believe that you're still writing. Because you're still reading this book, I believe that you still want to improve your craft. You have already displayed more discipline and desire than most people possess.

I'm proud of you.

DAY 175—Are you proud of yourself?

As I typed that last sentence in yesterday's essay, I wondered how *you* were feeling about your work. Do you realize how rare the discipline to write a book really is?

Back when pterodactyls flew, I took a couple of correspondence courses (yes, on paper) through Writer's Digest School. I found them very helpful and I have, in fact, tried to provide for you some of the things I learned from the experience. Today, however, these courses are taught online. I just hopped over to their website and found a course similar to one I took. It is for people who have a good running start on their novel—10,000 words and a synopsis—and it gives students the opportunity to submit this material and four more 10,000-word samples for personal review and critique by a published author.

What is the cost for this service? Well, the list price is $799, but there's a coupon code at the top of the page for a 10% discount, so let's say that the cost is $720.

I'm here to tell you that $720 is a bargain-basement price to review and critique 50,000 words, and I am not telling you this because I think that the teacher will be giving students short shrift because the price is low. Also, remember that the school is going to take a healthy cut of that $720, so the teacher's pay will be even lower per word.

How have they stayed in business for decades? My wonderful teacher inadvertently gave me that answer when she said that I was a rare student, because I actually finished the course. In other words, most people cannot make themselves finish the book they've dreamed of writing, even when they have $720 on the line. In a way, they subsidize the people who do stick with the program, and that's probably as it should be.

This book cost you nothing like $720, so if you have come this far, it is not because you don't want to waste your humongous investment. It is because you have the diligence to do what it takes to follow your dream.

I hope you're proud of yourself.

DAY 176—Remember all those people who pay for writing courses and don't finish…

…and remember that you are not one of them.

DAY 177—Check-in

If you're on pace, you're on page 140. Did you get there?
    If not, why not?

DAY 178—Do your characters whisper in your ear?

Although you've made an excellent start, you are still just beginning your book and you are just beginning your career as a novelist. It takes a while to become comfortable with your characters. At this point in the process, you might not always know what words would naturally come out of their mouths in certain situations.

By contrast, I've been writing Faye and Joe so long that their conversations constitute a key turning point in my book development routine. After I've researched and meditated and written a synopsis and discussed the plot with my editor and researched some more, there comes a day when I hear them talking to each other in my head. That's when I know that the time has come to sit down and write.

I'm just beginning a new book now, and I'm looking forward to the day when I overhear yet another conversation between the two figments of my imagination whom I love the most.

DAY 179—Look back at your characters' beginnings now and then

As I said yesterday, you are just coming to know your characters. If, like me, you are writing a series, you will have years to make their acquaintance. Even if you're not, you will still spend a lot of intimate time with them as you construct this book. You will know them much better when you reach the end than you did in the opening chapter. I suggest that you look back now and then to see whether their character traits have shifted too much in the intervening chapters.

Most people who know me are aware of the characters in the Star Trek universe, even those who do not share my lifelong passion for Kirk, Spock, and all their friends. Spock, in particular, has a place in our popular culture that is defined by his calm and apparently emotionless logic. Trek aficionados, however, have seen the original series pilot, *The Cage*.

Spock is the only character who survived from the pilot to the eventual series, but his character is recognizable from the start. Still... there are differences. When aliens steal two female members of the landing party, he bellows, "The women!!!" in a most unVulcanlike display of shock and anger. And when he sees a charming flower that emits a ringing sound in the breeze, he is so delighted that he smiles. In the actual series, Spock only behaves in this way when he is under the influence of mind-altering alien spores. He doesn't even behave this way when someone has stolen his brain. The early writers clearly didn't have a firm grasp on who Spock would eventually be.

Dragging this conversation back to your work, consider your characters' words and behavior in the opening chapters of your book. Are they still appropriate for those people, as they have developed in your mind and in your writing? Do you need to tweak those scenes to represent the characters' true selves?

DAY 180—Mary Anna's Random Writing Rule #10: Constantly check your characters' motivations

As you write, ask yourself this important question now and then: *Why are these people doing these things?*

When you're in the throes of developing a story, you know what needs to happen before the book comes to an end. Maybe your character needs to quit her job and move to Texas, because the man you've created to be the love of her life lives there and she can't exactly fall in love with him if she hasn't met him.

Well, you can't just shove her toward Texas with no motivation. People don't quit their jobs for no good reason. You need to give her ample reason to make that leap, or your readers will think she is flighty or impulsive or irresponsible or maybe she believes she is just so damn competent that she knows she can get a job anywhere, any time, and in any economy. The important thing to remember is that you must think carefully about how to create a character who is believable when she does such a thing.

In my last book, I needed to put Faye and her child in danger, far from help. Faye is an intelligent and rational woman, and I cannot allow her to do something that would, in mystery readers' circles, render her "too stupid to live." It took some planning and several false starts before I crafted a series of events that made Faye walk into known danger willingly, because she believed that she had no choice.

(These days, it's even tougher to accomplish this, because you have to neutralize your character's cell phone. Otherwise, most books would end with, "And then he called 911.")

You cannot just shove your characters around where you want them to go. You have to make them want to go there.

DAY 181—And another thing about motivations...

There are certain storytelling conventions that make me very tired. One of them is the instant love affair. You know I love classic Star Trek, but even when I was watching it on afternoon reruns as a teenager, I noticed that Captain Kirk could spot a curvaceous alien (plausible), chat her up with a few smooth 23rd-century pickup lines (also plausible), and be death-defyingly in love with her by the second act (not very plausible...not when you're talking about a man in his late thirties with a certain amount of romantic experience).

Along about that time, I noticed that the princesses in Disney movies gave me the creeps. They had a nasty habit of running off and marrying handsome men to whom they've spoken once or twice (Snow White), or with whom they've danced for an evening (Cinderella), or who are the first person they see after taking a hundred-year nap (Sleeping Beauty). This last example involves a woman falling in love with a stranger who sneaks up to her bed while she is sleeping and plants a big fat kiss on her. Creepy? I'd say so.

By contrast, the modern romantic comedy, while usually frothy and forgettable, is a relatively realistic model of real life. A man and woman see each other. Perhaps they are attracted and perhaps not. They meet and things don't go according to plan. After many misunderstandings and false starts during which they get to know the real person behind the cute exterior, they wind up together. The Disney movies make this formula seem like Dostoevsky. If you can rise above this (or any) formula, then you're aiming for art, and for this I applaud you.

Do you have a romance in your book? Is it clear to your readers why these two people are attracted to each other? Please tell me that they have other things in common besides being charming and photogenic. If you intend for them choose to spend the rest of their lives together, please give me some idea of what motivates them to do so.

DAY 182—My final word on motivation

Please don't tell me that the bad guy in your book kills people for no other reason other than that he's crazy. Yes, that happens in real life, but it's not enough motivation to support a novel with a plot more complex than this:

1. Evil Guy kills a pretty woman he sees in the supermarket because he's crazy.

2. Evil Guy kills two pretty women who had car trouble on a deserted road…because he's crazy.

3. Valiant Police Dude cannot solve the crimes, which make no sense because they are crimes of opportunity with no discernible motive.

4. Evil Guy kills three pretty women who are walking home drunk from a party, and he continues to kill random pretty women in increasing numbers until Valiant Police Dude coincidentally happens to be nearby when one of them screams. Fisticuffs ensue and Evil Guy falls from a high place and dies. Probably.

The End

Ladies and gentlemen, that ain't a plot. It's a sequence of opportunities for the eventual movie to depict beautiful young women screaming, bleeding, and dying. If that's your story, then your crazy Evil Guy had better be Norman Bates, and even Norman Bates had the mother of all motivations to go stark raving bonkers.

If you and your Evil Guy are going to kill people on paper, then please (please…please) do it for a good reason.

DAY 183—My actual, I'm-really-serious-this-time, final word on motivation

If you write a scene involving two teenagers creeping out into the woods on a moonless night, carrying nothing except a flashlight with a dying battery, then please (please!) tell me what motivates them to do such a stupid thing when they know that there's a killer on the loose. Yeah, sex is a powerful motivator, but the possibility of being eviscerated is a powerful demotivator. You're going to have to work hard to make me go along with that story.

DAY 184—Check-in

You're nearing the hundred-and-fifty page milestone. Why don't you celebrate by printing the thing out again? Riffle through all those pretty pages. Smell the ink. (Does printer ink smell?) Stand there and look at the pile a minute.

Then write today's page, print it out, and put it at the bottom of the pile where it belongs. We'll do something with all that paper tomorrow.

DAY 185—That's a big pile of paper there...

Unless you've got the day off, it's going to take you more than one day to read a hundred-and-fifty pages. Even fast readers don't have time or energy to sit down and plow through that many pages on a workday. No worries. Those pages don't have legs. They'll be there when you have time for them. But let's presume you've got a little time today. Write today's page, print it out, and slide it under the bottom of the pile, then start reading.

As you read, ask yourself some questions.

Do your characters behave consistently as themselves? Even those characters who are flighty need to be consistently so. If you're not sure whether the people in your book are consistent, go back and read those character sketches I made you write. (Aren't they useful? You're welcome.)

Have you given your reader a clear sense of the time and place where the action occurs? No one wants to feel lost in space during a book's critical opening chapters.

As you read, do you feel that you're in control of subplots and minor characters? It's easy to lose them in the confusion of plot development in the middle of a book. Ask yourself whether there are any characters who have disappeared without a trace. If so, there's a good chance that you've let a subplot languish too long. Go back, wake it up, and braid it into the storyline.

At this point in the book, you should feel a strong undercurrent driving the action toward the climax. If you're me, you have a pretty good idea what that climax will be. If you're one of those bold people who hates planning ahead, then I feel sure that you ignored my advice to write an outline and thus you *don't* necessarily know where the story's going. In that case, it's even more important for you to feel a narrative force pushing the story forward. It is very easy to bog down in the middle of a book, but a great story won't let you do that.

If you listened to me and wrote an outline, drag it out and read it. How does it compare to what you actually did? It's okay to depart from your outline, but it's a good idea to revise it periodically, so that you'll have it to provide structure when those hard plot development moments come.

Now, quit asking yourself these questions, relax, and enjoy reading the opening chapters of your book. Since you probably won't have time to finish it today, I'll give you some more time tomorrow.

DAY 186—You're still reading your opus...

Yesterday, I gave you a laundry list of details to worry about while you were reading the draft of your opening chapters. Today, forget the details and look at the big picture.

As you read, ask yourself whether the narrative hangs together. Have you repealed the laws of cause-and-effect and, if so, did you intend to do that? Even when you write flashbacks...especially when you write flashbacks...you must know the path through time that you want your reader to travel.

Look for spots where the plot drags. Why? Have you stuck in too much descriptive detail? Have you held back as you wrote the big scenes, afraid of being too dramatic or emotional? Did you fail to follow through on those big scenes, letting the characters absorb the enormity of what just happened?

More importantly, ask yourself the biggest question of all:

Are you enjoying this book?

If not, don't despair. This is your chance to figure out the problem and fix it.

Now, either write today's page, or know that you're going to need to catch up eventually.

DAY 187—You've read your opus, and you've had a chance to sleep on it

You finished reading your manuscript yesterday, so your subconscious had a chance to chew on it while you slept last night. I'm willing to bet money that you've already had a thought about a scene you want to add or some dialogue that you'd like to deepen.

It's difficult for me to tell you what to do about the things your subconscious is telling you, because I don't know what they are. All I can tell you to do is to trust the process.

I believe that your subconscious is far more involved in the work of writing fiction than it seems when you're in the throes of drafting a book. It *feels* like your conscious mind is thinking and planning and dreaming up something new for your characters to do. Nevertheless, I think your subconscious is always whispering into your conscious mind's ear.

Yesterday, you filled your conscious mind full of your story, as it stands now, then you went to sleep. Pay close attention to any ideas that you get today, because they probably come from a place that you can't access directly. Give those ideas serious thought.

Trust the process.

DAY 188—Just look at it...

Put the printed copy of your manuscript next to your computer. As you work, look at it now and then. Let that impressive stack of pages make you feel all warm and fuzzy while you write today's page.

DAY 189—Things I've Already Said That Bear Repeating #8: Surprise your readers, then let them enjoy the moment

There is a moment in every book, when the characters and the reader all recognize that something important has occurred. It is as if they all say in unison, "This changes everything!"

Use those moments. They are like the afterburners on a military airplane. Your story can be cruising along, strong and swift, but when your reader realizes that something has happened that casts a new light on everything that has already happened, that story gains a sudden burst of power and speed.

Choose carefully where you will place those scenes in your narrative. They are powerful tools in pacing the story. Drop them into passages or chapters that sag and feel the afterburner kick in.

DAY 190—Famous surprises and turning points in literature and popular culture

I thought it might be fun to list ten memorable literary and cinematic and TV plot developments here. These are moments that take a plot that is traveling a path that readers/viewers feel they can anticipate and propel it in another direction. Do you have any comparable moments in your story? Do you see any potential to add them?

1. Darth Vader's announcement that he is Luke's father and Obi-Wan Kenobi's announcement that Princess Leia is Luke's sister. George Lucas pulled a neat little stunt in withholding those bits of information as long as he did.
— Motion pictures *The Empire Strikes Back* and *Return of the Jedi.*

2. The death of the tenth and last occupant of the island, begging the question of who could have killed them all.
— *And Then There Were None* by Agatha Christie

3. The revelation of Rebecca de Winter's true character, calling into doubt everything that the second Mrs. de Winter has seen and heard since arriving at Manderley.
— *Rebecca* by Daphe du Maurier

4. The shooting of J.R. Ewing, followed closely by the revelation that an entire season of *Dallas* had been dreamed by Pam Ewing.
— Television series *Dallas*

5. Beth March's death, an event unsuspecting readers in the 19th century would not have anticipated in a book written for young people. And it still kicks modern audiences in the gut.
— *Little Women* by Louisa May Alcott

6. The death of Piggy, which heralds the final collapse of the "civilization" built by child refugees of an adult "civilization" that is also in collapse.
— *Lord of the Flies* by William Golding

7. The death of Spock, in an act of logical self-sacrifice that is so characteristic of the Enterprise's Vulcan science officer.
— Motion picture *The Wrath of Khan*

8. The suicide of Romeo, based on his mistaken belief that Juliet has died.
— *Romeo and Juliet* by William Shakespeare

9. Jody Baxter's recognition that his family will starve if his cherished pet deer Flag eats their corn crop and his assumption of the responsibility to kill Flag.
— *The Yearling* by Marjorie Kinnan Rawlings

10. Scarlett O'Hara's recognition that she loves Tara, her home, more than she could have understood before it was threatened by war, and that she will do anything to keep it.
— *Gone with the Wind* by Margaret Mitchell

DAY 191—Check-in

How many pages have you written? The official pace would put you at 154, but maybe you're one of those people who works in bursts. Maybe you were ahead of the pace a few weeks ago, but you've fallen behind. Or vice versa.

No matter. Write something today. Even a few sentences will put you a few sentences closer to achieving your dream.

DAY 192—How are you holding up?

If you're like me, when you get this deep into a book, you don't want to take time for anything so annoying as exercise. Do yourself a favor. Stand up and stretch your arms to the ceiling. Lean down and touch your toes. (Or try.) Swing your arms in a big circle. Your body's thanking you now, isn't it?

DAY 193—Remind yourself why you're doing this

We all have our own reasons for writing. Maybe you want fame or fortune. Maybe you need to get the demons out of your head and onto the page. Maybe you just have a story that needs to be told. Write down your reason. The day will come when you need to haul that piece of paper out and remind yourself why you want to write.

DAY 194—First-person point-of-view: Up-close and personal

Sometimes I feel like I'm a little hard on you, ordering you to chain yourself to your computer and write. I believe I shall make amends with a conciliatory gift. I shall ruminate a bit more about point-of-view issues, then tomorrow, I'll give you a free sample of some of my own work. And maybe I'll do it again later...

First-time authors often choose a first-person point of view, because telling a story while pretending to be the viewpoint character is very empowering. It also doesn't require a novice writer to handle multiple points-of-view, and it reduces the amount of dialogue, which can be tricky. First-person narratives feel immediate and real.

My books, so far, have been written in third-person, with occasional passages in first-person, because I find first-person limiting for novel-length fiction. Sometimes I need to look through a different character's eyes, because my main character just can't see what I need her to see. Many classic works of fiction are written in first-person— *The Great Gatsby*, *Gulliver's Travels*, *Rebecca*—so you should feel free to pursue that avenue if it appeals to you.

For me, first-person works best for short stories. First-person stories feel like a real person has sat you down, poured you a drink, and spent an evening telling you about an important event in his life. (As opposed to a first-person novel, which better be good, or else the reader is going to feel like somebody poured him a drink and launched into a story that lasted for two days.)

When I write a first-person short story, the characters often take over, telling me things that I didn't know when I sat down to write. This happens with my novels, but it can be scary. When unplanned things happen during the writing of a 95,000-word opus, I feel like the repercussions down the line could be simply huge. If I'm writing a 7,500-word short story, I'm much more likely to say, "Cool. Let's see where this goes."

This is why I have twice sat down to write a story, only to have the character tell me within a few paragraphs that he or she was gay. In both cases, this revelation enriched the story immeasurably. In one story, "Starch," the protagonist, Nurse Crain, was a lesbian in the 1950s, which in that day meant that she would likely never have children of her own. When circumstances required her to behave heroically in order to save the life of a child, her emotional reaction was very specific to her situation. That little girl, Rachel, will never live with Nurse Crain but, in a very special way, she is *hers.*

In "Mouse House," which I have excerpted later in the week, the narrator holds a job that requires the utmost discretion. As a closeted gay man, he has a great deal of practice in this area. He is, in fact, so discreet that he never tells the reader his name. This personal trait has made him very, very good at what he does for a living, but it has cost him relationships that he didn't want to lose, and it is about to cost him the love of his life.

In another story I'll excerpt later, "Twin Set," my narrator tells you what she believes, but it is up to you to decide whether what she tells you is true.

I think my choice to tell these three stories in the first-person was the right one. See if you agree.

DAY 195—Excerpt from "Mouse House" by Mary Anna Evans

If Peter Pan had expired less flamboyantly or, better yet, if he had not expired at all, the murder of Paolo Arrezzo might have remained forever unsolved. If Peter Pan had stayed alive, it is possible (though unlikely) that Mr. Arrezzo's death certificate might always have read "cardiac arrest." Medical examiners tend to take special care with the post-mortem examinations of high-level Mafia officials who find themselves without a pulse at the tender age of 42, but there are many chemicals capable of rendering one dead. While the crime lab would certainly have looked for the poison that left him face-down in his apple strudel, some of them are damn hard to find unless you know precisely what noxious agent you're seeking.

Young Mr. Pan's cause of death was much easier to pinpoint. When a human being covered in fake fairy dust leaps out of a castle window, trusting that his safety cable will guide him gently to the ground, it's best for that cable to be in one piece. I was in my office, using a dozen security cameras to scan the excitable crowd below the unfortunate Pete, when the cable failed and sent him to his fate.

Parents snatched their children—some of them teenaged and quite large—and carried them bodily toward the park exit. Within ten seconds, Main Street was a bottleneck with the potential to kill hundreds of panic-stricken guests. In the array of security monitors, I could see my staff, efficient and well-trained, leap into action. Opening seldom-used gates, they began funneling guests down into the basement that serves as the backstage for the biggest show in the world. Each guest who was shuttled through the basement and out an emergency exit was one more person who would not trample someone else or be trampled themselves. If our luck held, Mr. Arrezzo and Pete would be the only people to die in the park today.

Two deaths in one day. In a single morning. Mr. Arrezzo had expired over breakfast, and Pete had been flying the pre-noon show designed to welcome latecomers into the park. It was also timed to make the earlybirds stop in their tracks and wonder whether it wasn't time to grab an overpriced hot dog for lunch. The sooner they ate, the sooner the Corporation would have a chance to sell them another meal.

I pitied the PR chief. The Corporation does not appreciate publicity that can't be manipulated into a favorable slant. That's why they hired me. Good security does not make news. It is invisible. While my job application said all the right things—a degree in criminology, fifteen years of law enforcement experience, and specialized training in surveillance technology—my interview won me the job.

My employers have a deep and abiding knowledge of psychology. If you doubt that, spend a week at the park sometime. Ride all the rides once for pleasure, then ride them again for understanding. Watch how they use costumed characters and mildly humorous films to distract you from the fact that you just spent half-an-hour standing in line outdoors. In Florida. In August. Then ride all the rides again. Make an effort *not* to look where they want you to look. Ignore the charming dolls chanting about how small the world is, and look for the underwater tracks that branch off from the ride's main line. Where do you think they go? To a maintenance area, of course. When some destructive kid carves his name in a boat's shiny finish, somebody's got to hustle that watercraft to the repair shop. Maintaining the illusion of magical perfection is tough when more than 70,000 imperfect human beings might troop through the park on any given day.

Now, ride something else and look for tell-tale gaps in the scenery where a door might hide. If some idiot stomps on your daughter's finger while they're clambering into one of those fake mine cars, do you think they're going to let you carry her, screaming and crying and bleeding, out the front entrance in front of all those waiting guests? Nope, they'll send a cast member to spirit your whole family away through a hidden exit, down into the basement where you'll find a friendly nurse with a first-aid kit and a lollipop for your young one. Hell, they might even send a dwarf to the emergency station to apply the antibiotic ointment.

My point is this: I've never personally met a colleague who admitted to being a psychologist, but I'm convinced the Corporation employs a whole staff of folks whose sole purpose is to keep 70,000 people happy every day. (I wish somebody would turn them loose in the Middle East. We might achieve peace in our time.) I am convinced that those psychologists are intimately involved in the hiring process, and I believe that is why I was hired for this job. I am a man of utmost discretion. I consider the ramifications of my words and my actions. If anyone is less likely to say something stupid to the press or to a law enforcement official, I don't know who that person might be. I communicated that quality to my interviewers five years ago, and I was rewarded with my dream job. Two rather theatrical deaths made today a more difficult day than most, but I love my work. I knew I could handle this.

DAY 196—How'd that point-of-view work for you?

Clearly, I'm happy with my choice of first-person point-of-view for "Mouse House," seen through the eyes of a nameless character. Do you think the story would have been better, written in second- or third-person point-of-view? Should I have given him a name? Is this discussion of point-of-view giving you some insight into the way *you* prefer to tell a story?

DAY 197—What about your work?

Have all your projects been written from the same point-of-view? Can you think of a project other than the book you're currently writing that you might consider re-writing in a different point-of-view? Would you consider trying a new point-of-view for a future work? (Don't start it now. You've got enough to do. But make yourself a note for later.)

DAY 198—Check-in

We're in the middle of dissecting the concepts of point-of-view, using my very own stories as guinea pigs. I'll only interrupt this discussion long enough to say this:

You should be on page 161.

DAY 199—Another take on point-of-view

Excerpt from "Starch," by Mary Anna Evans and Lillian Sellers—

In 1954, the word "nurse" was a female one. We worked among women. We were taught by women. We trained at an all-female school that required us to live on-campus—with women, of course. It was an odd time and place to be a lesbian, and this was particularly true for me. I had, at that time, never even heard the word "lesbian," and thus had no idea that I was one.

In those days, on-duty nurses were addressed by their last names, so I was known as "Crain." I liked the notion of dispensing with "Mrs." and "Miss," and all the social baggage that separated women outside the hospital into single girls, married ladies, and old maids. The doctors we served were, without exception, male, and we were expected to stand when any of them entered the room, just as gentlemen outside the hospital rose out of respect for ladies. I positively reveled in this perversion of the prevailing custom. If anyone was ever born to be a nurse, I was.

I loved the uniform, white and severe. I kept mine starched so stiff that the collar chafed at my neck. Even our caps were starched to the texture of cardboard. My dark hair was no longer lank when I pinned it up beneath that old-style cap. Its medieval lines suited my strong features and, while I was still not pretty when I wore it, I was surely memorable.

Only one thing could have made me give up my cherished whites. When I was offered a job as a surgical nurse in the OR, I accepted on the spot, even though it meant that my working life would be spent in a nondescript scrub dress. Surgery is a life-or-death proposition, every day. This job was a chance to make people well, every day. People that might have died would roll out of my OR into decades of life. Every day. How could I turn that down? I spent the rest of my career in the OR.

And that is how I found myself face-to-face with bloody, messy, intentional death. Murder.

DAY 200—How did that excerpt work for you?

The excerpt we read last week from "Mouse House" was written in the first-person. So was this excerpt from "Starch." Do you think I achieved my goal of making the two narrators individuals? Did I accomplish another important goal, using the narrator's voice to set the scene without committing an info-dump that would stop the story dead cold?

Do you have some mental visual image of Nurse Crain? Good, because I wanted you to.

Do you have some mental visual image of the narrator of "Mouse House"? If you do, that's well and good, because I want him to be real to you, but I don't think a visual image is important in this case. I certainly didn't give you one, so if you have one, it's all your own.

Tomorrow, I'm going to give you one more story excerpt, showing you the way I introduced yet another character, one who is very different from Nurse Crain and the "Mouse House" narrator. As you will see, you find out quite a bit about her without learning her name, although I do reveal it later in the story, in my own good time. Instead, we learn the name of her sister Bailey. And we begin to get a sense of the things that may have pressured a beautiful and brilliant woman to do murder...

DAY 201—One last first-person excerpt, for your perusal

Excerpt from "Twin Set," by Mary Anna Evans—

Bailey's shadow fell over my life less than a minute after I was born, when she shoved her way out of our mother's womb. The doctor laid me down—tenderly, I'm sure—to look after her more pressing needs. Once Bailey's airway was cleared, her oxygen-starved complexion shifted from death's-door blue to baby-girl pink, and our pediatrician became the first to utter the refrain that has haunted us for thirty years now: "I don't think I've ever seen a pair of twins who are so absolutely identical. They're mirror images of each other." At least, that's how our mother always told the story.

In the meantime, I waited—quietly, according to Mother—until all of Bailey's needs were met. Then someone found the time to wipe the birth blood off me and welcome me to the world.

Having begun my life smeared in blood, perhaps I shouldn't have been surprised when I woke up half an hour ago, covered in a sheet heavy with the stuff. Perhaps it would have been better if the blood were mine.

◊ ◊ ◊

It was the movie that triggered the attack. There can't be any doubt. Hardly a week ago, I lay curled in this very bed beside Mack, watching a movie about a twin who committed a murder and tried to pin the crime on his brother. The handsome investigator was stumped because DNA testing can't distinguish between samples collected from identical twins. Or identical triplets or quadruplets, for that matter. Even if one twin's DNA mutates after conception, the difference is usually undetectable by forensics labs.

I was troubled by the knowledge that my sister might also be absorbing this dangerous information, so troubled that I lied to Mack. I told him I needed to run next door to Bailey's apartment to retrieve a sweater, or I'd have nothing to wear to work the next day.

"You girls should just knock down the wall between your closets. I don't think either of you ever wear your own stuff," Mack had said, reaching his long arms overhead and stretching every muscle on a body that was well-blessed with them.

Mack was half right. I never wore my own stuff, because Bailey's closet was always full of my clothes and hers, too.

I let myself into her apartment without knocking and found her watching political commentary on PBS, but it was an obvious ploy. I sensed that she had anticipated my arrival and changed the channel, and Mack's death proves that my intuition was right. Twins know each other in ways that are somehow more than natural, but still not supernatural. How else can I explain what has happened? Seven days ago, the television detective told me that Bailey and I are indistinguishable to a crime lab, and now Mack is dead.

◊ ◊ ◊

"Fingerprints," the handsome television detective had observed, "are formed after conception, in the womb. They are truly individual. Even identical twins have unique fingerprints."

Too bad Bailey is so careful to bleach her hair to the exact shade of platinum that I prefer. This means that both of our bathroom closets are equally well-stocked with rubber gloves. They do a great job of protecting our hands from peroxide. It is highly unlikely that she would have been barehanded when she slipped into my apartment, slid my chef's knife out of a kitchen drawer, and slid it through Mack's ribs into his heart. Several times.

I should have seen this coming. Our history is littered with stolen boyfriends and headless dolls. And now Mack is the latest casualty of our lifelong battles.

DAY 202—Behold, the beautiful monster...

Did I give you sufficient physical description for you to develop a mental picture of Bailey and, by extension, the narrator Haley? Are you clear on Haley's feelings for Bailey? Do you think Bailey's feelings for Haley are a mirror image of her sister's resentment? Are you curious enough to want to read on?

DAY 203—Diagnose your wounded characters.

The editor of my first novel was disturbed by the callous behavior of one of my characters, saying that it wasn't plausible. I cooperatively did a web search for the characteristics of various personality disorders and diagnosed him, saying, "Look! That's how sociopaths behave!"

If you're having trouble wrapping your brain around a troublesome character's motivation, do some armchair psychology and give him a diagnosis. If you ask me, an ethereally beautiful woman who would kill the man her equally ethereally beautiful sister loved, out of sheer jealousy, is both a sociopath and a narcissist. Damaged people are interesting. Where are your characters' wounds and scars?

DAY 204—One last thought on point-of-view, for the moment

When watching a movie, I jump when a character is shot. I weep when she weeps. When fake blood spews across the screen, I feel queasy. Effective first-person point-of-view has the same effect. In fact, the best third-person point-of-view is also that immediate and personal. Do your characters' feelings give you a visceral response?

DAY 205—Check-in

How many pages today? 169? Did you know that 169 is thirteen squared?

Is this pertinent? No. Engineering school simply reconfigured my brain to notice such things.

And now that I've checked my math, I see than you should really be on page 168, and I can't think of anything interesting to say about 168. Tomorrow, though, you'll be on page thirteen-squared.

DAY 206—Lost in time and space

If you're like me, you are so deep into your book's narrative by now that you have lost track of time—both yours and your characters. Sometime after writing the midpoint of my novels, I usually realize that I don't know what day it is in my fictional world. When that happens, I know that it's time to construct a timeline.

Someone asked me recently if I storyboarded my books. No, and I only have the dimmest idea of what storyboarding is. I do write those long, involved, for-my-eyes-only outlines that I've described, but stories evolve between outline and finished book. If they don't, then maybe we should just publish our outlines and be done with it.

I've learned to take a stab at a timeline when I'm outlining. I try to have some idea of the passage of time, so that I'll know when Faye has done enough for one day and she really needs to sleep. I don't record the consumption of every single meal, figuring that you'll presume she grabbed fast food or slapped together a sandwich if I don't tell you specifically that she ate. And I do not inform you when anybody goes to the bathroom, unless there's a darn good plot-related reason. If it's not part of the story and it doesn't drive the plot, then it is omitted in the name of streamlining.

The roughed-out schedule that's implicit in my outline shifts as I write, but I'm just not rigid-minded enough to force myself to think out the plot on a minute-by-minute level before I start a book. Once I have a rough idea of when important things in the narrative are going to happen, I plunge ahead. Eventually, I become so lost in time that I am forced to page through the manuscript, making notes on when this day ends and that one begins. The editor of *Artifacts* made me write her a scene-by-scene timeline. I have hundreds of scenes in a 300-page book, so this was an arduous undertaking. My natural style is tight third-person with multiple viewpoints, meaning that one scene may occur simultaneously with the next one, as two or three or even more people observe the same thing at the same time and I shift from one person's thoughts to the next.

This exercise taught me that I was using the multiple-viewpoint technique to manhandle time itself. By letting one character point a gun, then having another watch in horror, then having another see that she is in the line of fire, then letting the second one try to take the bullet for the woman he loves, I can spend a nice leisurely page or so exploring this turning-point moment in short rapid-fire scenes, without losing the tension necessary for such a situation.

But it is really hard writing a timeline for a sequence like that.

While I was writing *Findings*, my lack of a sense for the day of the week in Faye's world became a serious problem. I needed for Faye and Joe to go to the rare books library, which would ordinarily be closed on Sunday...so it was really important to know whether it was Sunday yet.

Then I wrote the climactic scene and I realized that I had three boats floating around those Gulf islands, and it was essential that I remember where they were all parked...moored...docked...whatever. I needed to make a boat location log as part of my timeline, because when one boat blew up and left Faye stranded, I did *not* want to hear from somebody after publication, saying, "If she'd just walked down to the beach where Joe dragged his john boat ashore in Chapter 12, then her problems would have been solved."

Of course, if I'd planned the passage of time in more detail when I started the book, all this fussing around could have been avoided, but I am only half-engineer. I am also half-artist, and I work the way I work. Now, go map out the timeline of your own book, before your characters start meeting themselves, coming and going.

DAY 207—I need a time stamp

In my last essay, I discussed the necessity for a timeline at some length. I did not discuss the practicalities of how to implement that timeline.

The editor of my first book, *Artifacts*, would periodically make a marginal note that said merely, "I need a time stamp." Oh, how wonderful it would be if we could insert self-updating date and time stamps into the margins of our books. If a reader became confused, he could just shift his eyes slightly to the right or left and see that, in the book's fantasy world, it is 2:00 pm on Thursday.

Alas. That's just not the way it is.

There are straightforward ways to mark the passage of time. I've read books that gave the date and time at the beginning of each chapter. I don't recall whether I've ever read a book that gives the date and time at the beginning of each scene for the entire book, but I'm sure it's been done. For a thriller, I think such a ticking clock could be a very effective device.

The closest I have come to that ticking clock was in *Effigies,* which takes place during the week of the Neshoba County Fair®, near Philadelphia, Mississippi. Everything in Neshoba County revolves around that fair, so it only made sense to break the chapter when the day changed and to make a note at the beginning of those chapters that said something like, "Saturday, Day 1 of the Neshoba County Fair®." Usually, though, it's better to be more subtle about such things.

My books generally take place over a continuous sequence of days, so I don't have to let the reader know that a week has passed since the end of the previous chapter. I try to let people know when Faye sleeps, and I might make note of what meal she has just eaten, in an effort to let them know what time it is. Since she works outside, I can use long shadows to indicate that is late afternoon and short ones to indicate noon.

The day of the week can be tricky to establish, since people don't go around saying, "Hello! It's Tuesday!" They do, however make notes that they have an appointment at 2 pm on Tuesday, so when Faye keeps such an appointment, then my readers know what day it is. They also say things like, "Tomorrow's Sunday. Do you think the rare books library will be open?" And working people are very vocal in their appreciation for Friday.

My advice is to look for opportunities like those, where it is easy to establish the date. It might be less convenient in the next chapter, but your readers are smart. If you just told them that it was Friday, and your characters haven't slept since then, then it's probably still Friday.

DAY 208—Things I've Already Said That Bear Repeating #9: Could your book take place anywhere else?

As I've said before, story possibilities exist that take place in random, unidentifiable places. If the point of your story is to dramatize the soul-killing interchangeability of cities where inhabitants are cut off from every scrap of nature, then go ahead and make your city unidentifiable. I would argue, however, that almost every other book would benefit from a setting that is tangibly real, even if that setting is imaginary. Wonderland and Narnia are not real, but I feel as if I've been there, because Lewis Carroll and C.S. Lewis took pains to provide descriptions that touch all five senses.

You've got half a book in your hands now. Read it, and see if it gives you the feeling that you've been someplace else...someplace wonderful.

DAY 209—A very selfish nag

If you are not writing at your desired pace, would you please step it up? I'm looking forward to seeing my name on your acknowledgements page.

DAY 210—The muddle in the middle

I love starting a new project. When the project is short and manageable, like a short story, I usually just toss the idea around for a while, then plunge in. When the project is book-sized, I prepare. I spend a month or so reading for a living, searching out books and websites that tell me more about my setting or about my subject, just like we did during the first month of this book-in-a-year project. Then I make an outline. And *then* I plunge in.

The first 75 pages or so of a new project seem to write themselves. In fact, if writing an exciting beginning *didn't* flow easily, I'd question whether I'd done my job during the preparation stage, and I'd go back to reading for a living for little while longer.

Similarly, the last 75 pages of a book seem to write themselves, with the words tumbling onto the computer screen as fast as my fumbling fingers can type. If they didn't come easily, I'd worry. Each of the previous pages was written expressly to set up those last exciting chapters. Difficulty writing a book's climax is almost certainly a sign that it's just not time to finish it.

But what about those middle pages? For me, some of them are just back-breaking to write. (Mind-breaking? Finger-breaking? Whatever... you know what I mean.)

So what's a writer to do when she finds herself stuck in the muddy middle of her book? I do two things: I rely on my outline, and I keep slogging.

The beauty of an outline is that you know where you're going. (Aren't you glad you wrote one?)

If you find yourself in a mushy spot, point yourself toward the next big scene in your outline, and do whatever it takes to get there. Push your characters toward the location of that scene. Write the dialogue that will get them ready for the action in that scene. Give them the knowledge that they're going to need when they get there.

Do these things, even if you feel like you're just forcing your people to do as they're told. Do them even if the action feels clunky or limp. Write the transitional scenes that will get you where you need to go, even if you know in your heart that they are awful...*because you can always edit them later.*

When I come back to those awful transitional scenes during the editing stage, a couple of things happen very frequently. First, I usually find that a lot of the narrative is unnecessary. I can just surgically remove ninety percent of the ugly and troublesome text, and the story still works. Still, I needed to write that ugly and troublesome text in order to generate the all-important ten percent. And second, I often find that many of the scenes that seemed ugly and troublesome aren't really so bad. With some honing and polishing, they turn out to be good enough to stay in the book, after all.

Don't be afraid to write bad stuff. You can always fix it later. Sometimes writing the bad stuff takes you straight to the good stuff.

DAY 211—Mary Anna's Random Writing Rule #11: Um...

There really are no rules. But you knew that already.

DAY 212—Check-in

A hundred and seventy-five pages...wow. That's a nice round number, and a really big one, too. If you're shooting for our goal of a book of modest length—270 pages—then you're way past halfway. Even better, you're within a hundred pages of the end. It's all downhill from here.

Okay, that's not really true. You've still got a lot of work to do to build anticipation for the climactic scenes, but still. A hundred and seventy-five pages is a lot of pages. Be proud.

DAY 213—No head-hopping allowed

A few years ago, I was re-reading *Gone with the Wind* for the first time since I began writing, and I found myself startled. One minute, I was in Scarlett's head, looking around at the glory that was pre-war Tara. The next minute, I was looking through the eyes of one of the Tarleton twins. I felt like I had whiplash.

It seems that point-of-view was handed differently in Margaret Mitchell's day. Nowadays, no editor worth his or her salt will let you get away with head-hopping. If you need to change viewpoint characters, you can do that, but you should not do it willy-nilly, just because you're in the mood. Current practice requires you to remain in one character's head for the entirety of a scene. To change viewpoint characters, you should end the scene you're writing and begin a new one, which will be viewed only through that new character's eyes.

Have I recently read a very successful book that broke this rule? Yes. But every single instance of head-hopping yanked me right out of the story, which was not that author's intent. And when I'd been yanked out of the story, I did not think, "Cool! That was an effective strategy!" I thought, "Was this person's editor asleep?"

Am I saying that you can never break rules of style or grammar in fiction? Of course not. But you need to have a good reason and you need to be extraordinarily sure of yourself. If you're writing something experimental and literary, you have some latitude here, but you do not have *carte blanche*. Know what you're doing and why you're doing it, or you risk looking sloppy. Even if you're writing something more traditional or commercial, you have my heartfelt approval to experiment, but don't break the rules just to break them and, for heavens' sake, don't break the rules because you don't know what they are.

DAY 214—You look tired

I gave you a day off...oh...about fifty pages ago, give or take. You're probably overdue for another one.

Put your feet up and do something brainless. Watch TV. Play a video game. Pet your poor neglected cat. Muse on the fact that other people do this all the time. Try and fail to pity yourself, because you're a writer. You don't have time to sit around and be brainless.

Tomorrow, when you're writing a double quota to catch up after succumbing to hedonism today, you'll be glad to be the kind of person who is driven by the desire to do something hard and who has the tenacity to finish it.

Enjoy your day off.

DAY 215—Are you feeling refreshed and peppy?

Good. Because now you need to write two pages to make up for yesterday's vacation.

DAY 216—Kicking the cliché habit

When you read your work, are you sometimes smacked in the face with a worn-out old phrase...or two...or oh, dear Lord...even more?

Brain scientists have shown that our minds fall into familiar grooves. When we speak or write, we reach for prefabricated thoughts, because it is so much easier than reinventing the wheel. I would argue that clichés aren't particularly undesirable in casual conversation, unless they are so frequent as to annoy the listener. They communicate the speaker's intent in a way that the listener can easily understand. There's nothing wrong with that. Clichés are not, however, a creative way to communicate.

Those of us who earn our livelihood with words feel inspired to do better than to simply regurgitate canned phrases. If I cannot find my own way to tell you something, why should I expect you to listen? We writers delve deep into the language for new ways to say things, in hopes that you will respond by finding new ways to think.

Does this mean that I never unconsciously resort to clichés? Oh, heavens no. I'm human, and I don't think there's any way to root every last cliché out of 95,000 words of prose...not unless I plan to devote a decade to each book. Go ahead and send me a catalog of every overused phrase in my body of work, if you feel that you must. I'll try not to use any of them again, but be assured that I know without looking that they are there.

A few days ago, a reader told me that she particularly enjoyed a sentence I wrote in my first book, *Artifacts*: "Providence tends to repay a man in the coin he hands to others." Then she asked, "Is that yours? Is it original?" I could only answer "I hope so."

Unintentional plagiarism is not so different from dredging my memory banks and coming up with a cliché...except using something that belongs to another writer is simply wrong. Obviously, I hoped that I hadn't unintentionally used someone else's pithy observation when I wrote about Providence and her coin. In this case, I also hoped that the sentence was original simply because I liked it.

I did a web search and could find nothing remotely similar to that sentence. This prompted me to breathe a sigh of relief. It's mine...I'm pretty sure it's mine...good heavens, I hope my brain didn't take a lazy trip down a well-rutted road and fetch that idea from somebody else. Because, while slapping a cliché into a book now and then is lazy, it's not unethical.

By contrast, taking someone else's idea violates one of the most timeworn phrases of all: Thou shalt not steal.

DAY 217—Speaking of clichés...

Take a few minutes and read a random chunk of your book. Circle any clichés that you see. Make a star in the margin beside any clichés that are so noticeable that you can't possibly live with them. (You knew I was going to make you do this, didn't you?)

Now, choose a key word or phrase from each of those clichés and search your document. Try not to flinch when you see that you've used each of them seven times. Just replace them with something more original and make a list of tired figures of speech that you'll never, ever use again. Until the next time, and then you'll need to root them out again. They're persistent little beasts.

DAY 218—Clichés are for everybody… let's enjoy someone else's misery

Pick up a book that you have read and enjoyed. I want you to read a good little chunk of it. Set a timer for one hour, so that you don't read so long that you don't have time to write today's page.

As you read, look for clichés, and keep notes of all that you find. I guarantee that you will find some.

Does it make you feel better to know that even the greatest author has to fight against the urge to use prefab language?

DAY 219—Check-in

Let me see. Where are you supposed to be in your monumental writing task? Page 182?

You have long since introduced your characters and set up the conflict that is now driving your narrative. You have probably spent the last hundred pages or so exploring that conflict, deepening it and making it appear that your characters' problems can never be resolved.

I suggest that you spend some time in meditation to determine whether there is anything else you can do to make their lives worse. Give them one more disaster, but not a random one. Make it a disaster that is closely linked to everything that has gone before. Give your plot one more turn of the screw.

Your characters might hate you for your cruelty, but your readers won't.

DAY 220—How can you be cruel to your characters? Let me count the ways…

A good protagonist makes it easy for a writer to be cruel, and writerly cruelty can drive a gripping plot. A good protagonist wants something so very badly—a home, a lover, world peace, safety for a beloved child, a Red Ryder BB gun. If you spend the entire book thwarting that desire —and you should—then you have great scope for authorial cruelty.

There are opportunities for secondary cruelty, as well, and a good plot is all about prolonging the agony. Therefore, Dorothy doesn't only suffer from her desire to leave Oz and go home. She agonizes over the Wicked Witch of the West's cruelty to everyone, even the winged monkeys. She is outraged over the humbug Wizard's deception. She is distraught to realize that, by going to the home she misses so desperately, she will be leaving friends she has come to love.

Isn't that a far more interesting story than a simple tale of a lost girl looking for the road back to Kansas?

DAY 221—What is the most effective way to be cruel to your characters?

Consider the timing of your protagonist's abuse.

Perhaps your plan is to deprive him of everything he cares about, until there is nothing left but the final conflict. (And perhaps you are writing about Harry Potter...) My advice to use is to time those body blows carefully. They will lose their impact if they all fall at once. Let them rain down at an ever-increasing speed, then let the heaviest blow strike when you need your character to be bloodied but not broken. Let it drive the climactic scenes.

J.K. Rowling stretched out her cruelty to Harry Potter over seven books. She took his parents. She took his hope of a happy home life. She took his beloved godfather. She took his friend Cedric and, with him, his last scrap of the innocent belief that children are always protected. She took his father figure and mentor, Professor Dumbledore. And all this was just a warm-up.

In the final book, she took one cherished friend after another. She rattled the foundations of Hogwarts, the only true home Harry had ever known. She threatened the entire wizarding world with subjugation under the personification of utter evil...He Who Must Not Be Named...Lord Voldemort. Finally, she took Professor Snape, who had protected Harry for his entire life, without his knowledge, then she gave Harry that knowledge so that he could appreciate the full tragedy of Snape's story.

She did not—and this is important—take Harry's free will. She did not force him to sacrifice his life for everything and everyone he held dear. He did that on his own. But she led him to that point, one disaster at a time.

Did we look away, unable to bear the boy's suffering? No. We did not. We trusted the author to give us a satisfying resolution. And she did.

DAY 222—Is the story flowing smoothly?

You're deep into the mid-section of the book, heading for the ending. When you get close to the end, you'll know, because the story will take hold of you and you'll know exactly what needs to be done to finish it. Until then, you'll probably need to wrestle with it.

Don't forget what I've told you before. If the story's not flowing smoothly, ask yourself questions. How are your characters feeling? How would you behave if you were in their shoes? What changes in their circumstances are required to make them behave the way you need for them to behave.

Let them tell you the answers.

DAY 223—As you write, take care of your most essential business asset

When I sold my first book, I made the business decision to pump a lot of my income back into publicity. This made sense to me, because I was not starting a business that required me to rent a store or buy inventory or hire employees (although a secretary would be nice) or build a manufacturing facility. I really have no other business asset beyond myself and the copyrights to my existing works.

I would have been hard-put to produce those works without my trusty computer, so that's an important tool. A printer is also a nice thing to have. I've got a lot of consumable supplies like paper and envelopes and ink cartridges and such in my office. At any one time,

I've got hundreds of dollars of inventory of books I can sell when I do speaking engagements. But that's about it, as far as tools go.

Here's the way I see it. Stories are my only product. I am my only employee, and my brain is the only tool that I really can't do without. It behooves me to take care of that brain and the body in which is resides. Yet as a person who has been a mother for twenty-six years, I'm really not good at taking care of myself. It's very hard to do that when there are three people running around who really and truly are more important to you than you are to yourself. But I'm trainable, and I'm working on this conundrum.

This makes me think of the old story about two men having a woodcutting contest. One man worked tirelessly for four hours straight, chopping down one tree after another. The other man disappeared for a few minutes every half-hour.

The first man felt a bit superior. He was bound to win, because the other guy wasn't man enough to work for an hour without taking a break. Yet at the end of the contest, the "lazy" man won, because he had cut more wood. The loser asked him how this was possible when he had taken so many breaks. The winner told him that he had taken no breaks. He had spent that time sharpening his ax.

So I'm trying to learn to sharpen my ax. I've upgraded my diet lately—lots more organic veggies, a little less of my beloved caffeine, fewer meals out. I'm exercising more, taking walks and learning to dance. I'm putting music back in my life, playing piano and singing and going to concerts. I have ambitions to learn to meditate, but I have a storytelling brain. It never shuts up. Truthfully, it's very noisy in here. Still, maybe I can learn to diminish the deafening roar a little.

Today and in the days to come, my friend, I wish for you a little time to sharpen your ax.

DAY 224—I haven't given up on the sharpen-your-ax metaphor

Before you write your pages today, make a list of things that restore your artist's soul. My list includes playing the piano, gardening, having dinner with friends, and singing. What's on your list?

DAY 225—Writer's Block: Pretend like it doesn't exist

Writer's block is a perennial topic of conversation among writers. It's entirely likely I'll write about it again. It's comforting for a discouraged writer to hear a colleague say, "You're just having a bad day. You'll get past it."

Imagine me giving you a pat on the back.

Truth be told, talking about writer's block makes me a little nervous, so I try not to think about it. I'm a little superstitious that way.

When I do public appearances, I get that scary question all the time: "Do you get writer's block?" Or, even worse, I get the scarier question that presumes I've had that problem and that I will again: "What do you do about writer's block?" It's a particularly common question among new writers, and I think it's based in fear. Fear that the asker will start a project she just can't finish. Fear that she will reach into her subconscious for a story and find it empty. Fear that she is not good enough.

I always answer the question honestly, giving the asker the respect he or she deserves, but part of me wants to say, "Stop it! Stop giving your fear a voice."

I started my family when I was very young, only 23. This was about the time I started pursuing writing seriously. I have never had the time I needed to get my work done. I've scheduled my writing time around naps and preschool and piano lessons and driving teenagers to the mall. It has been frustrating at times, yes, but it means that the stories were building up in my head, waiting for the moment when I could sit down and type.

If you're feeling blocked, maybe you should walk away from your project for a couple of days. Feel free to ignore the arbitrary schedule imposed on you by this book. You're an artist. You can't be forced to create, just because of some number on the calendar. (Not unless you have a contract and you've written your deadline on that calendar...)

A serious writer is never truly idle. The story pieces shuffle around in my head constantly, and when they fit together, I know—even if I've got my hands in a sink full of dirty dishwater at the time.

My children are growing up and flying the coop. I only have one left at home now. The day is coming when I will mold my days around what *I* want and need to do. This may mean that the work comes less easily, because I won't have that forced time away from the keyboard for the stories to germinate. I hope not. I'd rather trust that all the life experience I've been cramming into the space between my ears will continue to feed my storytelling soul. Trust, after all, is a much better mindset for an artist than fear.

If you're a writer, I invite you to forget that the phrase "writer's block" was ever coined. Trust your ability. Trust the process. Trust yourself. Just sit down and write.

DAY 226—Check-in

You should be on page 189. If not, what are you doing to get there?

Are you writing every day? Honestly?

If your life truly won't let you make a habit of daily writing, decide what you can do. Renew your resolve and do it.

DAY 227—Things I've Already Said That Bear Repeating #10: Research widely and randomly.

You may recall my affectionate term for the research process: "Reading for a living." I encouraged you to read widely while you were plotting your book. After I have a general idea of where my story is set and what it's about, I hit the library and the internet and the bookstore early in the writing process. I read about my setting's history. I look at maps and photographs. I read first-person references like memoirs or letters. And I crawl randomly around the web, following my nose and satisfying my curiosity. There is no need to stop this process, just because you've begun writing your book.

You should never stop ferreting around for material that will make your story feel more real. If you do enough of this, I guarantee that you will find details that flesh out characters and generate the kind of subplots that will keep your book from sagging in the middle.

DAY 228—Another selfish nag

Do you know why I'm so intent on seeing you finish this book? Because I'm hoping you'll write me a cameo role for the eventual movie. So get to work.

DAY 229—If you're going to write me that cameo role...

...here's a hint. I sing better than I act, and I act better than I dance. So if you want to write me a scene where I'm sitting on top of a piano, weeping over a man who has done me wrong and drinking straight out of a bottle of bourbon while I sing, then you can go right ahead. It's far better that I sit still and sing than that I should try to dance in front of a camera.

DAY 230—Mary Anna's Random Writing Rule # 12: Everybody has a past

We are all affected profoundly by the things that have happened to us. Very few other things *do* affect us more than our pasts. Our genes do, certainly. The things that are happening to us right this minute affect us, but the minute passes so quickly that those events immediately become part of our pasts. The things we worry might happen in the future affect us, but our worries are shaped by the things that have already happened. Doesn't it seem obvious that we need to understand our characters' pasts in order to write their stories well?

Earlier in this book, I asked you to write character sketches. I think it's wise for you to look at those now and then. As you write, you're naturally going to learn more about your characters, so it wouldn't hurt if you revised those sketches as time goes by.

I know. You're thinking, "She wants me to work on the book every day *and* waste time doing character sketches that'll never see the light of day? She doesn't ask for much, does she?" To tell you the truth, I don't keep a lot of formal notes. My characters take shape in my head. Nevertheless, you're just starting out, and you might want to at least consider keeping track of your own characters in actual written documents.

However you construct your characters' pasts, you must constantly compare their reality against the story you're writing.

Does it make sense for a woman who lost her father when she was a child to be attracted to much older men? Yes, it does.

Does it make sense for a woman who was badly burned as a child in a house fire that killed her brother to be careless with lit cigarettes? Maybe. Maybe not. In either case, I suggest you think carefully about that woman's relationship with fire. It almost has to be an important element of your story.

Look at the story you're writing now. Do the actions of every last character make sense, based on what you know about their pasts?

DAY 231—A thought about your protagonist's past

There's no law against giving your main character some of your own traumas and weaknesses. There's actually no law against using *all* your traumas and weaknesses. They can have your more pleasant memories and character traits, as well. Your protagonist can be a mirror image of you, if that's what you want to do. It's not like you're going to sue yourself for defamation of character.

As an artist, I prefer to create new people to populate my imaginary world. Some of them might have my klutzy approach to athletics or my affinity for children or my interest in music, but only as a part of a personality that is largely *not* me nor anyone else I know. Somehow, I feel that to lift a character completely from real life is cheating.

Therefore, I encourage you to consider giving one character the life you *wish* you'd had and another character some nightmarish experiences you hope you never have. Ask yourself how these things in their pasts have shaped the people they came to be.

And yes, I know that you're pretty far down the path to finishing your story, but it's never too late to get a new understanding of its inhabitants. That understanding will help immeasurably when you edit the book, and sharpening your skill at giving your characters a fictional but believable past will help you with all the books you're going to write in the future.

DAY 232—Happy unNew Year!

In keeping with my habit of celebrating holidays with you whenever it suits me, let me wish you a happy new year. Ignore the calendar. Ignore the fact that you may not agree with my opinion that the new year begins on January 1. Any day can begin a new year, so let's celebrate this one.

In recognition of this fictional holiday, I'm going to make a list of suggested un-New Year's resolutions for you. Accept the ones that work for you, reject the rest, and add anything else that will help you focus on your goal.

I will write every day. (You knew I was going to put that one first, didn't you?)

I will read the works of other writers. Even if I don't enjoy them, I'll still learn something.

I will not be afraid to rewrite heavily. Just because I edit something doesn't mean the old stuff was bad. It just means that I think I can do better.

I will find someone I trust to help me edit my final draft before I submit it, because I am well-aware that nobody is perfect.

I will hone my skills of observation, taking time to do nothing but look around and store up experiences to use when I go back to writing.

I will not tolerate any weakness in craft from myself. If I don't know how to use punctuation properly, I will learn. I will remind myself that grammar is not scary. Most of the important stuff is taught in elementary school. I will approach this matter with confidence and acquire the skills I need.

I will listen to people who criticize constructively, but I will ignore people who are just looking for an opportunity to tell me I'm no good.

I will write my book, dammit.

DAY 233—Check-in

Let me see. You should be nearly 200 pages into your opus by now. I hope you're damn proud of yourself.

Hey! I used profanity in my last essay, too. What's getting into me?

I must be drunk with the joy of knowing that you're charging ahead with the book you've always dreamed of writing. Carry on! Make me proud!

DAY 234—Brace yourself for Reality Check Week.

When you let your newborn baby book toddle out into the world, you are taking a huge risk. And what are you risking, exactly? Bad reviews? Poor sales? Post-partum depression?

Well, yeah, but you're risking more than that. You're taking the risk of looking stupid in public. Are you a hundred-percent sure that your blue-eyed villain doesn't suddenly turn brown-eyed on page 247? If you're not, you should be. This week, I'm going to talk you through your reality checks, so that you don't have that awful moment when you're reading an email accusing you of changing a secondary character's name in mid-story...and you realize that the nitpicky reader is *right*.

Try to maintain at least a tenuous grasp of reality at all times.

DAY 235—Reality Check: Not even an idiot would go in a dark basement while a murderer is rampaging nearby

In mystery circles, we have a tradition of calling characters who venture into the woods while a serial murderer is on the loose "Too Stupid To Live." I have rewritten whole sections of books after I realized that Faye would never do the things I've written for her to do. The plot required her to do these things, and my life would have been much easier if I gave up and let her be stupid, but Faye is *not* stupid. If I need for her to be in mortal danger, then I need to figure out a way for mortal danger to sneak up on her, because she is not going to go looking for it.

I'm going to put this in bold type, because it's important: **Your characters must have their own reasons to act.** If you make them do illogical things that conveniently support the story you want to write, then your reader will notice. The last thing you want is for a reader to ask, "Now why'd he do *that*?"

If your character finds himself mistrusting something his wife says, then you as the writer will need to establish a relationship between them that makes this mistrust realistic. Your reader needs to buy into a scenario in which your character is suddenly terrified of this woman who has shared his bed for fifteen years. In any ordinary relationship, he would respond to a bizarre comment from her by saying, "What you just said didn't make sense. Can you clear it up for me?" If, instead, he packs a bag when she's not looking and heads for the hills, you're gonna have to convince me that he's got a good reason.

If your war hero disobeys orders, make me understand why.

If your seventeenth-century colonial American female protagonist goes against her father's will and the teachings of her church, then you must have already shown your readers a character who is either very strong or very foolhardy. And you are probably going to need to make your readers watch while she suffers the consequences of being uppity in that place and in that time.

Don't let your characters be Too Stupid To Live or Too Illogical To Be Believed.

DAY 236—Reality Check: Consult the weather report

Early on, did you establish what time of year it is? I write stories set in the American South and my character works outdoors. If I tell you she's shivering and she's in Florida, then it's probably December or January. (Actually, I usually just go ahead and say, "It was warm for early January," or "Faye needed to finish her Christmas shopping," because I believe in making life easy for my readers, but you can do it your way.) If I tell you that she's in Florida and she's sweating, then I need to give you a little more information. It could be May. It could be October. It could even be March. If I tell you it's so hot that she can't breathe, it's probably August, but July is a possibility.

However you manage it, let your reader know the time of year. Then keep track of it. If your story lasts for two weeks, then nothing will change. If it lasts for two years, then you need to keep track of the seasons. Otherwise, your readers will be lost in time, and they'll tell you about it. You do not want to get an email that says, "It doesn't get dark until after nine in June, so your killer was offing people in broad daylight."

DAY 237—Reality Check: Is your character superhuman?

My character, Faye Longchamp, is five feet tall and she weighs a hundred pounds. I have established that she is tough, strong, and fast for a woman the size of a hummingbird, but come on. She still ain't Wonder Woman.

When I need for her to exert herself in a crisis, I try to maintain a sense of reality. In *Artifacts*, she needs to move a desperately wounded and bleeding friend up a narrow flight of stairs. She manages, but it's not pretty. She has to drag him, and he leaves a lot of his blood behind. There's simply no way that tiny Faye could move this man without a trace. Later, when she needs to move him across a steep roof during a hurricane, she has the help of a brawny man, and the job is still almost too much for them. As an artist, I enjoy the challenge of working within these constraints. If Faye could easily outrun and outfight the bad guys, what kind of story would I have?

I'm small, too. I'm bigger than Faye, but I ain't Wonder Woman, so this helps me write her character's motions. I use the strength of my lower body to lift, and I use the leverage of my not-insignificantly-sized hips to shove heavy objects where I want them to go. If your character is built differently than you are, give some thought to how he or she moves. You don't want your husky private eye to run like a girl.

If you put some effort into imagining yourself in your characters' bodies, I think you'll find that they behave in a more true-to-life way.

DAY 238—Reality Check: What day is it?

The calendar offers you an opportunity to slip up that is so subtle, so slight...why, it's almost diabolical. Are you always aware of what day of the week it is in your characters' world?

If not, then you risk sending a government worker to work on a Saturday. You risk having your devout Catholic private eye go for three weeks without attending mass. You could look back and realize that your schoolteacher victim went to work for seven days straight before she died.

It's not hard to make a note in your manuscript every time the day changes. This little habit will help you avoid so many problems...and it's not too late to go back and do it now.

DAY 239—Reality Check: What time is it?

Your characters are going to have days when they wish they hadn't gotten out of bed. If you've done a good enough job of making their lives miserable, in preparation for a grand finale that resolves all their problems and leaves them happy and victorious, then those miserable days are going to be very full. Your main character, in particular, may be moving from place to place and having important conversations with other characters. Maybe she's even running from the law or her lover or a purple alien with an evil-looking probe.

I suggest that you map those days out. You want to make sure that she's not driving five places and having an adventure at each of those places, all before lunch. Even worse, you do not want to say that she's driving from Santa Monica to Hollywood unless you know that she has enough time to do that, and you'd better take the time of day and traffic conditions into account. People will notice, and they will tell you if you're wrong.

And no, I don't know how long it takes to drive from Santa Monica to Hollywood, so don't look to me for that answer. You know how to operate the internet. This is both the beauty and the curse of the World Wide Web. You can answer any question in seconds...and your readers know it. If you make a mistake that could have been avoided with a simple web search, their confidence in you will be shaken. They will stop trusting your imaginary world.

This is the last thing a novelist ever wants to see happen. Check your facts.

DAY 240—Check-in

You have written over two hundred pages, and I'm glad. Nobody can write the story in your head but you, and I'm happy to be part of helping you get it out into the world. Someday, someone will read it. They will enjoy it or be horrified by it or be touched deeply by what you have to say. Keep going.

DAY 241—Have you tried to picture someone reading your book?

This won't be of particular help in writing today's page, or tomorrow's, but maybe it'll distract you from the pain of writing a book's middle. (Or maybe you're loving it. Different people experience things different ways. But I always find the middle to be a mushy agony.)

It took me many years to find someone willing to publish my fiction...many, many years. I wrote. I submitted. I got rejected. I got an agent. Still, I got rejected. Then I finally sold *Artifacts*, and I was launched immediately into the process of editing it and promoting it and even into the arcane details like building a website and getting an author photo made.

In all those years of seeking publication, I never thought much about what it would be like when somebody actually read the thing.

In April 2003, the day came when I went to church and somebody said, "I started *Artifacts* yesterday and I'm about halfway through."

I don't know what emotion I was expecting at that moment, but it wasn't terror. It just hadn't occurred to me that people I knew would buy my book and read it and maybe hate it. In a week, I'd be back at church, looking that poor woman in the face and wondering whether she was thinking, "Ew...that was a terrible book."

I eventually got over it, and I do think she liked the book, but try not to join me in my neurotic suffering. Spend some time today picturing people enjoying your hard work, and remember that there's no way to get from here to there that doesn't involve writing today's page. Even if you don't write it today, you're gonna have to write it eventually.

DAY 242—Go ahead and try to develop a writer's thick skin

One day people are going to read your work. Agents will read it and reject it. Editors will read it and reject it. When it does eventually see print, reviewers will render opinions over which you have no control. People you don't even know will send you emails, explaining how you could have written a better book.

The response to all art is subjective. There is no work of art that is universally beloved. I feel certain that there are people who detest the Mona Lisa.

My advice is to listen to your critics, because they may have a point. Try to objectively sift the helpful criticism from the stuff that just festers and burns for no good reason. Make good use of the helpful criticism and let the rest go.

This is impossible advice to follow, but it is good advice, and I suggest that you give it a try.

DAY 243—Mary Anna's Random Writing Rule #12: Don't be afraid to grow

We all have our own writing style. Some people will like yours and some people won't. Variety is the spice of life, and all that.

This doesn't mean that your style can't grow and change. Stick-straight, waist-length hair might have been stylish when your mother (or even grandmother) was a teenager in the 1960s, but I sort of hope she doesn't wear her hair that way now. Try to imagine a forty-five-year-old man still sporting the mullet he wore as a high school student in the Eighties. If Jon Bon Jovi can cut his hair, you can re-evaluate your writing style now and then.

My agent, Anne, tells me that she was so intrigued by my writing style when she read the first page of my first novel, *Wounded Earth,* that she went around her office, showing it to people and asking their opinions. Some people really liked it and some people really didn't. This doesn't bother me. I think it is far better to trigger a reaction in people than it is to have them read your work and say, "Meh."

That page attracted the attention of the agent I still retain after nearly fifteen years. In its way, it changed my life. Let's look at it:

> Babykiller was meticulous in all things. It was his defining quality. Attention to detail was the key to longevity in his chosen profession, and Babykiller had been in business a long, long time.
>
> Most of his competitors from the early days were dead or in prison, and he couldn't claim responsibility for all their misfortune. No, they had simply chosen a dangerous line of work. He was well on his way to outliving a second generation and he was considering retirement. At least he had been, before the oncologist's verdict. Retirement planning seemed so futile when death was certain.
>
> Babykiller had created a life out of certainties. He left nothing to chance. He made no mistakes—at least, he made no mistakes that were obvious to the cretins who purchased his services. He had built a seamless organization that ran like a Volvo. It was reliable. It required little maintenance. It was safe. It was boring as hell. Even if his organization survived him—and

he cared very little whether it did or not—it was a plain-vanilla sort of legacy for a man of his caliber.

Anne commented specifically on the way that I varied the lengths of the sentences. They range from the word-economical "It was safe," to that 30-word behemoth at the end of the passage. I have a tendency toward labyrinthine sentences full of commas and long words of Latin derivation. To me, interspersing terse bursts of no-frills communication is an antidote for a style that might feel flabby without them. Sometimes, a short sentence is all you need. Brevity works.

Check your own style to see if an occasional change-of-pace might do it some good.

DAY 244—Mary Anna's Random Writing Rule #13: Another kind of variety

I used a lot of words in that last post, telling you to vary your sentence lengths in order to keep your readers interested. I don't need a lot of words to point out to you that this works for words, too. Sometimes "enumerate" is the right word. Sometimes, it's better to just say "count." It's your book. You get to decide.

DAY 245—You look tired

Step away from your computer and take a walk. Your body will thank you, and I have a feeling that your subconscious will take the opportunity to work out some knotty plot problems for you. Enjoy the break.

DAY 246—Things I've Already Said That Bear Repeating #11: The novelist's most important questions

Whenever you're stuck on a plot point, think of your character's motivations. When you don't know where you're going to go with the story next, ask yourself this:

What is this person's problem?

Then ask yourself, *How will he try to solve it?*

Soon enough, you'll know what to do.

DAY 247—Check-in

Oh, good heavens. Did you ever think that you would see page 210?

No?

I did.

DAY 248—Verbs rock!

Once, my dear friend Bev Browning decided she wanted to write a novel without using verbs.

Bev is a brilliant writer, and perhaps she achieved this feat, but Bev is a ghostwriter. She can't tell me who she ghosts for, so I can't tell you. Still, if anyone can write a novel without pesky things like verbs, Bev can. As for mere mortals like you and me, dear readers, we should leave such projects to crazy people like Bev. Oops. I meant to say, "We should leave such projects to true professionals. Like Bev"

I see a common flaw when I review manuscripts that are nearly, but not quite, ready for publication. The narrative feels flabby, and flabbiness often has its roots in the overuse of descriptors. Excess adjectives and adverbs are like fat. They obscure the lean muscularity of your prose. They jiggle when your story walks.

With that metaphor in mind, compare these two sentences:

"The saggy skin of her face hung loosely down her neck, floppy and pale."

"Her jowls jiggled when she walked."

Now, that first sentence isn't really terrible. It might even work, in the right story, provided the sentences in the immediate vicinity weren't equally flabby. It also might work if I cut out two of these four words: "saggy," "loosely," "floppy," or "pale."

But the second sentence *jiggles*. You can feel the motion of this large person. This sentence sets up a host of possibilities for characterization. Is she trudging through life, weighed down by burdens and by her very own body? Or is she upbeat, striding through this world and doing what must be done, aware that strangers sneer at her floppy jowls? I, for one, want to know.

When you edit your work, do a complete read-through with an eye toward word choice, particularly verbs and nouns. A sentence can exist without adverbs, adjectives, conjunctions, interjections, and prepositions, but it ain't a sentence without a verb and (almost always) a noun. (Despite what Bev says.)

Never miss the opportunity to trade a weakly modified noun like "saggy skin" for "jowls." And never miss the opportunity to trade a flabby verb for a verb that jiggles.

DAY 249—Nouns rock, too!

If verbs give a reader a precise sense of movement and action, nouns give a precise sense of what a thing *is*. If you call someone a girl, a woman, a female, a lady, a doyenne, an ingénue, a coed, a grandmother, a dame, a vamp, or a bitch, then you have said something about the person in question. You have also said something about the person describing her or about the time in which she lives.

Is the air around your characters moving in such a way that you would describe it as a breeze? A gust? A windstorm? A zephyr? These are single-word descriptions that you can actually feel on your skin.

Finally, please notice that "girl," "dame," "vamp," and "bitch" are all words of a single syllable. It isn't necessary to use twelve letters and five syllables to boil a description down to a single word. It is only necessary to use the right word.

DAY 250—Yet another nag

I have a deep dark suspicion that you might be behind the pace. Why do I think that? Because you're well into the middle of your book, and there's where the demons be, me matey. Arrrh. (Can you tell that I just wrote a book about pirates?)

Put your hands on the keyboard and type.

DAY 251—Scene by scene

Are you conscious of how you build your scenes, and how you use them to build your book?

Most modern fiction is constructed as a sequence of scenes, each told from a single point-of-view. A story of a day in the life of a ten-year-old, for example, might consist of a scene at the breakfast table told from the student's point-of-view, then a scene from his mother's point-of-view as she waves good-bye to her son getting on the school bus, then a scene from his morning spelling class and another set in the school cafeteria, both told from his point-of-view. And so on.

When I'm editing at the scene level, I read the piece through at least once with a single goal in mind: making sure every scene really needs to be there. I ask myself whether a scene advances the plot or deepens characterization or injects an important sense of realism by improving the reader's perception of the setting. If a scene that shows our hero eating Rice Krispies does none of those things, then it has to go, no matter how well I described that nutritious breakfast's snap, crackle, and pop. I'm not really happy unless a scene accomplishes more than one of my goals as a storyteller.

Remember...if a scene serves no function other than to highlight the beauty of your prose, then it doesn't get to stay. Make your lovely prose work for you or make it go away.

DAY 252—One way to think about scenes

I don't think of scenes as separate from one another. In my mind, when the screen in my reader's head goes dark at the end of one scene, it immediately lights up with the next scene. Stopping one scene and starting another is just my way to shift the reader's attention from the happenings experienced by a character in one location to events that take place in another location or at another time.

I think of all these self-contained scenes as a string of pearls, flowing gently into one another and taking the reader along for the ride.

DAY 253—Another way to think about scenes

Nobody thinks linearly, moving from one thought to the next in an orderly progression of time and space. We flit from one thing to another. We sit in church and meditate on what we need to put on our grocery list, though we are occasionally called into the here-and-now when we are expected to stand and sing a hymn. A story that features a character sitting in church might begin with a scene where she sits in her usual pew. Then it might cut to a scene that recalls the last time she sat in that pew, with the husband who just left her the day before. Then it might cut to a scene that depicts their final argument. And then, in quick succession, to scenes that show their first date and a party where she saw him speak quietly to the woman with whom he cheated. There might be a scene where she imagines telling him what she thinks of him, or a scene where she imagines shooting him while he sleeps

You could tell an entire short story during the time when she sits alone in that pew, culminating in a scene where she rises with the rest of the congregation to sing the final hymn, but she is so far from the reality her body inhabits that she just can't manage to find the right page in the hymnal.

The ability that the scene break gives you to move through time and space is a very potent tool. Fit your scenes together carefully, like the parts of a finely crafted piece of furniture, and even a story that is crafted of twenty different scenes will look seamless.

DAY 254—Check-in

You are 217 pages into your book. Good gracious. Did you think you would ever get this far? Pat yourself on the back, write a page, and print that puppy out. It's time to admire the pile of pages. Go ahead and fondle it a little, if you want to. Nobody's looking but me, and I understand how you feel.

DAY 255—You've got some reading to do

I'm going to give you three days to read your working draft this time and, no. You don't get to take a break from your daily pages. If you want to work ahead, though, and write extra today, then you can knock off writing and just sit down and read. It's your call. Just don't think that the need to look back and read what you wrote is an excuse to stop making forward progress.

By this time, you should feel like a horse heading back to the barn after a long day with a cowboy on your back. You're ready for somebody to relieve you of that heavy saddle, and you can smell the oats. Your goal is in sight and you're moving a little faster all the time. Don't lose that momentum by breaking the habit of writing every day. Write your page, then settle down and read for a while.

DAY 256—Keep your focus on the climax

Even if you paid no attention when I urged you to outline this tome, I feel certain that you've figured out where you're going by now. You are only a few chapters from the end, so surely you have a darn good idea what that ending is going to be. This does not mean that there are not still surprises in store for you.

More than once, I have reached this point in a book, so near the climax, only to have a pair of secondary characters look at each other and find true love. I had a firm idea of what was going to happen to the main characters, but these bit players sneaked in out of nowhere and stole a scene or two. I love it when my made-up creations develop minds of their own. It makes my job so much easier.

Surprises aside, I'm pretty sure you know what is required to wrap this book up tight. Maybe someone is about to admit their love, or maybe an important character is going to die tragically, or maybe a detective is preparing to solve a murder, or maybe a child is about to be thrust into manhood. It's *your* book. I don't have to tell you the climax. You *know*. All you need to do is get there.

As you read, look for things that interfere with your goal of getting from the beginning of your book to that imagined ending. Take a red pen and make notes in the margin, but keep them brief. You are not rewriting or line editing. You are just noticing places where you want to remind yourself of things like, "This descriptive passage needs to be tighter," or "Where did this character come from? He's been out of the action for eighty pages."

Wait until you're finished to fix these things. At the moment, you are just drawing yourself a road map for later, when you're ready to edit the whole book.

DAY 257—Did your plot morph into something else since you wrote page 1?

How well does what you wrote match what you *said* you were going to write?

Be honest. It's really okay if you deviated from your outline. You're the artist and you're in charge. But don't fool yourself. If the book in your hand is about something else, or even somebody else, than you planned it to be, now is the time to acknowledge it.

Why now? Because if you write the climactic ending that you always planned, it might not match the book that you actually wrote.

Once you've finished reading your draft, haul out that outline you wrote weeks and weeks ago. Does it look like the almost-book in your hands? If not, how does it differ? Do you need to revise the outline before you plunge ahead to the end?

If so, buckle down and do that revision, even if it puts you off your schedule by a few days. Better to write a good book in 371 days or 96 days (or however long it takes) than to hold yourself to a schedule that yields a bad book.

DAY 258—We hold these truths to be self-edited...

Modern technology has revealed to us that Thomas Jefferson edited the Declaration of Independence down to the last individual word, even as the ink was drying.

Who among us is really surprised to hear that? Still, seeing a photo of the rough draft of the Declaration of Independence, complete with Jefferson's edits and the comments of Benjamin Franklin and John Adams, is enough to give this history buff cold chills.

If Thomas Jefferson didn't get it right the first time, why should we be hard on ourselves when our first drafts aren't everything we'd hoped they'd be? Editing is an important part of our art form. In fact, it could even be viewed as an entirely separate art form, requiring the use of an entirely separate set of skills. To edit one's own work requires clarity of thought and the ability to take an unbiased look at a piece of work that was created directly from one's heart and soul. Editing requires an unwavering belief that a story can made better, and it requires the judgment to recognize when a story has reached in its final form.

When Jefferson asked John Adams why Jefferson should be chosen, between the two of them, for the job of writing the Declaration of Independence, Adams said, "'Reason first, you are a Virginian, and a Virginian ought to appear at the head of this business. Reason second, I am obnoxious, suspected, and unpopular. You are very much other-wise. Reason third, *you can write ten times better than I can.*" (The italics are mine.)

When you doubt the importance of typing letters onto your computer screen, day in and day out, remember what words can do. They can influence. They can convince. They can deceive. They can flatter. They can wound. They can heal. They can foment war. They can wage peace. And when an uncommonly brilliant writer finds himself standing at a turning point in history, pen in hand, words can change the world.

DAY 259—A few world-changing pieces of writing

As a follow-up to yesterday's tribute to the Declaration of Independence, I'll list a few world-changing texts. We're fiction writers, and most of these aren't fiction, but they did profoundly change the way people think and act. Add a few texts of your own choice, then meditate on the power of our chosen art form:

The Magna Carta

Martin Luther's *Ninety-Five Theses*

The Bhagavad Gita

Uncle Tom's Cabin by Harriet Beecher Stowe

The Art of War by Sun Tzu

The Torah, *The Koran*, and *The Christian Bible*, the last one both for its religious influence and for its place in history as the initial product of Gutenberg's great invention.

The Prince by Niccolò Macchiavelli

Analects of Confucius

The Constitution of the United States of America

The Republic by Plato

DAY 260—Can you name three works of fiction that influenced your own work?

Make a list of your inspirations and keep it by your computer. Or even under your pillow. Here are mine:

1. *To Kill A Mockingbird* by Harper Lee

Ms. Lee's very personal description of the segregated South of her youth sang with her love for her adored father and the flawed people around him and even for the flawed world where they all lived. My work features a biracial protagonist who grew up in the 1970s South, and all my books are set in the 21st century South. Faye was born in 1968, eight short years after Ms. Lee's book was published.

I like to describe Faye's world as a place where the past is receding, but it is not yet dead. The people in Faye's world are descendants of the people in the world that Harper Lee created for Scout Finch.

Despite the fact that she is not white, the social changes that have taken place during Faye's lifetime mean that she can live a life that her grandmother could not have imagined in the mid-20th century, earning a Ph.D. and starting a business and marrying a man of a different race. Nevertheless, the fact of her race is always with her, and old prejudices do still linger in unexpected places. I think these things make Faye and her stories deeper and richer than they would have been if I had not given her a biracial heritage.

2. *The Source* by James Michener

This novel chronicles the lives and work of archaeologists working in the Middle East. I admired Michener's technique of telling the archaeologists' present-day story, while alternating it with stories from the past associated with the artifacts they uncovered. My Faye books have their own structure, but they do owe a great deal to my admiration for Michener's way of letting the artifacts tell the story. It is no accident that *Artifacts* is the title of the first Faye Longchamp mystery.

3. *The Martian Chronicles* by Ray Bradbury

I couldn't tell you the plots of these short stories. For me, the plots were not the point. I was simply stunned by the poetry of Bradbury's language. I had always loved science fiction, but before reading *The Martian Chronicles*, I had seen it as separate from literary fiction. From Bradbury, I learned that the quality of a work of prose has very little to do with its subject matter and everything to do with the author's command of our incomparably beautiful and powerful language.

DAY 261—Check-in

If you're on-pace you're in the vicinity of page 224. If you are, I'm curious as to how you've accomplished that feat. I'm not a creature of habit in my day-to-day life, but in my work life, I am. I take my daughter to school every weekday morning, and when I get home, I sit down to my computer. If I had a day job, my writing time would be shorter, but I think I'd still have a time of day when I pursued my writing dream.

Other people work better when they can schedule a big block of time and work, to the exclusion of everything else. They might borrow a friend's vacation cabin for a weekend and type their fingers bleed, and maybe they'd get as much done in a weekend as day-to-day writers like me get done in a month.

Others are totally random, writing when they see a block of free time on their calendar. This approach takes a lot of discipline, because it's easy to look up and notice that six weeks has passed since they wrote a word.

How do you handle your writing life?

DAY 262—Mary Anna's Random Writing Rule #14: No, it's not perfect, but leave it alone for now

I'm finicky about my work. I am a recreational editor. I can kill a lot of time paging through the current work-in-progress, changing pretty good words into just right words. It upsets me to see that I've missed a typo. It's very hard for me to give myself permission to be a flawed human being.

Nevertheless, that urge to make everything absolutely perfect can prevent a perfectionist from ever finishing anything.

When I start work for the day, I scroll back a few pages to see what my characters are doing and thinking, and I read those pages to get me in the right mindset to start writing. I might twiddle with a word or two, but *I do not let myself get so caught up in the need for perfection that I exhaust that day's writing time without generating anything new.*

At this point in your manuscript, you should be feeling a narrative drive toward the conclusion. Go with it. Fling words onto the computer screen with abandon and edit them later. Right now, just let your story be itself. You can polish it later.

DAY 263—I said something really important yesterday

It is something so important that I'm going to copy it here with no further commentary. (And if you have been noticing my tragic case of chronic logorrhea, you will know how much effort it cost me to omit the commentary.)

> I do not let myself get so caught up in the need for perfection that I exhaust that day's writing time without generating anything new.

DAY 264—Be careful, people will talk: Dialogue and narrative techniques

By now, you're far enough into your book that you've surely written a lot of dialogue. How's it going? Do your characters sound like human beings when they talk? Can you advance your narrative smoothly, using your own style?

Ever-perfect grammar can sound ridiculous in dialogue, but transcriptions of actual speech show that real-world dialogue is too random and repetitive to use unedited in fiction. Complicating matters is the fact that people breathe. They interrupt themselves and each other. They pause to think before answering a tough question. It's not easy to replicate these rhythms when writing fiction.

As you develop your craft, you'll want to pay close attention to the individual voices of your characters as you write dialogue, but you must also be aware of your own narrative style. Each writer has a unique voice. Even when you were doing your first-grade writing assignments, you had a voice.

I think some writers anguish about finding their voices to the point that the doubt affects their work. Even worse, that doubt causes them to give up their work. That's not what we're here to do today. So my first piece of advice regarding developing your narrative voice and your style for writing dialogue is this: "Don't worry too much about it. Just write what you hear."

Stay tuned through this week for more advice on this subject.

DAY 265—How does your voice look?

It is important for a writer to read intelligently. You should first appreciate a piece of writing for the information it conveys or the story it tells. Then you should take some time to consider how the writer chose to arrange the words on the page. And the physical arrangement of those words *is* a part of the amorphous thing we call "voice."

How long are the paragraphs? How long are the sentences? How complex are those sentences? Are the words in those sentences long and Italianate or are they short, blunt, and Anglo-Saxon? Even some poetic figures of speech can be detected visually—assonance and alliteration come to mind.

The rhythm of a dialogue passage is a very visual thing, even more so than the rhythm of a narrative passage. You can see a rapid-fire exchange of harsh words, simply by those words' layout on the page. A leisurely conversation between lovers just won't look the same.

DAY 266—Every word you use is a conscious choice

When you read the work of others, consider how the author chose a vocabulary appropriate to the piece. A first-person narrative offers an unparalleled opportunity for characterization by word choice. Every line in the book is dialogue. Every descriptive passage in the piece is filtered through the narrator's eyes. If something is described, it is because your protagonist considered it important enough to describe. The words used in that description can only be the words chosen by that character. Choose well.

Whether you're writing in first-, second-, or third-person, narrative passages describing setting and action offer you the opportunity to work like a poet. I often suggest that writers begin solidifying an important narrative passage in their minds by making a list of "perfect words" that communicate the feeling they're trying to convey. Nobody's going to yell at you if you don't use every last one of those words. In fact, using every last one of them is probably overkill. Still, making that list will help you gather your thoughts in a way that only another writer will understand.

DAY 267—You don't want to hear this, but...

...I believe that a writer's voice evolves through time and practice. I was told early in my fiction-writing life that I had a very strong voice—something that is a double-edged sword, since a noticeable voice is also a voice that some readers might dislike—but this was not early in my *writing* life. I had already spent eight years as an environmental consultant, which is a profession that has no product other than its reports. I wrote reports and proposals and marketing plans, day in and day out. Before that, I wrote a master's thesis in a matter of months.

This work experience has made me utterly comfortable at the keyboard. Couple that with the fact that I won the high school typing award, thanks to many years spent at a piano keyboard developing my eye-hand coordination, and you'll understand why I say that I don't even think about the physical process of writing. It feels as if I am beaming my thoughts onto the screen. (Fortunately for me, I took two years of high school English under the late and lamented Mrs. Garner, so those thoughts are already grammatical. This is a great timesaver.)

When you reach the point where you are not thinking about the process of getting words on the page, and when you reach the point where you know exactly what you want to say and can compose it on the fly, you'll probably find that you write in a voice that cannot be mistaken for anyone else. Yes, it will take some time, but you can look forward to it.

DAY 268—Check-in

Where are we? Page 231? At 250 words per page, that's almost 60,000 words. You could call that a book. Some famous books have been that short. I think *Jonathan Livingston Seagull* and *The Old Man and the Sea* are even shorter.

In most cases, I think you need something upwards of 60,000 words to develop a plot with some depth, but still. If you're still working at the pace we set out the outset, you have shown that you have the endurance to be a novelist. Is that cool or what?

DAY 269—Listen to your story sing

When I'm polishing my craft, I like to draw from other art forms. I'm a musician, so music often informs my work. Everything I've mentioned so far during this week of focus on style—the arrangement of the words on the page, the length and complexity of sentences, the length and floweriness of words—all these things give your prose an intrinsic rhythm and melody.

Everybody has their own work habits, but I can't work in a room where a television or stereo is playing. I don't tend to read my work to myself aloud, though it's a great technique that many wonderful writers use, but I do hear the words and sentences in my head as I type them. I don't like other words and music to compete for my attention.

As you read your story, does it have the feel of a piece of well-developed music? Does the pacing of your words reflect the action? A leisurely walk should be told at a different pace than a desperate race against time in an ambulance loaded with a critically injured child. Have you used your choice of word length and sentence length to force your readers to consume the story in *your* natural rhythm, not theirs?

In your rush to get your story on the page, don't forget to listen to the sounds it makes.

DAY 270—Things I've Already Said That Bear Repeating #12: Villainy is endlessly entertaining

Who is the villain in your story?

Or perhaps it would be more comprehensive to ask the question this way: *Who or what is the antagonist in your story?*

It is certainly possible for a book to feature a non-human antagonist. Science fiction thrives on marauding aliens. Zombie stories focus on the undead. In a far more literary vein, *The Old Man and the Sea* pits its protagonist against nature itself. Still, in most cases, the roadblock between a book's main character and happiness is generally embodied in human form.

Hannibal Lecter.

Simon Legree.

Satan.

(Notice the sibilance in those names. The sounds of the letters "s" and "l" just sound snakelike and slimy. Perhaps that is why these guys have those names.)

People love to watch evil at play in the same way that they love to ride roller coasters. They want to explore this thing they fear, but they want to do it without being destroyed themselves.

Now, as you finish the first draft of your book, is a good time to consider your antagonist. Are his or her motivations clear? He might be insane—Hannibal Lecter, for example, likes to eat people—but are his insane machinations clearly presented? Are those motivations consistent? Do they drive the plot?

Most important of all, at this stage of the game: Are the antagonist's motivations central to the book's climactic action? (Which you should be writing right about now...)

If not, your climax will feel weak. Worse, it will not feel inevitable.

If you do this analysis and find that the role of your antagonist needs to be tweaked, just make a note to yourself to do it later. Write the book's final big scenes as you know they need to be, then go back during the editing process and fine-tune the character motivations that will lead you there.

You'll know you got the villain right when she scares even you.

DAY 271—Yet another selfish nag

Have you written my cameo role? If not, then do so. Right this minute. Then finish the darn book before I get so old that even Hollywood's makeup artists cannot render me fit for the silver screen.

You'll need to make her a slender brunette of a certain age with a thick southern accent. Or, if your novel is set in Bolivian among Bolivians, you'll have to make her mute, because I'm not much of an actress.

If you love me, you'll write me a romantic scene with Brendan Fraser or Robert Downey, Jr. or, in a cougar-ish vein, Chris Pine. (I'm no cougar, but I'm enough of an actress to behave like one, ever so briefly, in the service of great art.)

I'll bet you're feeling inspired now, so go write yourself a book.

DAY 272—Writer's block? Trust the process

When I teach, I am invariably asked questions about writer's block. Do I get it? How does one cure it? Is it inevitable?

I never know whether I should reach out and hug the terrified questioner, murmuring, "It'll be okay, really," or whether I should just reach out and shake the person and say, "Get a grip!"

Sometimes I think that worrying about writer's block is a symptom of a bigger problem. I think that some people think of WRITING as something that is so deeply important and larger-than-life that it must be written in bold, italicized capital letters. Well, it *is* important. It's my chosen art, and maybe it's yours. But if I write something stupid today, or even if I don't write today at all, nobody will die. No civilizations will fall. The sun will not fail to rise or set.

Writing should be fun. It should be the thing that helps you shake the world's pettiness aside. It should be something you anticipate fondly while you're taking care of the boring, odious tasks of daily life. If you're like me, the stories pile up in your head while you're doing those boring and odious tasks. They're waiting to burst out when you finally...finally...get a chance to sit down and write.

All the things you did yesterday, while you were waiting to have time to write, and all the things you've learned and all the life you've lived are bottled up in your head. You can trust that when you reach into your creative well for stories, something will be there. As I've already told you, my late father liked to say, "No education is ever wasted," and my father was always right.

Feeling blocked as a writer doesn't mean that you have nothing to say. I think it means that you have let your anxieties tell you that you have nothing to say that is *good enough.*

The cure? Write anyway.

DAY 273—Writer's block, revisited

I talked about writer's block yesterday, but it's difficult to exhaust the subject. Maybe this is telling. I can write all week about not feeling able to write. Perhaps the difficulty when a writer is blocked is that he or she simply needs to find the right subject, something that invokes passion or excitement. Or maybe, in the case of writer's block, outright terror.

I was once on a panel with two other writers who had published many dozens of books between them, and another writer who was about as far along in his career as I was and who was just as serious about it. During the question-and-answer period, the conversation kept veering toward the question of writer's block. People genuinely wanted to know what we did when inspiration didn't come.

We tried serious answers.

"Trust the process."

"Write whether you feel like it or not. The act of sitting down and beginning a project will trigger that mysterious part of the brain that sends you your stories."

"Write through the tough parts. Yeah, maybe you'll get a book that has a slam-bang beginning and a can't-miss ending, with a bunch of saggy parts in between, but you can always edit. That's what revisions are for."

These answers did not mollify the crowd, so we went for humor... black humor, which is usually quite truthful underneath the sarcasm:

"I have a contract. My contract has a due date on it. Every day, that due date gets closer; thus, I write whether I feel like it or not."

"When I need inspiration, I just look at my credit card bill."

If your goal is to be a professional writer someday, perhaps your inspiration should be pretending you have a contract with a due date on it, or imagining that your royalties might someday make a dent in that credit card bill.

I don't think I'm done with this subject, so we may be talking about the quest for inspiration again tomorrow, but I think I'll leave you with this thought today—

Don't let your mind get in the way of your art. When the nattering voices in your head tell you things you don't want to hear, drown those voices out with the clattering of your computer keys.

DAY 274—Don't wait for inspiration, but trust that it will come

I am an engineer to the core. More than five years of training so demanding that it could pass for a brainwashing exercise will do that to you. I have trouble accepting as fact things that cannot be proven, but I don't want to live in a world without faith and miracles, so I work hard at believing in things not seen.

There are things about the creative process that I don't understand. How is it that I can slave over a difficult piano piece for weeks, then suddenly sit down and play it well? (Not perfectly. That would be a true miracle. But better than before and, as an amateur, that's all I can hope to achieve.)

How is it that I can go to bed with no idea what the plot for my book is going to be, yet wake up with an interesting premise that is actually plausible?

I cannot answer these things. I just believe that if you keep writing and you keep leaving yourself open to inspiration and you keep filling your head full of the information you need to make your book feel real, then the inspiration will come. And the book will come. And after that, inspiration will come again.

DAY 275—Check-in

Page 238. Are you there? Yes? If I were you, I'd start working big numbers like "page 238" into casual conversation.

You could say at random, "Yeah, I'm 238 pages into my novel. I'm not sure my hard drive can hold it." Or you could respond to your teenager's whine thusly: "You have a five-page paper to write by next week? Well, *I've* written 231 pages in 231 days. So there."

It's okay to start being insufferable, right about now. You've earned it.

DAY 276—There's gotta be a writing tip in here somewhere...

When I was researching my south Louisiana adventure, *Plunder*, I made an epic trip to the watery lands south of New Orleans that culminated in a good hard look at the results of the BP oil spill—-miles of absorbent boom, tons of sandbags, scads of helicopters, herds of clean-up ships, and more oil-stained marsh grass than I ever hope to see again in my lifetime.

One of the more dramatic moments in that trip came when I ran afoul of the law, receiving twin citations for fishing without a license and for committing this crime in waters that had been closed to fishing because of the oil spill. (I didn't know we were in restricted waters. Truly...)

The drama in this story arose when I found out that the penalty for fishing license-free is over $250. Gulp. And I still don't know the penalty for fishing in restricted waters, because that infraction requires the infractor to appear personally before the judge. Big gulp. This is not a small effort nor expense, not when the infractor lives nine hours away in Florida and she has a book coming out three days after the court date.

When the magnitude of my problem became clear, I decided it was time to beg Plaquemines Parish for mercy. The first step in this process should have been to call the phone number written on the citation, but I was denied. It was completely indecipherable. I still don't know what it said.

Since I know how to operate the internet, I looked up the parish government's phone list and started calling people, asking sweetly for help. After talking to six people in six departments, including two judge's offices, I finally found myself talking to a nice lady at the District Attorney's office. I told my sad story for the seventh time. (I lived far away, my mother was very ill, I was a single parent...all of these things were true.) She asked if I'd ever been convicted of a fish and wildlife violation. I said, "I don't even *fish*." And I don't. This one-time legal infraction was one of those peer-pressure mistakes that you warn your children about. "But everybody else was doing it..."

Then she said I might qualify for a diversion program. I'm a little foggy on the details. I had to pay something to be in the program, but it was way less than the fine would have been. Then I had to fill out some paperwork, follow some instructions carefully, wait for some undetermined probationary period, then my record was wiped clean. I am now as innocent as a newborn babe.

I cannot tell you how happy I was not to be folding a quick trip to New Orleans into my busy life, as much as I want to go back there sometime soon.

So how can I slap this experience into some kind of shape that will make it look like a writing tip? Hmmmm.

Spending an entire morning navigating Plaquemines Parish's government felt a lot like doing book research. Sometimes, you ask somebody a question and they send you to someone else, who gives you a half an answer that turns out to be wrong. This stage can go on a long time, but it's important not to quit. While I was writing *Effigies*, it took me a long time to track down some Choctaws who were willing to talk to me, but it would have been a much poorer book without their input.

Whatever it is that you need to know, somebody knows the answer. Crawl over the internet, make some phone calls, check out some library books, and know that a labyrinthine path to that answer is common. Sometimes you have to earn your answer. Sometimes you learn important things while you're on the path.

And sometimes, you find somebody who's willing to put you in an amnesty program that will wipe your permanent record clean of any evidence that you were ever an interstate hunting and fishing criminal.

DAY 277—In honor of the things I learned on my way to being an interstate hunting and fishing criminal…

…I shall tell you something really cool that I learned while researching a book. It has not found its way into a book yet, because I have not yet written a book that would be enhanced by this tidbit of information. This leads me to your helpful writing tip for the day: Just because it's cool doesn't mean it belongs in your book.

While researching *Effigies*, I had need to learn about a particular cave in Mississippi. Now, Mississippi is not known for its caves, but internet research told me that there was a book called *Caves of Mississippi*. I was immediately possessed by a burning desire to see this book, but there were no copies available through online bookstores, used or new. If you've shopped for out-of-print books, you'll know that most of them are for sale *somewhere*. The price might be exorbitant, but you can get a copy if you want it bad enough. But I couldn't get a copy of *Caves of Mississippi*. (And I still can't. I just checked.)

After much searching, I located a copy in the library of the University of Southern Mississippi…which is in Hattiesburg, my home-town. And I needed to go there to see my mother. Score!

Soon enough, I was ensconced in the USM library with the coveted book in my hands. It was a little saddle-bound text of less than 100 pages that had been put together by the state speleological society in the early 1970s, and I thought it was absolutely beautiful. Within minutes, I had found and read the listing for Nanih Waiya Cave, which readers of *Effigies* will know something about. Being me, I couldn't just read those few pages and immediately relinquish this thing I'd sought so tirelessly.

I flipped through the book, reading about caves that had housed failed tourist attractions and caves hidden deep in woods owned by private individuals and caves that were hardly more than mudholes. One cave was singled out as being unusual, because it was in sandstone, rather than the more common limestone.

This cave was not small, perhaps the size of a suburban family room. It was located in a cow pasture, in an outcropping of sandstone with a heavy concentration of salt of the sodium chloride variety. You know...table salt. Those of you who know cows can probably see where this story is headed.

This cave did not arise from the usual geological forces. No. This cave was licked out of the rock, over many years, by cow tongues. And, before that, probably by eons of deer tongues.

This tidbit of information has been useless in the production of my books, thus far, but I do occasionally speak to groups of middle-schoolers. When I think I might be losing them, I trot out the cow tongue story. It is guaranteed to make the boys snicker and the girls go, "Eeeewwwwwww!!!!!"

DAY 278—I've had other bookish adventures, besides being an interstate hunting and fishing criminal

I like visiting the places where my stories happen. I'm sure I advised you to do the same, pages and pages ago. If your story is set on Mars, you're outta luck, but if it's set someplace that you can reach for the cost of a tank of gas and a night at the Holiday Inn Express...come on. Live a little.

Effigies takes place on and near the Choctaw reservation near Philadelphia, Mississippi. I spent quite a bit of time in Philadelphia, after I realized that this was my first book set in a real place, and I was at great risk of getting something *wrong*. I went to the Mother Mound of the Choctaw, Nanih Waiya, several times, but I was stymied by my inability to find its companion mound, a natural geological feature with a cave inside it. (This was the cave that prompted the search for *Caves of Mississippi*, chronicled in loving detail in my last essay.)

I got directions to the cave mound directly from the lips of the Choctaw's tribal archaeologist, and *still* I couldn't find that mound. Frustrated, I stopped at a convenience store located on a lightly traveled road, way out in the country, and asked why I couldn't find the sign pointing to the cave mound.

"They took down the sign when they closed the state park...after the killings," said the man behind the counter.

"Killings?" I asked with professional interest, being a mystery writer and all.

"Yeah. Some people got killed at the state park. One of them was in a wheelchair. It was bad. After that, they just shut the thing down and locked the gate."

I said, "That's too bad," and prepared to leave, figuring I wasn't ever going to see the cave mound, but he wasn't finished.

"But I have the key."

Before I could even process the question of why someone at a nearby convenience store would have a key to a state park that had been closed due to killings, he continued. "Do you want to go over there?"

And he handed me the key ring *with his truck key still on it*.

Sometimes, I really miss living in Mississippi.

Then he re-thought his action, and I thought, "I guess he realized that even polite and ladylike women can still steal trucks. Modern life has come to Mississippi, after all. That's sad."

But no. He wasn't thinking of his truck. He was thinking of the polite and ladylike woman.

"I'd better lead you over there. If you go too far, you'll drive over a culvert that's trying to cave in. It won't hold up that big car of yours. You'll have to park and walk from there."

I had borrowed my mother's humongous and shiny red Cadillac, and I have no doubt that it would have caved in any suspect culvert, so I agreed to follow him. He got in his truck and drove away slowly, so I could follow. (I guess he had an extra set of keys.) Then, he showed me where to park and, drove away, telling me to lock the gate behind me. Because of the killings and all.

The road was broad and well-paved with gravel, so the walking was easy and it was impossible to get lost. Still, that road led deep into the woods. Considering that I was alone in a sizeable state park, it occurred to me that, though I'd been further from civilization before, I'd never been further from civilization *alone*. That walk might well be the furthest I've ever been from another person.

I listened to hawks shriek and pileated woodpeckers cry. As I approached a small wetland, I saw a great blue heron rise up, a stone's-throw from where I stood. A second later, I walked through a muddy spot in the road and saw that the heron's footprints were huge, the size of my hands or bigger. Just past the wetland, the cave mound rose up in front of me, on the bank of a wide creek.

It was tremendous, and it looked very much like the human-built mounds that dot North America, broad and flat-topped. I can imagine the Choctaws, stopping in their migration to admire it, then choosing to settle in that spot and build a mound of their own, not far down the creek...a Mother Mound that would stand for two millennia and more.

Caves of Mississippi had told me that there were multiple entrances to the mound's cave, but I only found one. Hurricanes Katrina and Rita had recently blasted through the area and there were many downed trees on the mound's flanks. I presume they covered the other entrances. The one I found was small and damp and utterly unappealing. Besides, I hadn't brought a flashlight and, though my hips would have probably fit through the opening if I'd opted to slither in, I wasn't completely sure. (Those of you who have read *Effigies* will know where my imagination went with that.)

I climbed the mound. I surveyed the creek and the countryside. I communed with long-dead Choctaws. And then I walked back to the Cadillac and I returned the nice man's truck keys and I went home happy, because I'd had an adventure.

Effigies is a much better book because I went places I'd never been while I was writing it. Please grab opportunities for adventures, large and small. They will improve your writing, it is true, but they also make the kind of memories that you will want to keep you company when you are old. I think writers live interesting lives, not because their lives are any different from other people's, but because they notice the interesting things scattered among the ordinary.

Go. Be interesting.

DAY 279—Considering style

If you do not already own a copy of Strunk and White's timeless guide for writers, *The Elements of Style*, get one.

It's cheap. It's a quick read, and it is the purest distillation of advice to practical-minded writers that I know. Once you've read it, you will remember its succinct advice forever. It's been around for more than fifty years for a good reason.

E.B. White, of *Charlotte's Web* fame, wrote this book as a tribute to a beloved professor, William Strunk, Jr., who had compiled a slim volume of aphorisms like "Omit needless words," and "Be clear," that White had found useful in his writing career. White edited Strunk's work into an easily assimilated guidebook for scribblers everywhere, and I'd like to thank him for it.

There. That's all I have to say, and I think I've followed Strunk and White's dictum to "Be clear," so I believe I shall quit.

DAY 280—Strunk and White, once again

The most famous dictum in Strunk and White's *The Elements of Style*, and one that beginning writers of my acquaintance most need to assimilate is "Omit needless words."

Continuing to type after making that point would be oxymoronic, so I shan't.

DAY 281—Avoid a succession of loose sentences

Strunk and White warn their readers against "a succession of loose sentences," and I applaud the notion. For what is bad fiction, if it is not a succession of flabby sentences, loosely connected in a way that has little connection with logic?

The venerable men had a particular type of loose sentence in mind, those very common sentences that consist of two independent clauses connected by a conjunction or a relative.

"Suzy went to the grocery store, and then she went the mall. She bought a purple sweater, and she got a manicure. The sweater made her look fabulous, while the lavender fingernail polish suggested by her manicurist did not. Suzy would have liked to tell the manicurist this, but she did not." And so on.

This is not a fascinating story. At least I *think* it isn't a fascinating story, although it might be if she encountered a famous rock star at the grocery store who asked her to dinner, thus sending her to the mall in a paroxysm of joy that spurs her to buy new clothes and paint her nails lavender. But even if a fiction-writing genius could craft a fascinating story from Suzy's everyday activities, it wouldn't sound fascinating unless those sentences were recast into some interesting and varied structures.

There is nothing wrong with a two-word sentence. The Christian Bible incorporates a famous two-word sentence that could hardly be more emotionally affecting: "Jesus wept."

There is also nothing wrong with a sentence that meanders along for half a page, provided that the writer has a grasp of grammar and style and provided that writer has the discerning ear of a musician. William Faulkner had those abilities, and he could stretch a sentence into any shape that amused him.

And Strunk and White were capable of prompting me to write a page of prose expounding on their simple rule: "Avoid a succession of loose sentences." We should all be so provocative.

DAY 282—Check-in

Let me see. Where are we? Page 245?

(See how quickly I did that math? That's what an engineering education will do for you.)

And what was our goal? Page 270? Let's do some more math. What's 270 minus 238?

Dang. You're within 32 pages of the finishing line. It's time to put on that last-minute burst of speed and power.

DAY 283—Make me feel something

How's your book coming along? I mean...really. How are you doing with it? Is the story keeping you up awake at nights, because you're eager to plunge through to the end? Or does it leave you cold?

I'm currently reading a book that I'm not enjoying much. I'm not going to tell you its name, because I think I'm the only person on the planet who didn't like it, but this experience is prompting me to think a lot about why I like what I like, as a reader of fiction.

I'm a lifelong compulsive reader. If my hand falls on a piece of printed material, I'll read it.

This doesn't mean that I'll like it.

My current encounter with an unlikeable book has made me take a close look at the book in question. What's my problem with it?

Well, I think it's poorly edited, but that's not the author's fault and...do you know what? A story doesn't have to be polished to a bright shiny sheen to make me turn the pages, not if it's well-paced.

I think my real issue with this book is the protagonist. He just doesn't seem to care much about anything.

Lovers come and go, and his response is a resounding "Whatever..."

I'm told that he's passionate about his profession, but I never feel it. I'm learning from this experience that I need to feel a connection with a character if I'm going to connect with a book. And if that's going to happen, the character needs to feel something.

Because I'm all about improving my own work, I took a fairly impartial look at my own work in response to this revelation. I'm into

the seventh installment of my Faye Longchamp archaeological mystery
series and, though Faye's a loner, she has a pretty decent list of things
that she cares about. She's passionate about archaeology and history
and about the lives of the people who used the artifacts she digs up.
She's intent on restoring her own huge artifact, her family's 19th-
century plantation house. Most of all, there are people in her life whom
she loves deeply. I care about Faye and the things she cares about. I like
to think that my readers do, too.

In my latest novel, *Wounded Earth*, an environmental thriller
featuring Larabeth McLeod, I have a character who is being manipulated by those very emotions that make her most human. Wouldn't
you be angry at a madman who dumps nuclear pollutants into major
rivers? Wouldn't you need to stop someone who dumped a mutilated
animal on your doorstep, just to show you that he can kill endangered
species any time he damn well pleases? And wouldn't your heart freeze
in your chest when a man capable of such things threatens the person
closest to your heart—your daughter?

Mother love may be humanity's most primal emotion. My goal
when writing Larabeth's story was to make you feel her need to save
her child. You may or may not feel what I intended for you to feel
when you read her story, but I don't think your response will be,
"Whatever..."

DAY 284—Mary Anna's Random Writing Rule #15: Consider your loose ends

You really are nearing the end of your tale. Now's the time to think
back to any story threads that you dropped and haven't picked back up
yet. Where are all your secondary characters? Are there any people
who disappeared on page 110? Even if you started their storylines as
red herrings to distract readers from some arcane plot twist you were
planning, you have to play fair. Tell people what happened to Cousin
John or, if you've decided he wasn't so important after all, make
yourself a note to delete him when you edit the book.

Life doesn't always give us tidy resolutions, but people expect them
in their books. You may choose *not* to resolve a story line—it is your

prerogative—but do so consciously and know that it may frustrate your readers. Don't leave them wondering about Cousin John. They may have cared for him.

DAY 285—Get to the point

When you're this deep into a manuscript, it's good to have some guiding principles in mind as you work. It's very important to keep the notion of pacing in your forebrain. If, while you're writing, you have the feeling that the narrative is moving slowly, then I can guarantee that you'll find a problem with pacing when you eventually read the finished paragraph.

When I review manuscripts for aspiring writers, there is a problem that I see time and again in books that are right on the brink of being publishable. These writers have put some effort into the mechanics of their work, so there are very few errors of punctuation or grammar or spelling to point out. They've worked hard to develop their characters and plot, and they've written a complete manuscript.

(I find that actually completing the manuscript often translates into a writer who does everything else better—characters, setting, mechanics, and plot—probably because the discipline necessary to actually finish a huge project like a book carries over into all aspects of the work.)

The final hurdle that must be crossed to generate professional-level work is high, and it's hard for students to wrap their minds around, because it isn't as easy to point out as a misspelled word. Almost-publishable work generally lacks pacing. It isn't tight. And tight copy is like pornography. I know it when I see it.

So how is that helpful to you, who are so intimately entwined with your book that you can't see the forest for the trees?

On a larger scale, you must make sure that dry, boring exposition is not dragging your story down. Look at the opening chapter, in particular. How long does it take for something to happen? Beginning writers feel that they need to introduce each character and describe the setting and set up the action, all in the first chapter. Wrong!

How many people would have watched *Raiders of the Lost Ark*, if the screenwriter had opened the film at the university where Dr. Henry Jones was teaching, then described the Ark of the Covenant, then put us on the airplane with him to get to the jungle where he wanted to find a golden idol? Oh, and the unrepentant scene-setter-upper who wrote this engrossing flick would have probably spent that plane ride describing the idol and the booby traps that awaited Dr. Jones when he found it.

Yawn.

Instead, we moviegoers were plunged into danger and mystery and tarantulas and a honkin' big rolling rock before ever really meeting Indy. It felt like we were dropped out of an airplane. And we loved it.

When do you introduce your characters to your readers? After they're hooked. That, ladies and gentlemen, is what flashbacks are for.

Please, please, please do not describe your alien villain's elaborate military uniform to me before he whips out a blaster and threatens somebody with it.

DAY 286—Things I've Said Before That Bear Repeating #13: Make every word count

Pages ago...weeks ago...I advised you to write haiku to remind yourself of the importance of making every single word count. Now, as you're writing the final scenes of your book, that advice matters still more. These are the words that will stay with your readers when they put the book down. Make them count.

DAY 287—I just told you to make every word count, but...

...I didn't tell you to count every word. Back in the olden days, writers had to estimate their word counts based on an average number of words per typed page. Now, our word processing programs do this for us. This is a good thing, except it gives us an opportunity to exercise our neuroses with two measly keystrokes.

Try not to stop writing every fifteen minutes to see how many words you've written. It's not productive, it wastes time, and it keeps you from getting into that timeless state of "flow" that fosters concentration and focus. You've either written a bunch of words or you haven't.

I give you permission to check at the end of each writing session, but no more.

DAY 288—Decide what to leave out

Elmore Leonard famously said, "I try to leave out the parts that people skip."

Amen, Mr. Leonard. I recently read a book in which the author felt compelled to tell me everything his character bought when she went to the grocery store. He also seemed to feel that one can describe a character by listing three pieces of clothing: "She wore gray pants, a blue sweater, and a black jacket."

So here's your handy pacing-and-style hint of the day: Don't do those things.

Another common problem I see with stories that have pacing issues is that the narrative is being dragged down as the writer tells me what the book's setting looks like. Even a single paragraph of unrelieved description can be too much. These are the chunks of text that readers tend to skip. There are exceptions to this rule, writers whose prose is so beautiful and compelling that you can't stop reading even though nothing's happening, but those writers are rare. Until you're absolutely certain that you are the exception to this rule, here are some techniques to try:

Feather your description into a paragraph where something dramatic is happening.

Use description to give your dialogue a more natural rhythm. People don't always talk in rapid-fire repartee. Some people speak more deliberately. They pause to think, sometimes even in the middle of a sentence. If you insert a brief description of what's going on around the speakers, you don't have to say, "He paused to think." The pause will be there naturally.

Sometimes a character's interior life is in tune with events in the natural world. He's calm on a balmy summer day. Her feelings are tempestuous during a hurricane. And sometimes there's a dramatic contrast between what's going on inside and outside a character. Use those relationships to drive your plot and to depict your story's setting. Your readers will care more about the natural world when you relate it to a person.

When writing description, use language as carefully as a poet. You may think of four beautiful words. Use the most precise one, and save the others for another time. And don't waste your time or your readers' patience on words that serve no function.

There should be no scene in your story that doesn't serve a purpose. A scene entirely devoted to establishing a setting does serve a purpose, but it's a perilously slender one. A story's pacing improves dramatically when each scene serves more than one purpose—for example, it acquaints us with a character and presents him or her with an obstacle to overcome.

DAY 289—Check-in

The goal for today is page 252, but I don't even care how many pages you've written. If you're still with me, then you are serious about your work. Even if circumstances have kept you from reaching page 252 by now and then reaching the end of the book in less than a month, I think that you will get there, and soon.

I believe in you.

DAY 290—Some more helpful hints on what to leave out of your narrative

If you decide that you do need to put this stuff in your book, be sure that you have an excellent reason:

There is no need to tell me when your character goes to the bathroom.

It's okay to skip the stuff that happens between waking up and going to work. Tooth-brushing, breakfast-eating, and commuting are pretty much the same for most people, unless they flip on the morning news and see that an atomic bomb has fallen on Cleveland.

There is no need to include the pleasantries we use to greet people:

"Hello."
"How are you?
"Fine. You?"
"Fine. How's the wife?"

These exchanges obviously provide some kind of social glue, but they are mind-numbing

You don't have to chronicle a character's progress from one place to another. If he stands up from the dinner table and we next see him on the back porch talking to his dad, we're going to presume that he pushed back his chair, walked across the room, opened the door, passed through it, then closed the door behind him.

In other words, feel free to boil your character's actions down to the important stuff. In most cases, your reader's agile mind will follow along and fill in the blanks. If you have indeed skipped too much detail, the generous friends who read your book in manuscript will tell you where you need to add details back in.

DAY 291—I bet you think I'm going to nag you

It's too late to nag you now. You're so close to the end that you can taste it. It is no longer possible that you won't finish this book. If you tried to quit now, you would explode. Go. Write. Enjoy yourself.

DAY 292—Using the rhythm of your narrative to pace your story

Except for short stories written in real time, where events take place at the same pace at which a reader is experiencing the story, the pacing of a tale is completely independent of the speed that things happen to the characters. You can make a 100-meter foot race last for an hour by viewing the scene through the eyes of each racer and most of the participant, one at a time. You can flash back to the childhood of the frontrunner. You can spend ten pages exploring the agony of the racer who falls and breaks an ankle.

The ability to control time is one of the novelist's most potent tools. If you feel that your story lacks emotional heft, look for your most dramatic scenes and try to think of ways to make them last longer. Milk them for all they're worth. If your story is dragging, check to see whether you really need to take your readers into the bathroom where your protagonist is brushing her teeth. Maybe you want to skip the morning entirely, because the bad guy doesn't come on the scene until after lunch.

You are in control of the pacing. You can hold back the hands of time. Remember that.

DAY 293—Pacing the climactic scene

If you are writing a very literary domestic drama, your climactic scene might be a heart-stoppingly painful moment with very little movement or action.

A man's lover walks out the door and his heart breaks.

This is the stuff of great tragedy. I just described it in a single sentence, but I don't want you to do that in your book. Your readers will feel cheated. Give them a moment to absorb the way the empty room looks and the way his life, now empty, suddenly feels.

Conversely, the climax of a thriller might involve non-stop action involving fisticuffs and acrobatic martial arts moves that defy the laws of physics. I would argue, however, that these flashy tricks are not enough. I would argue for an ebb-and-flow in that action.

Let your readers feel the flash of pain as a knife grazes your heroine's shoulder. Let them experience the moment when she succumbs to pure terror, then pushes it aside and readies herself for one last assault. Describe that last desperate bid for life as slowly and lovingly as a film that has switched to slow-motion.

Consciously manipulate the pace of your book's climax so that your readers have time to feel what your protagonist feels. This is their payoff for sticking with you for hundreds of pages. Give it to them.

DAY 294—Like a horse heading for the barn

At the end of the day, a tired horse knows where he can find a warm stall and some hay. Weary as he may be, his pace picks up a bit when he turns toward home.

I imagine that's where you are in your writing life today. You see the end of the book. You know it will feel so good when you get there. The writing is coming easier and faster.

I don't want to distract you from that good feeling, so I'm going to be quiet now.

DAY 295—Take care of yourself, especially now

I'm feeling especially maternal right now, and that's saying something. I've been a mother for more than half my life. I don't know what it's like to *not* feel maternal any more.

I know that you are not thinking about food or sleep or exercise while you are in the throes of finishing your book. Nevertheless, you cannot live on chocolate and Coca-Cola, consumed at two in the afternoon on a Saturday while you're still in your pajamas. Trust me. I've tried.

Even more, I hope that you aren't trying to emulate all those authors of classical novels who pickled themselves in ethanol. If chocolate and Coca-Cola cannot sustain life, then tobacco and alcohol and things not legal assuredly cannot.

Feed the body that houses the brain that spawns your deathless prose. I want you to live to write another book.

DAY 296—Check-in

Are you on page 259 or thereabouts? If so, you don't really need to check in with me. You know your book is nearly finished better than I do.

DAY 297—Make them feel something and they will miss you when you go

Now is not the time to obsess over whether you have thoroughly explored the deep questions and overarching theme that you intend your book to communicate. You're going to be finished with the thing in a week and a half. When that happens, you'll read it, and then you'll know if you said what you wanted to say.

Right now, you have to focus on writing an ending that makes sense with what has come before. When you're writing the final scenes in a white-hot frenzy (and something tells me that you're writing more than a page at a time these days), the only thing you can reasonably be expected to do beyond that is communicate emotion.

How do you want your readers to feel when they close the book? Should they feel a sense of resolution and justice? Wonder? Regret? Romance?

The closing pages of your book should be suffused with your chosen emotion, or the desire for it. If you give your readers a satisfying emotional release, they will forgive almost everything else.

DAY 298—Saying good-bye

After the climax, you know that you should just go ahead and quit this book already, but it's hard. You've got subplots to tie up. You have secondary characters to tell good-bye.

Go ahead and do these things. Your readers want to know how Great-Aunt Jezebel resolved her problematic subplot. Just don't take too long to tidy things up. Nobody cares about Great-Aunt Jezebel quite as much as you do, so give her one last moment in the sun, then quit.

DAY 299—Mary Anna's Random Writing Rule #16: Clear your mind and write

As you near your book's conclusion, you may be tempted to overthink everything.

Don't.

If you've done your job, and I think you have, then you have set up an ending that is inevitable. Just write it down.

DAY 300—Are you thinking about your next book?

I know what you're thinking. You're thinking, "That woman is nuts. I'm struggling to finish this beast, and she wants me to think about another book? If she were standing here, I'd kill her."

Don't kill me. You didn't quite understand my question. I wasn't saying that you *should* be thinking about your next book. I just asked whether you *were*.

As I wrote my first book, *Artifacts*, I was terrified that I didn't have enough material in my head to finish it and, even if I did, I was absolutely sure that I would never again have another idea that could support an entire book. Never, never, never. Who was I kidding? How could I ever have a career as a writer if I never had another good idea again?

Yet as I finished *Artifacts*, I found the idea for *Relics* bouncing around in my brain. I ran with it, though I was still convinced that it was my last idea ever, and that I'd never, never, never have another one. Yet as I finished *Relics,* I found the idea for *Effigies* running around my head. At this point, I learned to trust the process. I'm currently letting the idea for my eighth Faye Longchamp mystery germinate, because I know that the ideas want to come, if I will let them.

So don't read today's essay and feel pressure from me to be thinking about your next book. Just know that my own experience tells me that you may find that book coming to you, unasked. Relax and let it happen.

DAY 301—While we're talking about where ideas come from...

I have author friends who hate it when people ask, "Where do you get your ideas?" I don't mind. I actually like answering the question. It's interesting to trace an idea back to its roots and try to figure out why I got that particular idea at that particular time.

I find that my subconscious speaks up when I've got my conscious mind tied up with a routine task that doesn't really require much thought.

Washing dishes.

Gardening.

Driving.

These things all work well. Playing the piano would seem to be a good idea-generating activity, but I find that it requires too much thought and attention. My subconscious can't come out and play when I'm actively trying to remember how many sharps are in a piece's key signature.

Driving is my best idea source, but stop-and-go around-town driving won't do it. I need an all-day road trip, and I need to be alone or in the company of someone who isn't chatty. The setting for *Artifacts,* a dilapidated and abandoned plantation house, sprang into my mind as I drove west across the Florida Panhandle on I-10. Before I reached Alabama, Faye's character was well-developed and I knew who the murder victim was and why she died.

A couple of years later, I was driving down I-10 again, and the plot to *Relics* leapt into my brain. I can't explain to you how these things happen. The creative process is a mystery of its own. It fascinates me, but I wouldn't presume to explain it. Sometimes I just have to go with the flow, and sometimes that flow is straight down an interstate highway.

One day, somebody's going to catch me in a weird mood when asking the time-honored question, "Where do you get your ideas?", and I'm going to tell that person the truth: "I find them lying in the ditches on either side of I-10."

DAY 302—Where did I get the idea for this book?

Several months ago, I was writing up my notes to teach a writing workshop, something I've done many times since *Artifacts* came out in 2003. I enjoy teaching writing. I feel like I can connect with my students on a personal level, and I enjoy telling them the things I wish I'd known in 2003...or 1997...or even 1984.

It occurred to me that I probably had half a book tucked into my computer's memory. I had recently made a foray into ebook and print book publishing, so I knew how to get it quickly into the hands of people who could benefit from my experience. Once I realized these things, I sat down to write and you hold the results in your hands.

Some books germinate slowly, and some just beg to be written. This book begged me for my time and attention. I'm glad I listened.

DAY 303—Check-in

You should be on page...oh, never mind. You're finished for all practical purposes. Carry on.

DAY 304—Famous last words

You are poised to write the last pages of your book. At the end of those pages will be the book's last line. Many pages ago, we talked about the importance of a strong opening line. We've also talked about the need to close each scene with a sentence that is at least strong enough to signal that you're finished, for the time being. A scene-closing line should really do more than that. It should make your eyes dart forward to the next scene.

A chapter-closing line should do the same thing, but more so. It should signal the end of something important, and it should point toward something even more important. It should ask...no, it should demand...that the reader turn the page.

The sentence that closes a book should do even more. It should reflect on the adventure that your characters and your readers just shared. If you are writing a series or are thinking of at least a sequel, it should let the reader know that these characters have more stories to tell. And if this book is a standalone, the last line should provide a sense of closure and, not incidentally, it should make the reader feel the need to read more of your work.

Here are some examples of closing lines from some of my short stories. I hope they'll help you get a grasp on the emotion you'd like to leave *your* readers feeling.

As you head toward your book's ultimate sentence, I'll share with you the last lines of my books tomorrow.

Enjoy!

Later, when the sheriff and his people had come and gone, Garrett knew he would ask Wynnda if she'd like to help him leave the moonshine jug out for Frank.—"Land of the Flowers"

I was still weighing my options when the sirens sounded on the street below.—"Twin Set"

It's hanging near the tip-top of my own Christmas tree, right this minute.—"A Singularly Unsuitable Word"

After all, it does specialize in building places where the impossible seems real and dreams come true.—'Mouse House"

And I answer her, in my flat Tinseltown tones, saying, "I love you too, darling. And I always have ... ever since I first saw you wearing that stupid rubber monster suit."—"Low-Budget Monster Flick"

DAY 305—My own last words

It only seems fair to share with you the last lines to the books in my Faye Longchamp mystery series. And no, it is not an accident that the last word in each of the first three books is the same one...

She couldn't wait to show it to Joe.—*Artifacts*

Faye stroked his hair as she watched him sleep and wondered what she was going to do about Joe.—*Relics*

She hopped to her feet and hurried in his direction, calling out for Joe.—*Effigies*

"Marry me, Faye."—*Findings*

"Tomorrow. At Home. At Joyeuse."—*Floodgates*

Faye intended for Michael's first night alone with his parents to be spent at Joyeuse.—*Strangers*

DAY 306—What will the last words in this book be?

I have no idea. But you could sneak a look at the last page...

DAY 307—D-Day: You're done!

Today's the day. If you've kept to the pace you set for yourself on Day 1, you'll type "The End" today.

By now, I'm sure you know that I am chock-full of advice for you on how to edit your book and how to market it and how to get it out into the world. But let's save that for later.

Today, I want you to hit "Save," (or, if you prefer to remain in the mid-twentieth century, rip the last sheet of paper out of your black manual typewriter. The action still has a certain dramatic flair.) Go outside and enjoy the sunshine. Hug your loved ones. Let someone buy you a drink to celebrate. If no one volunteers, pour yourself a glass of champagne.

You've earned it.

CHAPTER 6—YOU FINISHED IT. NOW WHAT ARE YOU GOING TO DO WITH IT?

DAY 308—Take a celebratory day off

I have workaholic tendencies, it is true, but even I would not suggest that you begin editing your book one day after finishing it. Do something relaxing and mindless today, preferably something that involves fresh air. Enjoy yourself, with my good wishes.

DAY 309—Okay, it's time to edit this thing

It's entirely possible that you believe the book you just wrote is perfect in every way, a coherent whole that could only be diminished by changing a single word. I know that there are people who believe this about their work, possibly many people, although most of them have too social skills too finely developed to let them actually admit it. I did have a conversation with a man who took up half-an-hour of my time in a bookstore, telling me about his struggles in finding an agent who understood that not a single word of his book could be changed. It has been years, but I have no doubt that this man is still unburdened by an agent or publisher. Or readers, for that matter. (And no, he did not buy any of my books, either.)

You're going to want to spend some serious time editing the book that you just invested months in writing. Perhaps you can get it done in the weeks left to you in this year we're spending together, and perhaps you'll need a little more time. It's okay to take that time. Please don't let the rough jewel that you just created go out into the world without giving it the precision cut and polish of a master jeweler.

If at all possible, get the opinion of trusted readers, the more the better. If you can afford a professional editor, consider getting one, but

I also encourage you to distribute it among selected friends whose taste you trust. Then let them read it while you do the hard work of self-editing.

I've said this before, but if you have any doubts about your grammar and spelling, now's the time to get a book or take a course. Language skills can be learned, and they are the tools of your trade. I have never seen an unpublished book that was evidently written by a person with really poor mechanical skills which I thought would be publishable if only the grammar were corrected.

I have a theory that the logic required to construct a complex sentence is related to the logic required to construct a plot. In other words, you will not be wasting any time you spend in gaining or polishing these skills. You will be developing an important brain function.

I think math does this for your brain, too, but I'm not going to assign you any algebra homework.

You're welcome.

DAY 310—Print the thing out. Yes, it's gonna take some time and cost some money.

I'm a big believer in editing in multiple formats. Reading a book on paper just looks different from reading a book on the computer screen. You will see typos on paper that you won't see in fifty read-throughs on the computer. And vice-versa. So burn some paper and printer ink and electricity and time, so that you can get the thing printed out, or burn some money and pay a copy shop to do it.

I like to bind my manuscripts for editing, usually by printing onto pre-punched paper and putting the printed sheets into a 3-ring binder. If I'm using a copy shop, I might get them to bind it in a more fancy way, but it really doesn't matter. I'm just trying to approximate the feel of reading a physical book. I'm also trying to avoid dropping all those pages in the floor. Some people, my agent included, prefer a printed manuscript in single-sheet form, when she's not reading them with her e-reader. Different strokes for different folks. Just print it out, and start reading if you still have time.

(I don't like to leave you Luddites out. If you wrote the beast in longhand or on a typewriter, now is the time to type it into a word processing program so that you have an electronic copy. This goes without saying if you're planning to self-publish, either in ebook or print form, because you must submit electronic files. Traditional publishers and agents require bits and bytes now, too. But I'm sure you already knew that.)

DAY 311—I just want you to read it

Read your own book as if you just checked it out of the library on a whim. Read it for pleasure. If you're honest with yourself, you'll recognize that it feels flabby, somehow. You will be fighting this feeling throughout the editing process. Every time you read that book, you should be identifying useless adjectives and prepositional phrases that say nothing. Deleting such things should give you a feeling of great power! Indulge yourself!

DAY 312—Things to bear in mind while you read

I've already talked a good bit about reading your own work critically and about editing in general. It wouldn't hurt if you went back and looked at some of those essays, but I'm going to harvest the best advice from earlier in the book and put it here. You're going to be flipping around in your own book. I might as well try to minimize your need to flip around in mine.

Does every scene have a purpose?

Are your "big" scenes spaced in a way that maximizes excitement and minimizes boredom?

Now that you're reading it all at once, does the chronology make sense?

Did you follow your outline? If not, are you happy with the result?

Does your protagonist change? How?

Does every scene end powerfully? How about every chapter? What about the entire book?

DAY 313—Look at the big picture first

Before you start looking for misspelled words and before you start twiddling with sentence structure, look at the overall flow of your story. Does it grab you from the first chapter? Are the characters immediately engaging? Do they grow and change as the complications build toward a peak at the climactic scene?

Now, before you find yourself embroiled in making every last word perfect, consider whether you want to do big-picture editing. Are there any scenes that, quite frankly, need to go? Or, thinking even bigger, are there whole storylines or characters that are superfluous? Now is the time to jettison them.

Some people naturally write spare and lean prose, but some throw everything into their stories, including the kitchen sink. There is nothing wrong with either approach. The "spare and lean" people can always flesh things out. The "kitchen sink" people can always clean things up later. I'm just telling you that this is the time to do those things. If you try to line edit now, you're wasting your time. You'll have to do it again after you do the broad-brush changes that you know you need to make.

I'll remind you now about something I told you many, many pages ago. More than once, I have realized that my story really caught fire in Chapter 2. This might have meant that Chapter 1 needed to go away, but in the two cases I'm remembering, I found that simply reversing the first two chapters fixed my problem. Shoving the original Chapter 2 to the front made the book interesting from the get-go. Keeping the material in Chapter 1 back until the second chapter meant that I could keep important background information in the book, without letting it stall that all-important beginning.

Take some time today to consider whether all your scenes are necessary and whether they are presented in the proper order.

DAY 314—Prioritize your editing chores before you start

If you know that you crammed 300 pages of story into 900 pages of prose, then you know that your primary editing chore will be cutting text without losing anything important to the plot. It would be foolish to waste time polishing individual sentences until you knew which sentences were going to stay. If, instead, you feel that your plot is overly spare and that you need to add some backstory for the protagonist and flesh out a subplot that feels a little thin, that's different. You should certainly concentrate on those things, but there is nothing inefficient about tightening up the prose as you go.

I suggest that you make a list of editing chores and prioritize it, so that you don't wind up leaving perfect sentences on the cutting room floor.

DAY 315—If you have an obsessive streak...

When I was writing *Artifacts*, I was concerned that I might reveal the killer too soon, leaving too many pages for the wrap-up. I began to wonder how professionals handled this issue. I gathered a big pile of mysteries and found the moment of the big reveal in each book, marking the page with a sticky note.

I found that there was a wide variation between mysteries and mystery authors when it came to revealing the killer's identity. Some followed the typical Golden Age pattern where the detective gathered everyone into a room and presented evidence so compelling that the killer confessed. And some included quite a bit of dramatic action after the climactic revelation, during which the killer was hounded toward justice. This second approach is my natural style. I found that both approaches could be effective, so I relaxed and followed my instincts.

Later, I became curious about how long it took for mystery authors to kill somebody, so I did the same exercise with the books' beginnings. Sometimes the body dropped on page 1. Other times, the author took some time to develop his or her characters before offing one of them, which has the advantage of giving the reader a chance to care about the one who died. I noticed an interesting pattern, in that first novelists frequently shed blood very quickly, while the same writers' later books might be more deliberate in their approach. I think this is due to the need for first novelists to catch an editor's or agent's or reader's attention immediately. Once a writer has earned his or her audience's trust and respect, more time can pass before mayhem ensues.

If you don't write mysteries, consider the major milestones common to books like yours. How do you want to structure any love story in your book? How soon will the characters meet? On what time scale will you develop their relationship? If you're writing a literary novel about a dysfunctional family, some of the elements of romantic plots still apply—meetings, arguments, misunderstandings, pain. Are you happy with the pacing of those plot points?

It never hurts to take some time to see how other writers have paced their stories. It is not plagiarism, not if you are honestly writing your own story. In fact, you may find that you want to do the *opposite* of the things you read in others' books. If you don't know what the writers before you have done, it is very hard to be fresh and original.

DAY 316—In all honesty...

Editing this book is going to take you a while. You need to read it through, pick it apart, slice it and dice it, put it back together, put it down, walk away, then pick it up and read it through again. Rinse and repeat.

If you short-change this process, you will be short-changing your-self. However, I don't think you want to read daily advice from me that says, "Read it through and fix the stuff that bothers you. Let it rest a couple of days. Now read it through again and fix the stuff that bothers you. Let it rest a couple of days. Now read it through again and..."

I'm going to move on and talk to you about the publishing industry and how to decide where your book fits into it. This does not mean that your book is finished and that you should redirect all your attention to getting it into the hands of readers everywhere. In all likelihood, it is not finished.

My suggestion for getting the most benefit from this book is to keep editing while you're planning your assault on the publishing world. I'll remind you periodically to do that, but you will, of course, be working at the pace that works best for you.

You don't want to be so obsessed with perfection that your book never leaves your hands, but it is far more likely that you'll be tempted to let it go too soon. Keep perfecting your book while you develop a plan for its future.

DAY 317—If you have literate friends, now's the time to call on them

If you have friends who like to read and whose opinions you trust, by all means, hand some copies of your manuscript around. You must, of course, be prepared for the possibility that they may have comments other than, "It's fabulous! When can I buy copies for everyone on my Christmas list?" Consider this your practice run for the day when your book goes out to reviewers who don't know who you are and thus have no reason to spare your feelings.

Let's talk about what you can expect from your friends. If they're readers, they're likely (but not certainly) pretty good at the mechanics of language. You'll be able to tell fairly easily whether you need to take seriously their comments on grammar and spelling and literary style. If they're readers, they also probably have a good feel for storytelling. If a man who has had his nose in a book since the age of six says that portions of your story drag, then I suggest that you listen to him. Most importantly, if someone whose opinion you respect suggests that you hire a professional editor, I think you should listen. Your friends can only be expected to do so much to help you whip your manuscript into shape.

If there are aspects of your story that required you to do research, then consider whether you have friends with expertise in that area. My series character, Faye Longchamp, lives on an island. She spends a lot of time running around in boats. I have friends who also spend a lot of time running around in boats, and I rely on them to help keep me from looking stupid.

All of these suggestions presume that your friends are helpful and kind. We all know that this is not always the case. Some people are opinionated. Some people are difficult. Some people are jealous. If you get the slightest inclination that you have a received a critique of your work that was not motivated by good will, throw it away. Do not make that person's problems into your problems.

DAY 318—Give yourself permission to make dramatic changes in your manuscript

Sometimes a whole page of text needs to go. You sweated over it. There's nothing wrong with it. It just doesn't fit into this book.

When this happens, remember that you are working on a computer. Nothing need ever be truly deleted.

Make yourself a separate file for deleted text. When you find yourself reluctant to make a needed cut, move those paragraphs that you're so loathe to lose into that file. When the book is done, read through the file full of deleted text. I think you will find that nothing in that file is critical to the book, but if I'm wrong about that, you now have options. Simply cut the indispensible text out of your deletions file and paste it back into the book.

Knowing that none of your writing need ever be truly lost is incredibly freeing.

DAY 319—Picture yourself as a diamond cutter

When I edit, I approach the job as if I were cutting a diamond. (Not that I actually know how to do that, but the metaphor seems apt.) The first draft is amorphous and raw. Something beautiful is lurking inside it, but much work will be involved in exposing that beauty.

In the early stages of the work, I might find myself whacking out entire scenes or writing new ones to complete a subplot that I inexplicably dropped in mid-book. I liken this to the stage where a diamond cutter takes something that looks pretty much like a dull white rock with rounded and random edges and forces it to cleave along planes that approximate the familiar shape of a cut jewel.

Next, I might find myself revamping dialogue to bring out a character's true nature. I might write entire paragraphs enhancing the setting's description or clarifying the passage of time. I might kill paragraphs that are chock-full of pretty prose, but which do not engage the reader's attention or advance the plot. I liken this to the cutting of precise facets at the exact angle that will best reflect and refract light.

Is the gem cutter finished now? No. Those precise facets must be polished to a high sheen. This is the time when you must attend to every word. Is it the proper word? Is it in the right place? Is it used properly in a grammatical sense? Is it spelled correctly? You may be dealing with 70,000 or 90,000 or 120,000 words, but that doesn't give you license to wield them carelessly.

Only when you've completed the final polish will you know how brightly your story glitters.

DAY 320—Give your outline a look-see

How does your finished book compare to the book you planned to write?

Don't panic if you deviated from the plan. You are an artist. You are in control of your artwork. The outline was for your personal use. It did not constitute a contract.

However, I do think you should look at the places where you deviated from the plan, and ask yourself why. Did you simply have a better idea? Did that better idea change everything, all the way to the end of the book? Or did you eventually work your way back to your original plan?

Did your characters grow and change in such a way that the action in the outline just made no sense any more? Did you uncover information while doing research that forced the storyline to change in order to make it mesh with reality?

Most importantly, ask yourself honestly whether the story, as written, is better than the story you had planned. If it is not, then you'll need to wrestle with the differences between plan and execution until you're happy with the outcome. If the story *is* better, then you should take it as proof that you've learned something about plotting as you wrote this book. You'll be able to take this new skill with you as you move on to your next book, and that's just cool.

DAY 321—Can a writers' group help you edit your book?

Many of you are already members of writers' groups, so you are in a good position to answer this question. Since you are still in those groups, I presume that the other members' comments were helpful to you during the drafting of the book. (And those of you who left unhelpful groups will also be in a good position to answer the question of whether you should let your peers help you edit.)

If your experience with the group has been unremittingly positive, then my only caveat would be to make sure that your fellow group members remain objective. If they supported you with encouragement and critique as you wrote your book, it is possible that they are as almost as close to it as you are. In other words, they might not be any more likely to see fatal flaws than you. Presuming this is not the case, then I suggest that you stay with a group that has worked for you in the past.

If you have been a lone wolf writer to date, should you seek a group of peer critics now? Maybe. You no longer have as much cause to worry about spending too much time critiquing the work of others and too little time writing. Mutual critique is your goal now.

If you do join a group, I would caution you against the same things that can make a writers' group harmful as you first draft the book. If you detect the slightest note of jealousy or arrogance in any of the members, run. There are people who will criticize your work harshly simply because it is not theirs. Anyone can see that they will be of no help to you.

Conversely, people who are not willing to criticize when necessary, for fear of hurting someone's feelings, will be of no help to you, either. "That was so good! I loved it!" is not a helpful critique. Devoting your limited time to a detailed critique of a group member's work, without getting a helpful critique in return, is not a winning proposition.

Another critical factor in choosing a group is the ability and experience of its members. If you have stuck with this book this far, and if you have finished your manuscript, then you do not belong among utter beginners. (Rejoice!) You will help them much more than they will help you and, though it would be kind of you, you don't have time for that. Neither do you belong in a group of authors with ten published books to their credit. (Yet.) Look for your peers or, if you're lucky, a group that's slightly more advanced than you are.

And, last, remember that writers' groups don't meet every day and that meeting time must be spent on everyone's work. The critique process can be slow when you're editing an entire book. If waiting for input from the group is hurting the momentum you gained by working through this book, then you should probably go your own way.

All that having been said, comments from a reader whose opinion you respect are pure gold. If you can find such a reader or readers in a group, then join up and give them your best effort in return.

DAY 322—If you're planning a series or a sequel, did you craft your book accordingly?

When I wrote *Artifacts*, I had no idea whether I would ever sell it. I certainly had no idea whether the eventual publisher would want a sequel, much less a series. Fortunately, I got lucky. Faye Longchamp is a sufficiently complex character to support as many books as I care to write about her, so ideas for future books in the series keep coming. Also, my decision to age her in real time over the course of the series— about a year per book—gives me a chance to send her back to graduate school and marry her off and force her to start her own business and just generally make her life interesting. Have you thought of what the future might hold for your character? If there's nothing in the current book that will prompt a reader to pick up your next book, just to see what happened, then maybe now's the time to correct that.

Fortunately for me, I don't have a strong need to sweep up every last loose end in my characters' personal lives at the end of the book. (I do feel a need to resolve the conflict at the core of the story, and writers do otherwise at their peril, but I don't feel the need to end every book with, "And they lived happily ever after.")

For this reason, I've had people ask me if I planned to write a sequel to *Wounded Earth*, although I have no such plans at the moment. I wrote that book as a stand-alone. The protagonist's romantic relationship is tied with a pretty bow at the end. Her relationship with her child is healthy and growing. She is clearly going to recover from the not-insignificant physical wounds I inflicted on her during the climactic scene. The villain is deader than Julius Caesar. What could I possibly do if I wrote another book about this woman?

Well...that dead villain left behind an assistant who may be smarter and more amoral than he was. This assistant has wisely retired to Brazil with enough money to sink an aircraft carrier, but he also knows which nuclear plants might or might not have been sabotaged and there may come a day when he needs to come out of retirement to take advantage of any potential mayhem. And if he should ever leave Brazil, he possesses sufficient charm to turn the head of my protagonist's pretty daughter, despite the fact that she was looking warmly into the eyes of a handsome FBI agent when we last saw her. Oh, yes, if I wanted to bring these people out to play thriller games again, I most assuredly could.

How does your book end? Did you leave room for another adventure with these people? Do you want to?

DAY 323—Summary Week: Producing a synopsis that won't make your agent sneer... or a publisher...or a potential reader

Whatever your marketing plan is for this book, you need to learn how to tell someone what it's about. How else will you entice an agent, publisher, reviewer, or reader into giving it a try? Unfortunately, novelists notoriously stink at summarizing their work.

We're going to spend a week talking about summaries and synopses and teasers and query letters, but we're really only talking about developing one skill: the ability to summarize your work in a way that makes the reader respond in the way you intend. In a query letter designed to interest an agent or publisher in your work, you only have a paragraph to say enough about your book's plot to entice the reader to ask for more. If that agent or publisher is willing to look at a synopsis, you get more space, perhaps a page or two, but you're going to have to tell your entire story, all the way to the end. Later, you'll need to construct something I call a "teaser," which is like bookjacket copy. It's designed to tell just enough of a story to convince a reader to choose your book over thousands of others.

These summaries vary widely in level of detail, but they all have a single goal. They are intended to point people in the direction of reading your work of fiction, but they are not in themselves works of fiction. They are sales pieces. Learning to write them well is critical to your career, but less critical to your art. I would argue that you don't really grasp your story if you can't analyze it, so the ability to synopsize is useful. Still, the main intent of these pieces is to sell. And this kind of writing is particularly difficult for novelists, which is why we're going to spend a week talking about it.

Writing a novel requires an author to put tens of thousands of words on the page. By comparison, a one- or two-page synopsis should be child's play. Why do most novelists find the synopsis to be the most dreaded part of the whole writing/submission process?

1. Book-length authors write long. It's what we do.

2. It's hard to fish one pithy paragraph out of 350 manuscript pages, because you are your book's mommy or daddy. You like it all.

3. You're afraid you don't know what your agent or editor wants, and that you'll choose the single most boring paragraph imaginable to represent your work. It would be much easier to cram it all in there and hope they see something they like.

To solve these problems, keep this in mind. There are many possible summaries for your work. They will vary according to your purpose and your audience. Know who will read the synopsis and what they want before you start.

A potential agent reads a query letter looking for a quick punchy description that will give him or her something to sell. The query letter does not necessarily have to tell the book's ending. If you are querying an editor directly, the situation is not so different. The editor is looking for a book that can be sold to the powers-that-be at his or her publishing house.

An agent who is trying to sell your book will typically write the cover letter that accompanies your manuscript to prospective editors. This letter will summarize the key points concerning the book and its potential sales. Agents should have personal knowledge of individual editors and houses so, ideally, this letter will be personalized to appeal specifically to the person being pitched. Since sales are an agent's livelihood, this letter will likely be slicker than yours, but if the synopsis in your query is excellent, your agent may draw from it. This gives you just a little bit of control over your own destiny.

A more formal synopsis typically accompanies the query letter. Sometimes an agent or editor will request a specific length for this synopsis. Unless otherwise stated, one to two pages is a good length. Like the query letter, this synopsis should be single-spaced. If sample chapters are requested, they should be in standard, double-spaced, manuscript form. This synopsis is not intended to sell the book to the end reader. It tells the *entire* story, including the ending, so that an editor or agent can see the plot of the book being offered. They will be reading the synopsis with the aim of determining whether the book will sell well to their target audience.

Later, you will want to be able to craft very different summaries of a type that I call "teasers." Any time you are trying to sell a book to an end reader—on your website, in your newsletter, in your dustjacket copy—you will need to be able to write a teaser.

But first, you must craft your query letter and synopsis well, because your book will never get a first reading if the agent or editor of your choice is not intrigued by the way you describe your work.

DAY 324—Summary Week: I have still more to say about synopses

After your book is contracted with a publishing house, you will have yet another opportunity to synopsize it, with different goals in mind. You will probably receive a lengthy questionnaire that asks questions designed to help the house's marketing department sell your book. My questionnaire for *Effigies* asked for a long synopsis of about 200-250 words, as well as a short synopsis of 50 words. Although my publisher called them "synopses," you might want to think of them as "teasers," in this case, to distinguish them from synopses that cover the entire book. For the long synopsis/teaser, I wrote something that could work as dustjacket copy, a description of the book of significant length that ends in a way that makes the reader want to buy the book. For the short synopsis/teaser, I pictured someone from my publisher's marketing department promoting my book to someone who only wanted to give them a few seconds to do it.

The material provided in the questionnaire is frequently used by a publisher's marketing department to prepare a "sell sheet" that accompanies review copies being sent to reviewers, bookstores, and the media. Again, if you provide good material, you have more control over the way your book is presented to important opinion makers. You will also probably put some version of these teasers on your website and in your press kit.

Every time you put together materials designed to sell your book, read them again with your current target in mind. For example, my books feature two multiracial protagonists and racial issues figure heavily in their plots. *Effigies* was released in February, which is Black History Month, so my press kits sent prior to that month included extra material highlighting the black history connection, in the hope that journalists looking for a timely tie-in would be more inclined to choose my book than another book with a generic topic. I was booked for at least two radio interviews as a result of promoting the Black History Month connection during the short time it was appropriate, so I saw results from this strategy. Don't miss an opportunity to stand out in the crowd by writing one synopsis or cover letter and using it, unchanged, forever.

Boiling the long teaser down to a very short teaser was a true challenge for me. I began with the long teaser, first cutting text that was obviously superfluous, but eventually cutting text that I would have termed essential. Faye's sidekick Joe was jettisoned. The description of the conflict that triggered the murder and all mention of other suspects—all these things are gone, but the less-than-bare-bones summary still communicates the crux of the book.

To give you a glimpse into the workings of the publishing world, I'm going to give you the actual text of those two synopses/teasers tomorrow and the next day, then we'll talk about them the day after that. I think both versions work. See what you think.

DAY 325—Summary Week: Your first real-life example

Long teaser for *Effigies*

Faye Longchamp and Joe Wolf Mantooth have traveled to Neshoba County, Mississippi, to help excavate a site near Nanih Waiya, the sacred mound where tradition says the Choctaw nation was born.

When a farmer, Carroll Calhoun, refuses the archaeologists' request to investigate an ancient Native American mound, Faye and her colleagues are disappointed, but his next action breaks their hearts: He tries to bulldoze the huge relic to the ground.

Faye and Joe rush to protect history with their bodies, if necessary. The situation grows more dangerous as Choctaws arrive to defend the mound and the farmer's white and black neighbors come to defend his property rights. Though a popular young sheriff is able to defuse the situation, tempers are short.

That night, Calhoun is found dead, his throat sliced with a handmade stone blade. Was he killed by an archaeologist, angered by his wanton destruction of history? Did a Choctaw take up arms to defend an embattled heritage? Neshoba County farmers have been plowing up stone tools for centuries. Did someone take this chance to even the score with an old rival?

The sheriff is well-aware that Faye and Joe were near the spot where Calhoun's body was found. The whole county saw their confrontation with him over the mound. And their combined knowledge of stone tools is impressive. They had motive, means, and opportunity. The only thing saving their skins is the fact that the same thing is true of almost everyone in Neshoba County.

DAY 326—Summary Week: Your second real-life example

Short teaser for *Effigies*

Archaeologist Faye Longchamp is excavating in Neshoba County, Mississippi. A farmer refuses her request to investigate a nearby Native American mound. She's disappointed, but his next action breaks her heart: He tries to bulldoze the relic to the ground. When his throat is slashed with a stone blade, Faye was near the murder site, she'd argued with the victim, and her knowledge of stone tools is no secret. The only thing saving her skin is the fact that these things are true of almost everyone in Neshoba County.

DAY 327—Summary Week: Did those teasers work for you?

If they did both work for you, give some thought as to why? If they didn't, then can you figure out why not?

When you set out to write your own summary or synopsis or teaser, remember one key thing: These bits of prose are designed to entice. You want to entice an agent to take you on, or an editor to accept your book, or a reader to devote hours of his or her life to you. Here are some guidelines:

> The first sentence should contain as much of the initial conflict as possible.

> Next, you want the reader to ask "What happened next?"

> Unanswered questions like "No one knows how..." are incredibly useful tools. (Each of the quotes in this paragraph is a phrase I've used in my own synopses.) Deepening the protagonist's initial difficulty—for example, surrounding Faye with people who "wish she would just go away"—also ramps up the tension

quickly. Then sealing the curiosity in the reader's mind with an ending that is fraught with peril—"the killer is still close at hand" or "her archaeological skills...just might save her life" will drive the reader to want to know more.

Once you've accomplished that goal—driving the reader to want to know more—it's time to stop. You're writing a synopsis, not a book. Leave your target reader wanting more.

DAY 328—Summary Week: The synopsis that started it all

When I was trying to figure out how to sell my fiction, I went out and bought a bunch of first novels, because I wanted to figure out what had prompted an editor to plunk money on the table and say, "You're hired." (This is an excellent exercise, for those among you who have an analytical bent.) In other words, I figured I might as well have a good idea of what writing strategies had actually worked for someone else.

Perhaps it has occurred to you that, as you write the query letter and synopsis that will go out into the world and sell your book for you, it might be helpful for you to have an example *that actually worked.* Here, in all its glory, is the plot summary that comprised the bulk of my original query letter to Poisoned Pen Press.

To give credit where credit is due, my friend Diana Tonnessen helped me craft and perfect this synopsis. She has many years of experience in writing and selling nonfiction and in teaching others how to do the same. If I'm very lucky, she'll decide to work with me on a book like this one for nonfiction writers.

With Diana's help, I got the attention of Poisoned Pen Press. I've been working with them for seven books now, and I'm very happy with my career. I wish the same for you.

Artifacts—Excerpt from query letter

Faye Longchamp has lost nearly everything except for her quick mind and a grim determination to hang onto her ancestral home, Joyeuse, a moldering plantation hidden along the Florida coast. No one knows how Faye's great-great-grandmother Cally, a newly freed slave barely out of her teens, came to own Joyeuse in the aftermath of the Civil War. No one knows how her descendants hung onto it through Reconstruction, world wars, the Depression, and Jim Crow, but Faye has inherited the island plantation—and the family tenacity. When the property taxes rise beyond her means, she sets out to save Joyeuse by digging for artifacts on her property and the surrounding National Wildlife Refuge and selling them on the black market. A tiny bit of that dead glory would pay a year's taxes. A big valuable chunk of the past would save her home forever.

But instead of potsherds and arrowheads, she uncovers a woman's shattered skull, a Jackie Kennedy-style earring nestled against its bony cheek. Faye is torn. If she reports the forty-year-old murder, she'll reveal her illegal livelihood, thus risking jail and the loss of Joyeuse. She doesn't intend to let that happen, so she probes into the dead woman's history, unaware that the past is rushing up on her like a hurricane across deceptively calm Gulf waters. The killer is still close at hand, ready to kill again to keep his secrets dead and buried.

DAY 329—Summary Week: And how, you may ask, do I intend to synopsize this book?

Well, I'm still working on it, but here is the current draft. Since I'm planning to publish this book myself, this should be helpful to those of you with a goal of independent publishing. For this use, I'll need a teaser-style summary for my website, my promotional materials and, probably most importantly, for the online bookselling sites. I'm not sure I'll have much of a need for a query of full synopsis, but if I do, I shall write one.

This synopsis has a single purpose: It must clearly explain why a person browsing an online bookseller should buy this particular book, and it must do so quickly, before the potential buyer clicks over to another site. See what you think.

Your Novel: Day by Day is designed to be an all-in-one guide to planning, writing, editing, and publishing a first novel, guiding a new novelist through the day-to-day details of the process. Its author, Mary Anna Evans, is an award-winning writer with eight novels, two nonfiction books, and a collection of short works to her credit. She says, "This is the book where I tell other writers the things I wish I'd known ten years ago." Work through this book of practical advice with Mary Anna, day by day and page by page, as she advises you on—

crafting a plot,

fleshing out believable characters,

organizing a novel's timeline,

crafting believable motivations for your characters,

editing objectively,

evaluating traditional and independent publishing options,

and marketing to agents, publishers, and readers.

Because she understands the importance of maintaining your own motivation during the arduous process of writing a novel, Mary Anna has chosen a narrative structure that will provide you with a written companion for a year's worth of writing. This book consists of 365 essays on topics that range from nuts-and-bolts writing tips to words of encouragement to periodic kicks in the pants. She has even included the actual synopsis she used to query her agent and to sell her first book. If she could sit with you, day by day, as you learn about this exciting art form, she would. Since she can't, this book is the next best thing.

DAY 330—Back to Self-editing: Give your computer a shot at the nit-picky details

The attempt of any word processing program to check my grammar and spelling irritates me to no end. For every word it identifies that is misspelled or out-of-place, the stupid thing flags twenty that are perfectly fine. (And it suggests replacements that would be laughable if I had enough time on my hands to read them all.)

Nevertheless, go ahead and run your spelling and grammar checker. It will force you to look at individual words in a way that most people can't, especially fluent readers of the type that typically become novelists. We become engrossed in the story and we forget to check each and every solitary word. It's entirely possible that you'll spend half-an-hour slogging through your manuscript and only find three actual misspelled words, but it's also entirely possible that you wouldn't have found them any other way.

It's a good practice to use all the tools at your disposal, no matter how flawed.

DAY 331—What is your publishing goal?

If you wrote a book for children with the sole purpose of giving it to your grandchildren, then you are in luck. It is startlingly easy and cheap to produce and print a paper book these days, and ebooks are easier and cheaper still. If you wrote a novel for a very small and highly specialized audience—perhaps you fictionalized the ghost stories popular among young people in your hometown—then you still might find that producing your own book or ebook is the obvious financial choice.

If you have your eye on a wider market, then you must decide whether your goal is to seek publication through a traditional royalty-paying publisher. Contracts with the big famous New York firms and with well-established independent houses are hard to come by, but if you can land one, you will have the benefit of their established distribution systems and publicity machines. Very few writers make bestseller lists and earn bestseller-level money, but that kind of success has in the past been more common with larger royalty-paying publishing rather than self-publishing or working with a very small publisher. This business model may be changing so I encourage you to do the research. Learn as much as you can.

The downside to the traditional royalty arrangement is that you get a fairly small percentage of the sales price of your books, and it can take a long time to finally see your book in print. If you are of retirement age, you might wish to publish your book yourself, rather than spending years that you'd rather not waste looking for an agent and more years waiting for the book to get out of the production process and get into print.

Smaller publishers exist, and more are emerging, who will handle business details like cover design and distribution and marketing, so you may choose this option, but you will then have to share income that would have been all yours if you had self-published. Perhaps that is a good choice, if it enables you to write more books. Smaller publishers will not have the distribution or marketing power of bigger ones, but they probably have more power than you do, and you will probably be more important to them than you would be to a publisher of many, many books. Some of these smaller publishers are ebook-only, so you will have to decide how important having a physical book is to you.

If you have a businesslike bent and believe that you can learn to promote and distribute your own work in a way that generates the income you desire, then self-publishing may be your best fit. Just be aware that being a publisher has little in common with being a writer. You are going to be learning two jobs at the same time, all while *doing* both jobs. Some people thrive on such a challenge. Only you know whether you are one of them.

I am in the unusual position of having my feet in several different publishing worlds at the moment. My mysteries are published by Poisoned Pen Press, a publishing house that is large by independent publisher standards, yet is clearly a small press when compared to the behemoths in New York. I have a nonfiction title coming out this year from a very large educational publisher, Pearson. And I am even now establishing a fairly sizeable self-publishing presence in Joyeuse Press, through which I am bringing out this book to join a list that already includes a novel, a full-length collection of short works, a mini-collection of three short stories, and six individually published short stories.

My industry is changing in front of my eyes, and I think it is important to consider the publishing options for each project carefully. Now is the time for you to do the same, and I recognize that the industry will be different in the two months between now and when this book hits the streets. And, though I will update it frequently—a huge benefit of self-publishing—it's almost a given that things will change again before you read it. If you make a habit of learning about your industry and applying what you learn to your own work, you'll be ready. Or at least you'll be as ready as a person can possibly be.

DAY 332—For traditional publishing, you need an agent

If you're going to go the traditional publishing route, I think you want an agent. Yes, I know that the ebook revolution is changing everything, but traditional publishers are pretty hidebound organizations. I know that they are trolling the bookselling websites, looking for successful self-publishers to snap up, but I also believe that they will continue to lean on agents to screen submissions. (Unless the tsunami that is the ebook revolution rolls over the entire industry and washes all the agents away...which could happen. If it does, I'll swim out of the tsunami debris and revise this book for you.)

Publishers and their editors prefer to work with agents, because the volume of work submitted by hopeful authors is just too great. If an agent whom they know and trust sends them a manuscript, an editor knows that it rose above hundreds or thousands of submitted manuscripts that the agent didn't think were marketable. In most cases, the editor and the agent know each other, and the editor knows that the agent has hand-picked a manuscript suited for his or her taste. These facts alone mean that having an agent will get attention for your work that it would not otherwise have gotten.

After the sale, an agent's job is to look after your financial best interest. My mystery publisher is rare, in that it works with many unagented authors. I elected to go through my agent anyway, because...well...I don't know what in the heck an option clause is and I don't know what my options might be in getting an option clause changed. Anne, my agent, does know these things, and she has negotiated a more favorable option clause for me on more than one occasion.

In 2002, I had no notion that my electronic rights had any real value, but Anne did, and my contracts reflect that. I had no idea that the advent of print-on-demand publishing technology might render old-style "out-of-print" clauses obsolete, but Anne did and my contracts reflect that, too. If you do elect not to get an agent, I suggest that you work with an attorney who specializes in such things. I'm certainly no attorney, so I can't give you legal advice in this book.

Be cautious in negotiating your book contracts, and consider having an agent do that for you. What you don't know could hurt you when the next new technology appears on the horizon.

DAY 333—How do you get an agent?

The short answer to this question is that you need to decide which agents interest you, contact them and offer samples of your work, then follow up if any of them express interest. Easy, right? It's just like selling anything: identify a prospect, demonstrate why your product is what that person needs, then follow up with answers to any questions they might have.

The hardest part is identifying the prospect. Which agent interests you? In this case, the internet is your friend. With the right web search, you should be able to identify who represents your favorite writers. It is possible, though, that they are not taking new clients or that they are not a good match for you in some other way.

Further web searching will show that there are free listings of agents on sites like Preditors and Editors. I suggest that you just type in a search string like "literary agent listings" and see what turns up. At this point, you are just surveying the marketplace. I think you'll eventually want to spend some money and join a subscription site like writersmarket.com or buy a book like Jeff Herman's *Writer's Guide to Book Editors, Publishers, and Literary Agents*, simply because the paid listings tend to offer more specific information. Back when I was looking for an agent, a book of listings was the only way to go, and I was an information freak, so I bought both the Herman book and *Writer's Market*.

Once you've gathered the information you need to narrow down your choices, decide what is important to you in an agent. I wanted someone willing to take on a first novelist. I needed an agent who represented thrillers and mysteries. I preferred someone who had an office in New York. I also wanted someone who would look at a work sample, instead of just a query letter, based on the logic that I had no track record and my work needed to speak for me. I knew that I was not willing to pay a reading fee, nor to work with anyone who charged me on any basis other than as a percentage of the money I earned.

You need to make your own list of priorities. After you identify the people who meet your requirements, it's time to approach them. (I presume that if you've reached this point in my book, then you've finished your book. Agents do not want to see unfinished novels. They want to be sure you can finish what you start, and it's very difficult to judge the quality of a novel's plot without seeing all of it.)

Unlike in the Dark Ages, when I was agent-seeking, most queries are made by email now. *You must follow the agent's submission directions to the letter.* If they say no attachments, send no attachments. If they say to limit your query to one four-sentence paragraph, do not send five. If they say you may send ten sample pages and your first chapter is eleven, send the ten pages. *Agents get a humongous pile of queries every day. Give them no reason to reject your submission without reading it.*

After that, you wait for a response. Be prepared for rejections. Be prepared for silence. Work on another project while you wait. And if they all say no, try again. I know of no one at the top of the publishing business who will tell you that getting there was easy.

DAY 334—Small publisher, no agent

As I've said, I think having an agent is the way to go, because I don't know the ins and outs of book contracts. Nor do I know the ins and outs of agency contracts. Please don't interpret anything I say here as legal advice. In any contractual situation, you must know what you're signing and seek legal help when it seems justified.

So what do you do if you're offered a publishing contract, but you have no agent? If the contract stands any chance of being lucrative, you can probably find an agent willing to represent you, just by sending out a few emails. If it is a very small publisher, then fifteen percent of the tiny amount you'll probably earn probably will not entice an agent to help you negotiate that contract.

In that case, you'll need to assess whether you're willing to pay an attorney to help you with the contract, even though your expected income may not justify those legal fees. You probably should take into account that you are selling a book that has no value now, but might have a great deal of value later. In the end, the decision is yours.

DAY 335—Ebooks for your friends and family: The easiest kind of self-publishing there is

Perhaps you wrote your book with no notion of a huge audience or big buckets of money. Perhaps you had a story that you'd told all your children while they were growing up, and you just wanted to write it down. If you can have a few dozen electronic copies to distribute to your kids and grandkids and nieces and nephews, that's all you'll need to feel that this project has been a success.

Or perhaps you wrote for a slightly larger group—your church or the residents of your hometown or the members of your state historical society. You are approaching the market size that might interest a small publisher. In fact, some historical societies have their own publishing companies. Still, if you don't see a realistic possibility that your book will sell at least several hundred copies fairly quickly, then you are unlikely to find a publishing house willing to spend the money to bring it to market.

Does this mean that your book is unworthy of publication? Of course not. It just means that you are unlikely to find someone who will pay the upfront costs of publication, in hopes of making money later. If you are willing to pay those upfront costs, or if you are willing do the labor yourself, then it is surprisingly easy to see your book in print. And if you're okay with your book only being available electronically, then the cost can be very low.

It is beyond the scope of this book for me to list firms and websites that produce ebooks, comparing services and costs. There are self-publishing guides on the market that can do that for you. My goal here is to help you write a good book, then point you toward publishing options, based on my own experience and not on an all-consuming review of the entire industry.

I personally used smashwords.com for my first foray into the electronic world. I have no doubt that there are other options for producing ebooks, so I encourage you to scour the internet for the situation that best suits you. For my purposes, I found Smashwords to be ridiculously cheap and easy. In fact, it was free. I spent a weekend formatting my manuscript according to their guidelines. I fumbled around in the graphics program that came with my computer and made a passable book cover. I uploaded the book and cover. I was done. And it was all free, because Smashwords makes its money by taking a percentage of income from books sold. At most, you might incur the cost of hiring an artist to prepare the cover, if computer graphics are really not your thing.

Once a book is uploaded, Smashwords will convert it into various formats that will work with almost all e-readers. The author can set a price or give the book away for free. Anyone who wants to read it can download it directly from Smashwords, so there's no need for you to worry about distributing it to other sales sites, if you truly are aiming at a small and well-defined market. You can just call your family up and tell them where to look for the book.

For writers who are not in it for the money, but who just want it to be available, Smashwords or another similar business can be a very good fit.

DAY 336—Printed books for your friends and family: They're pretty easy to self-publish, too

In recent years, the physical act of printing a book has undergone a tremendous change, and the chief beneficiaries are people who would like to publish a book without printing 10,000 copies. An important new technology is called "print-on-demand," often abbreviated POD, and the name means exactly what it says. If a publisher using POD technology receives an order for a single copy of a book, then that publisher can print and ship a single copy.

For those of you who only want a few dozen or even a few hundred books, this is a godsend. In the past, traditional printing generally made it financially unrealistic to print in quantities that didn't run into the thousands, leaving people who only wanted a few books with a garage full of dusty tomes that could never realistically be expected to leave their boxes.

Again, there are many entire books in print about self-publishing, and I don't have the space to lay out the pros and cons of all the options. I do, however, have space to describe my own experience with producing print books through createspace.com. (If you're reading a print copy of this book, then you are holding an example of their work.) I understand that lightningsource.com works similarly, although there are differences in distribution that will matter more to people seeking a national or worldwide audience than they will to people who are focused on a particular group of readers.

CreateSpace is associated with Amazon, which meant that getting my print books listed for sale on Amazon was effortless. My print books are also for sale directly from CreateSpace and I get more money when people buy them there, but as best I can tell, I am the only person who actually does buy them there. By opting for an extended distribution agreement (for a fee), I can make my books available in other online bookstores, physical bookstores, and libraries. In the interests of bowing to reality, I will say that the odds of a self-published book by an author without a track record being stocked in bookstores or shelved in libraries are low, but this extended distribution agreement at least makes it possible.

Like Smashwords' ebook production system, CreateSpace gives you the option to create your book yourself, in its entirety. Unlike my ebook publishing experience, I found that my layout skills were not sufficient to craft a good-looking interior or cover for a print book, so I paid a professional, Kimberly Hitchens at booknook.biz. This made producing a print book more of an investment than producing an ebook, but I'm talking hundreds, not thousands, of dollars for a book that is indistinguishable from books published by the big guys.

And even if your goal is only to make keepsake copies available to your family, your book is still online and available for sale, so people may find it and buy it. I'm here to tell you that royalties are very nice things to get.

DAY 337—Self-publishing for a larger market

It is not difficult to stretch beyond the self-publishing plans suggested in my previous two essays. If you self-publish ebooks through Smashwords, it costs nothing to offer them through the site's Premium Catalog, other than making the effort to ensure that the book itself meets quality standards governing things like layout and cover art. The Premium Catalog distributes to major vendors including Amazon, Barnes and Noble, Kobo, Sony, and Apple. Smashwords takes a cut of sales from those sites, so you may wish to work directly with some or all of the other sites, trading your time for the extra income. Other ebook distributors may handle these things differently so, again, I'd suggest a book on self-publishing or a solid time investment in searching the web, if you're considering publishing your own work on a grand scale.

My experience in marketing print books to a wide audience through CreateSpace has been similar to my experience in marketing ebooks through Smashwords. Opting for their Pro Plan ($39 up front and $5 a year) got me a cheaper cost per book, which makes sense when you're aiming at a wide audience. Opting for their Expanded Distribution Channel merely required me to join the Pro Plan and to make sure that my physical book adhered to certain standards, including trim size and page count. The Expanded Distribution Channel takes me into sales venues outside Amazon and CreateSpace's own site, including "retailers, bookstores, libraries, academic institutions, wholesalers and distributors," according to CreateSpace. It's up to me to get those other sales venues interested in my work, but I'm happy to let CreateSpace make me available to them.

Extrapolating this to other print self-publishing companies you might use, I'd advise you to shoot for the widest distribution possible, if that suits your goals. The worldwide web is...well...worldwide. You don't know where your potential customers are. My experience is that it is not expensive to make yourself available in a variety of venues. If you are being quoted exorbitant fees, find out what the company is promising. If they're not guaranteeing you the moon, move on. As you can see, these services are being offered cheaply, and a little research on your part should get you a situation that will work for you.

DAY 338—If you self-publish, you're in control. Make yourself look
    good.

I've just spent a good bit of time telling you that you can make an
attractive ebook or paper book all by yourself. And you can.

At the moment, I have seven ebooks on the market, with two more
in the works. My first three ebooks were short stories, which are priced
low and earn a low percentage for their royalties. I considered them a
pilot test for the whole process, speaking in engineering parlance. I
had already been paid for them when they appeared in print anthologies, so anything I earned was going to be gravy, but I also didn't
want to spend a whole lot until I knew what I was doing.

I did the covers myself. I prepared the books themselves according
to Smashwords' guidelines. I uploaded them. It was cheap and easy.
They have sold a few copies a month ever since. (One of them is
suddenly selling quite well. If this continues and the books on which I
earn more substantial royalties follow suit, I will be a happy woman.) I
think they look good enough, but I think it's obvious that they were
not professionally done. I plan to redo them at some point.

Next I published a full-length novel, WOUNDED EARTH, as an
ebook, using the same do-it-yourself method. It has sold somewhat
better than the short stories, because I have promoted it more. People
kept asking me whether it was available in print, so after some months,
I decided to make it so. As I've said, my graphics skills were not up to
the task, so I hired professionals to design the book's interior and
cover. This gave me the opportunity to change the cover for the ebook,
at no extra charge, so I did so. The new cover got excellent feedback
and for good reason. Any fool can see it is of higher quality.

When it came time to do my short story collection and this book,
my plan was obvious: hire somebody to make me look good. You must
develop your own business plan, and you can see that my business plan
was not, "Spend a boatload of money from the get-go." Assess your
own skills and your own goals and your own pocketbook, then produce
the most attractive package possible.

Your book is your face to the world. If you have chosen to be your
own publisher, you have the option of making it the best it can be.

DAY 339—A beautiful book isn't judged solely on its cover

It is implied in everything I wrote in my last few essays, but I'm going to state it outright here: When I say that your book is your face to the world, I am not solely talking about the cover. While your cover is one of your most far-reaching sales tools, it is not the only element of your book that readers may judge and find wanting.

The layout of your book is the first thing readers will see when they begin to read. You want it to be clean and easy to read. You also want it to look as much as possible like the books your reader is accustomed to seeing—generous margins, attractive typefaces, clean design.

Hitch, my book designer, mentioned hyphenation in passing recently. If she had not, I would not have known that she or one of her minions checks each hyphenated word to make sure it breaks in the proper place. She also adjusted the pagination of the epilogues I put at the end of each short story in *Jewel Box*, so that it would be clear where they end and where the stories begin. I am certain that there is plenty of information out there on how to make your book layout look good. All I'm saying is that, if you choose to do it yourself, be prepared to invest some time in learning how. People who find themselves annoyed by an amateurish-looking book are not people who will run out looking for your other books as soon as they finish this one.

DAY 340—It's time to read your book again

We've been talking about business issues. If you set your book aside during that time, it has been resting for more than a week. All the while, your subconscious has been chewing on it. I think it's time to pick it up and read it again.

You'll find that you get through it faster every time you read it. There is an advantage to that. If you repeated yourself, using a distinctive descriptive phrase on page 27 and again on page 235, you're more likely to notice now, when you're probably reading those pages just a few hours apart.

For this read-through, try to notice whether you've developed any tics. Did you use the word "ostentatious" ten times? Did you describe the heroine's eyes as "cornflower blue" one time too many? Did you describe the view through her kitchen window four times?

It's easy to lose track of what you've already said when you spend months writing a book. Let today's read-through be your chance to eliminate those redundancies.

DAY 341—Dialogue Q&A

Turning our attention to nuts-and-bolts matters, these are some of the questions I'm asked most often about dialogue:

Do I have to use "he said," or "she said," after every line? (This is called "attribution.")

No. In fact, it's best to consider each line of dialogue before you decide to give it an attribution. If the reader will know who is talking because of what the character says or because of how the words are said, then no attribution is needed. If the speaker can be inferred because the other person clearly spoke last, then again, no attribution is needed.

Some writers never use any attributions. Is that okay? Am I wrong or old-fashioned if I use them?

In my opinion, attributions exist only to give clarity to this question: "Who is speaking?"

If the context of the story answers that question, then leave the attribution out. But sometimes there are three or more people talking, and the conversation just gets confusing. And sometimes conversations are very long, and you don't want your reader to constantly be counting statements, saying, "Odd-numbered lines are Sally. Even-numbered lines are Mike." If you think there's any doubt, stick in a "he said," now and then.

What about descriptive attributions like, "he shouted," or "she said despairingly," or "he groaned"?

Don't do it! If the reader doesn't know your character is in despair by what she says or does, then you have a problem that will not be helped by using the word "despairingly."

What about dialect? Is it ever okay to specify nonstandard pronunciations?

Readers dislike dialect, because it's hard to read. It's also very hard to write dialect that doesn't risk sounding disrespectful to the character who is using nonstandard English. Nevertheless, no one speaks in perfect English all the time. I try to limit myself to one or two nonstandard constructions per character in a conversation, and I lean toward regionalisms—"I might could meet you at noon," instead of "I may be able to meet you at noon"—that don't sound as condescending to my ear as more blatant violations of grammar like "I seen a bear yesterday." Or, even worse, "I seen a bear yestiddy."

What are some techniques to control the pace of a conversation?

Rapid-fire short sentences convey a sense of urgency that leisurely conversation does not. By contrast, sometimes I *want* to slow down the pace. On those occasions, I will break up a character's words with a moment of observation. This gives me a chance to slide in a description of a character or the setting, without having to stop the narrative dead in its tracks. Here's an example from *Relics*:

> He ran his fingers through his short blonde hair. "I went to medical school because I wanted out of Alcaskaki. I wanted to see the world and I wanted to see it in style, with more money than a plain old family doctor would pull in." He spoke slowly, as if it were important that she understand the extent of his greed. "I was leery of a specialty like surgery. Can you imagine holding someone's life in your hands every livelong day? Dermatology was perfect. Acne and botox patients don't have emergencies. You just set your office hours, do your job, and go home. People will pay a lot to be beautiful."

Notice what I've done here. This is an educated man from the rural South. He speaks in Standard English, mostly, with quirks like "plain old family doctor" and "livelong day." I've managed to tell you that he's blond with the same sentence I used to slow down the narrative, so that you would feel his meditative mood. I manipulated the pace, while revealing more about his character, when I told you that "he spoke slowly, as if it were important that she understand the depth of his greed." This sentence also serves as an attribution in this two-way conversation between a man and a woman. There is no reason to add, "he said," or even worse, "he said meditatively."

If I had to choose one idea for you to take away from this example, it would be this: Make every phrase do double-duty...or triple duty.

This strategy is the best way I know to make a book feel tight and spare and perfect.

DAY 342—You're still reading...

...but you'll probably finish today. Pay attention to the inevitability of the ending. Does every event point toward an ending that has no choice but to come?

DAY 343—Working with an Editor: Someday, Somebody's Gonna Read This Besides You...

...and that person's gonna have opinions.

When you ask a person off the street to comment on your work, you can take or leave their opinions. Working with an editor is trickier. In the end, the book is yours, and a good editor will not insist on changes you can't abide. However, if you have a contract with a publisher, then the editor works for your employer. If you can't come to terms with your employer about the book it is paying to publish, then you may find yourself jobless. It's not so different from any other employer-employee relationship, really, except that your end product is art and you want it to be *your* art.

Let's presume that your editor is a reasonable person who knows the business, based on the fact is that he or she is still employed by your publisher. You should be able to discuss points of contention with a person like that, in a respectful way, and I suggest that you try very hard to see that person's point-of-view. In my opinion, having a good editor—and I do—keeps me from going out into the world with my pants down. (So to speak.) I can feel free to push my limits, maybe try an extended metaphor that might be brilliant and might just be stupid, because Barbara is there to keep me from making myself look bad.

You already know that I adore classic 1960s Star Trek. William Shatner is widely derided for his tendency to chew the scenery, and I understand why. Yet I suggest you look at some of those old episodes, if you have a chance. Being a science fiction actor meant that he had the opportunity to play a woman and an old man and a man under the influence of an alien toxin and a man who has just been stabbed in the back. There were times when his willingness to risk looking stupid resulted in moments of actorly brilliance. (In my non-expert opinion.)

In those cases where he went too far, and copious scenery got chewed, I blame the director for letting it happen. I would think that an actor who trusted his director could afford to take that risk, knowing that he would be reined in if he went too far. In my art form, the editor serves that role, and I am grateful for Barbara.

Someday, when you are having a disagreement with your editor and you want to take an airplane to her office and throttle her, take a step back. Be grateful that there's someone in your writing life who won't let you go out into the world with your pants down.

DAY 344—Should you hire a publicist?

I have been in the publishing business since late 2002. Most of that time, I have been without a publicist. I have always been aggressive about seeking publicity and, early on, I was considering hiring some-one to help me. I asked my agent what she thought and whether she could recommend anyone. She said, "Honestly, Mary Anna, you couldn't afford anyone who does as well as you do."

At times, I have ignored her advice. Because I have never been in a money-is-no-object situation, I have only hired publicists for specific projects with costs that I could control, instead of retaining someone to do all my promotion all the time. Some of those projects have included mailing promotional bookmarks to a targeted list of bookstores,

booking me for store signings and media interviews, sending promotional emails for a specific event, and making follow-up phone calls.

I'd like to tell you that the money I spent on those things was well-
spent, but most of it wasn't. I could have gathered those bookstore
addresses and mailed out the bookmarks. I could have booked myself
at stores and media outlets all over the country. I can, and have, done
promotional emails and made follow-up phone calls.

Most of the time, the people I hired worked hard, but the results
were small, relative to the money I spent. Sometimes, however, my
experience with publicists was egregiously bad. An example would be
the time I showed up for a radio interview...and found that the
interview was on a station for the blind. At the time, I had no books on
audio, so even if the listeners were intrigued with what I said, what
were their options?

I called my publicist to see what on Earth she was thinking. "Well,
blind people have friends who can read your books. Maybe they'll
enjoy your interview and talk to those friends." Maybe. But I think I
should have been told the situation before we drove an hour out of our
way and paid to park. Actually, I think I should have been told before
she charged her full rate—hundreds of dollars for one interview. Let
the buyer beware.

If you have some extra money and you have no extra time to
market yourself, then by all means hire someone to help you. If money
is tight, though, don't be discouraged. If you can communicate to a
media person why it is to his benefit to interview you, then you will get
an interview. If you can convince a bookstore owner that you can draw
some buyers into her store, then you will be booked for a signing. A
good publicist's experience and contacts can help you, but doing the
scut work yourself for a while will help you judge the quality of a
publicist's work when you do eventually hire one.

DAY 345—Shelf Space: It's always been important, but now you have
         more control

When I was just starting out, a veteran mystery writer told me that
sales and income would snowball over time and that most people hit

their stride with about the sixth book. (My sixth book came out about a year ago. Picture me standing by my mailbox, waiting for my snowballed royalty check to arrive...) Popular wisdom has long said that it behooved a writer to occupy shelf space, the more the better.

Between mysteries, I write short stories. I just finished a math literacy book. I'm writing this book. I've published essays and articles. The best thing a writer can do for her career is to write. There's no better way to get your name out there.

Unlike most things, modern life has made acquiring shelf space easier. Do you have a short story lying around that you couldn't sell or a published story to which you own the rights? Publish it yourself as an ebook. Do you have an original thought? Publish it in your blog or, better yet, submit it as a guest post to someone else's blog, so that you can introduce new people to your work. Do you have half-a-book's-worth of workshop notes on how to write fiction? Write the rest of the book and publish in a format not unlike this.

Writers write. Look for ways to get your work into the hands of people who will enjoy it.

DAY 346—How do you feel about public speaking?

First, let me say that there is no law that writers must be public speakers. If you have a public speaking phobia, all is not lost.

Nevertheless, I find it astonishing how often I find myself talking to a crowd. Why is that? Just because I can put words on a page in an entertaining fashion does not mean that I can put them together well while I'm standing in front of a crowd.

I guess it comes back to the notion that, in order to sell books, a writer must sell herself as an interesting person who can tell interesting stories. Hence, the need for us to stand up in front of a crowd at a library or bookstore. If this comes naturally, then the publicity part of a writer's job is going to come easily to you. If it does not, then you might consider joining Toastmasters or taking a speech class, preparing for the day that your book is on the market and people are dying to hear what you have to say.

If you're completely certain that you cannot do this, even with the help of the Toastmasters, fear not. You will need to become a social media maven, instead.

The internet is tailor-made for those of us who are adept with the written word. Start investigating your options now. I suggest that you start a blog and learn to promote it. By the time your book comes out, you'll have followers who are already interested in what you have to say. In the end, that may be more important than the ability to wow a library crowd.

DAY 347—Embrace the 21st Century's Narcissistic Vice: Google yourself regularly

Most writers are introverts, so it is God's little joke that our careers depend on getting our names and work and faces in front of as many people as possible. As you do personal appearances and web promotions and blog posts, you're going to want to see whether you're getting results from these activities. Because if you're not, then you can stop doing them.

As you build your web presence, I encourage you to do a web search on your name and on your book's name and on a combination of the two. This will be easier if your name is a little unusual. Going by my full name lifts me out of the densely inhabited ranks of "Mary Evans," and the second "a" in "Anna" distinguishes me from all the women named "Mary Ann Evans." (Yes, I know that George Eliot was one of them.) There are few enough women named "Mary Anna" in the world that I am frequently the first hit when you type in those eight characters. If I don't come in first, either the wife of Robert E. Lee or the wife of Stonewall Jackson usually turns up instead. (I do believe that I have the most Southern name in the world.)

These web searches will turn up reviews that you need to know about. They'll give you an indication as to whether the bookstore where you're appearing next week has done the promised publicity. Yesterday, I found the new *Publishers Weekly* review of *Plunder*. (They said it was "engaging" and "character-driven." Yay!) Several years ago, I found out that a very influential magazine for Young Adult librarians,

VOYA, had placed *Artifacts* on their annual list of Adult Mysteries with Young Adult Appeal. This information led directly to my writing two published academic articles, making several paid personal appearances and, eventually, publishing a book on mathematical literacy.

You know you get bored sometimes while you're sitting in front of your computer. It never hurts to Google yourself when that happens.

DAY 348—Are you sick of your book yet?

You should be. And if you're not, you're going to be. I don't think there's any way to polish a book into publishable condition, other than to read it, revise it, and ruminate on it.

So what's the goal for this read-through?

I want you to focus on the characters. All of them. Focus on the main characters, certainly, but also on the secondary characters, and even those with little walk-on roles. My guess is that you've lavished attention on your main characters, both protagonist and antagonist, and that you're feeling pretty good about their three-dimensionality. The secondary characters who interact closely and frequently with the main characters are probably shining in their reflected glory. In scenes where you paid special attention to your portrayal of the main character, you almost certainly fleshed out everyone else in the room, if only to make them better foils for your hero or heroine.

But the minor walk-on characters...they're tricky. You don't want to spend a half-page on someone who's going to walk away and never be seen again. Look for economical ways to make those throwaway characters memorable, in terms of personality, dress, speech patterns, or annoying habits. Try not to throw them away, in terms of storytelling opportunity.

One handy trick is to recycle those characters. Maybe your character bought a lemonade from a gossipy lady at the church social. If, later, you need to make your character want to leave his small-town roots and never come back, don't create a new character to knock on his door, complaining about how loud his teenaged daughter plays her music. Let the gossipy lemonade lady do it. If your readers see her once, then she's just an acquaintance, but if they see her in action again, they have a relationship with her. And this means that they have yet another strand in their relationship with *you*.

Never pass up an opportunity to deepen your relationship with your readers.

DAY 349—Is it clear why your characters behave as they do?

I hope that you have already examined your major characters' motivations from every possible angle. And I hope you know that you need to do this again as you read the book this time. You have probably already figured out that I'm going to ask you to do this for everybody, as you are reading today.

You should know why the lady selling lemonade at the church social is nosy. If at all possible, you should tell your readers or at least give them a hint. You should know why she's obsessed with your protagonist's daughter's loud music. Is it possible that she is agora-phobic and unable to leave the street where she lives, except to go to church? Might that contribute to a social isolation that would make her nosy? Might she be wondering whether it's too late to conquer her anxiety and go out into a world where she might meet a man and someday have a teenaged daughter of her own?

Can you see how the storytelling possibilities open up when you refuse to write off a character as "minor"? Some characters really are just bystanders, only seen when it's time to shove people into place in time for the next big scene, but make sure. You don't want to waste a unique character by using him as a momentary convenience, then throwing him away.

When you read your book this time, stop every time you see a new character. Ask yourself if there's anything you can do to make that character more three-dimensional and real.

DAY 350—The best piece of promotional advice I've ever received

Over the years, I've gotten myself on TV in five states and on the radio dozens of times, all across the country from Oregon to Florida, including six interviews in the number one U.S. market, New York City. I've gotten print coverage all over the country, including a cover story in a statewide magazine. Yet even I readily admit that I'm not as well-known as, say, John Grisham or others of his ilk. How did I do that?

I have the best luck with the media when I take the time to identify a particular broadcast station or print media outlet. I identify a show or column that relates to my work or to me, then I craft an email that explains what I have to offer *to them.*

"Hey, I've got a new book out!" is not very interesting to a radio host. Thousands of books come out every month. Why should yours be the one to get valuable air time?

If, however, you have a multiracial series character, as I do, you may be able to interest an interviewer who specializes in minority issues. If you can identify a show that markets to women, then you might succeed by pitching the strength and moxie of your book's heroine or, if you're female, you might be able to pitch yourself. I cannot tell you how many interviewers have led with the question, "How did you make the switch from chemical engineering to novel writing?" If you are pitching a program with a title like "Arts Desk," this would be the time to mention your glowing reviews and literary awards.

If you are visiting the area, say so. Many, probably most, radio interviews are done by telephone, but there is a special immediacy to live, in-studio interviews. If you can offer that, then do so.

The best marketing advice I've ever received came from my dear friend Bev Browning. She said that, while composing a marketing letter, I should picture myself sitting across the desk from my prospect. When I wrote a sentence that was of interest to him, I should picture myself handing the paper across the desk to him. If I indulged myself in a sentence that was of interest to me, I was to picture him handing the paper back to me, with a look of disinterest. In a perfect marketing piece, every sentence would result in me handing the letter to him.

To illustrate, here is a good sentence, by Bev's definition:

"Your listening area, Neshoba County, Mississippi, includes the setting of my book, and I recently received the Mississippi

Library Association's annual fiction award, so I'm getting good feedback from readers in your state."

And here is one of the worst sentences ever:

"Hey, I've got a new book out!"

DAY 351—You need a website. But you knew that.

If you have something to sell, you need a website. If you have a brand to promote, you need a website. If, for any business-related reason, you need people to be able to find you and reach you, you need a website. All of these things apply to a novelist.

Even if your book's not out yet, you might as well lay the groundwork for your web presence. Search engine optimization is a great mystery to me, but I do know that it takes a while for the search engines to find you. Why don't you give them a head start?

If you don't have a book out yet, you're going to need something of value to put on the site. Why don't you offer a short story for free? You can also have a page that allows people to sign up for the promotional newsletter that you're going to send when the book comes out. If they like the story, they might sign up. I'm guessing numbers will be small until you have a book, but it's a start. The main thing is to start building an online home for your fans.

In 2002, I built my own website, using Microsoft FrontPage. It took me a month, but I was damned if I was going to hire somebody who wasn't born to build my site when I was learning to program in FORTRAN. Because I am a writer and valuable content is what I do, my site has always been content heavy. I have the expected stuff, like synopses of the books and my bio and reviews and my appearance schedule and a media kit with downloadable photos. There's a link to my blog, and a separate page for contests. I also have lesson plans and reading guides for classes and book groups who are reading my books.

My homemade site wasn't beautiful, but it provided plenty of information and I was happy with that. The day came, however, when I was heartily sick of maintaining it and I hired a professional. The highly talented Ramon made my site beautiful and stylish and functional. (I have not asked Ramon whether he was born when I was taking FORTRAN, but I think not. I don't want to know.)

Take a look: www.maryannaevans.com

Ramon designed my blog to look just like my site although I think they're two separate entities, in a technical sense. (The difference is invisible to me, and probably to you, so he did a good job. If you'd like to get in touch with him, his email is developers@aardken.com.)

He also did a great deal to optimize the site and the blog for search engines, and this is an important point. I will not discourage you from doing your own site at first. It is certainly cheaper and even the least fancy site will communicate the basic information to an interested reader. The world has changed since I built my site myself, however. I think you'll eventually want someone who's search-engine-savvy to take care of your online presence, but that can wait, if your budget is like most people's.

I'll close with a fond memory of my days as my own webmaster. At the time, my son was 17 and very talented in math and science. (He is now a mechanical engineer, sayeth the proud mother.) During the month I built the site, I'd stayed locked in my upstairs office, so that my children would not hear the frequent cursing. When the site was functional, I finally came downstairs.

About a month later, I was updating the site. My son looked over my shoulder and said, "Mom. You know more about that than I do, and that scares me."

Never pass up the opportunity to surprise your children with your capabilities. Scaring them never hurts, either.

DAY 352—Climb aboard the runaway freight train that is the social media world

A disclaimer: I am not a social media expert. Being a curmudgeonly sort, I doubt the word of anyone who claims to know much about social media, unless they make their living doing it. And I doubt the word of a lot of people who *do* make their living at it. To me, promoting oneself to the teeming worldwide pool of internet users is something of a black art. Nevertheless, I have watched the struggles of bookstores and traditional media over my nine-year career (which isn't all that long) and I can see the future.

As much as I love bookstores and try to support them, relying on bookstores alone to sell your books in the future will be exceedingly dangerous. And as much as I cannot imagine a world without the newspapers and magazines and broadcast media of my youth, relying on them alone for publicity will be dangerous, as well. We're all going to have to use the internet to connect with our readers, and social media sites have the advantage of being free.

There are whole books and many web pages on this subject, so consider this as merely my attempt to persuade you to take advantage of all the education you can. At the least, you need a facebook author page and a twitter account. I have a Linkedin account that's fairly dormant at the moment, and I am a Google+ novice. There just isn't time in the day to write books and do all the tweeting and status updating that the experts recommend. We're all learning as we go. But anybody can see that building a long list of friends on facebook or followers on twitter gives you a long list of people to reach out and touch when you have a new book out. This can only be a good thing.

This advice is not original to me, and I have already given it to you, but it is one of the few bits of popular wisdom about internet marketing that I feel in my gut to be true. You don't want to be selling your books with every post and tweet.

You want to be getting to know people and letting them get to know you. You want to communicate that you are an appealing and interesting and helpful person. If you do, people will forgive you the occasional promotional moment, and some percentage of them will buy your book.

That is the extent of my social media wisdom. Good luck out there. I'll look for you in that worldwide teeming pool.

DAY 353—Blogs: Yours, mine, and theirs

I find blogs to be one of the more intriguing phenomena of the wired world. I think the advent of the internet will be seen to be as historically significant as the invention of the printing press, for many of the same reasons. Knowledge is power, and anything that disseminates knowledge to more people is culturally transforming.

When I sit down to write a novel, I can access almost any piece of information in the world without leaving my house...without leaving my chair...without lifting my hands from the same machine on which I write those novels. In years past, I would have needed to go to the library every time I had a question like, "Faye just dug up an arrowhead. She's in east Alabama. What does it look like?" Now, I can go to authoritative sources on the internet or, better still, I can email an expert directly and get an answer almost immediately that says, "It's brown. It will fit on her palm. It's called a Madison point." If I need information, the internet lets me go find it.

Blogs reverse that process. If I have information (or even an ill-considered opinion) that I want to share with the world, I can put it out there. If my blog posts are interesting enough and if I'm savvy enough about promotion, or maybe if I'm just lucky, I can reach an audience that is practically unlimited.

You're a writer. You cannot let an opportunity to reach the world pass you by.

So we've established that you need a blog. I don't even care what it's about. Maybe you have a hobby like knitting. Maybe you have strong political opinions. Maybe you really can't think of a topic of broad interest, except for writing. That's okay. Lots of writers blog about writing. That means that you'll have a lot of competition, but you need to go with what you know.

I blog about whatever suits me, including the Aerosmith concert I just attended or the fact that frost killed my impatiens, but the general theme of my blog is writing-related. Since I am now the proud author of a book on how to write, this is okay. In order to stand out from the crowd, I gave my writing blog a particular slant. I write about the behind-the-scenes process of making a book, from writing through the publishing process. Some of these stories are kinda funny—there was the time my cover designer confused the moon with the sun—and I think booklovers are interested in learning about the publishing industry's secrets, so it works for me. I call it "It's Like Making

Sausage...Sometimes You Really Don't Want to Know How Books Are Made..."

Here's the link: http://maryannaevans.blogspot.com

I am not religious about updating my blog, though I know I should be. There is that problem with not having enough hours in the day. But when I do blog, I hear from people. I see my book sales rise. (A little. If they rose a lot, I'd blog constantly.) I get subscribers to my e-newsletter. Blogging is a good thing to do.

And it's a good way to make connections. If you have interesting friends, invite them to guest blog. Their friends will visit your blog, and some of them will stay. If your friends have blogs, they will likely invite you to guest blog for them, and you will promote your post to your friends and fans. Connections get made, and that's good. When you have a new book out, you can do another guest blog for all those folks and call it a blog tour. Now and then, one of my posts gets picked up by other blogs with far more followers, and I magically get a huge publicity boost *with absolutely no time or energy expenditure on my part.* When you remember that there are not enough hours in anyone's day, you will realize how priceless that kind of exposure is.

Go ahead and blog. If nobody reads it, you'll get practice in writing quickly and coherently. If people do read it, you'll get free publicity. It's a no-lose proposition.

DAY 354—Make yourself look good

We've already established that you need a website and a facebook page and a blog, but you already knew that. How are you going to use these tools to connect with your readers?

Well, for one thing, you need to give them a human face, if you expect them to identify with you. You're going to need a publicity photo. In the old days, you used a head shot primarily to decorate the dust jacket and to get feature articles and broadcast interviews. The only people who saw it were journalists and the people who looked at your book's dustjacket and, if you were lucky enough to get print coverage, the people who read the eventual article.

Nowadays, your face is on view every time somebody looks at your website or your facebook page. (And please note the first half of the word "*face*book"...) If you want to be perceived as a professional, please, please, please do not lean up against a wall and ask your husband to snap your photo.

We are all sensitive about our looks. Most people who sell a book have been writing for many years, so they are not fresh-faced coeds. Their sensitivity ramps up with every wrinkle. People let this fear keep them from showing their face to someone who actually knows how to take a picture.

DO NOT DO THIS.

Readers do not care if you are beautiful. They care if you are interesting. Hire a portrait photographer who can take a picture that tells a story, and that story needs to be, "I am fascinating and you will love my books. Rush out right now and plunk down enough cash to buy everything I've ever written."

A good photographer is expensive, yes, but that money will come back to you in publicity. A professional photo will get you Twitter followers and facebook friends and newspaper coverage. It has gotten me (small-circulation) magazine covers and local TV coverage. Oddly enough, a good photo will get you radio coverage, although I can't imagine why.

When I sold *Artifacts*, I had the surreal experience of being asked on Wednesday if I could provide a photo by Friday, because the catalog was going to print. I begged off until Monday, but that still ain't much time. Fortunately, I have a friend who is truly a genius at portrait photography, Randy Batista. (If you can get yourself to Gainesville, Florida, book a sitting with Randy. He'll make you gorgeous. Truly.)

I called Randy in a white-hot panic and he worked me into his schedule. I called my hairdresser Irene in a white-hot panic and *she* worked me into *her* schedule. I found a walk-in nail salon and I walked in, just in case my hands showed in the portrait. (They did, so it was money well-spent.)

Randy asked me what I was going to wear and I said, "A business suit?" And he asked me where I wanted the photo taken and I said, "In the studio?" Randy said, "Um...no. Tell me about the book."

So I told him it was a mystery about a woman desperate to save her ancestral home, and he said, "I know the place. And we want you to look approachable, so wear jeans and a simple top. Maybe black, but gray would be better."

I take directions well, so I bought a gray sweater and showed up at the location shoot. Randy had chosen a dilapidated Victorian house as the backdrop. I liked it. Nevertheless, he saw the expression on my face and he asked me, "What's wrong?" and I said, "I'm forty years old and you're going to be pointing that thing at me." He grinned and said, with just a touch of a Cuban accent, "Don't you worry 'bout a thing."

The experience was exactly like the modeling footage you see on TV, with Randy crooning, "Lean into the light. Turn your pretty face toward me. More, more. No. Stop. There. Hold it! You're GORGEOUS!!!"

I'm here to tell you that every woman should get this kind of treatment at least once in her life.

I'll show you the photo in a second, but be aware that we were going for a mysterious look for a mystery author, so I'm wearing what someone has called my "Take your best shot, buddy," face. People have said that it doesn't look like me, because I'm a smiley sort, but my older daughter said, "Yes. It does. It looks like her when she's mad at me." And perhaps she has a point.

It is also possible that I look stern because this house was not in the nicest part of town. Periodically, a homeless man would pedal past slowly, calling out, "Aaaaayyyy...bay-beeee!"

I've recently retired this shot because I figured five books (and seven years) per photo was probably enough. Using the photo past that point would have been just dishonest, but look what Randy did for a forty-year-old mother of three:

And, seven years later, look what he did for a grandmother:

Just for comparison's sake, this is what you get when an amateur points a camera in my direction. (For reference, this picture was taken a few months before the photo directly above this paragraph.) It's not a particularly awful shot, and it's pretty close to what I think I actually look like, but it does not say "Run out and buy this woman's books!" to me. I think it says, "She looks like she might be a nice lady."

This expository photo comes complete with grandchild:

Trust me. If you're serious about your career, you'll hire the best photographer you can afford.

DAY 355—Remember to avoid being annoying...please...

When your book comes out, you are going to justifiably proud and excited. If any of your nearest and dearest do not support your efforts with praise and congratulations and purchases, if they can afford them, then I say shame on them.

However. There will come a day when their interest will wane. They simply cannot be as interested in your book babies as you are. They cannot come to all of your book signings. They may not even be able to find time to read your entire literary output.

Now, extrapolate this to the world at large, where there are vast numbers of people who truly have no reason to care that you wrote a book. These are the people to whom almost all of your sales will be made. Since you can't meet them all in person, most of your contact with these potential customers will be on the internet. As you learn to use the internet as a marketing tool, be aware that it is as easy to turn people off by a sales pitch as it is to turn people on. Probably easier.

If you already are web-savvy, then you have an idea of etiquette in the internet world. Some online communities, particularly those where books are discussed, have specific guidelines about how much self-promotion is allowed. Some communities do not allow you to mention your books at all. Others will only permit you to mention them in your signature line. Still others are looser requirements, but it is considered in good taste to announce a sales pitch by using words like, "BSP Alert!", where BSP stands for "blatant self-promotion."

Tread carefully in the early days, both in person and online, and know that you'll probably still offend someone by accident. In the real world, you may never hear about it, until you notice that you get fewer party invitations. In the virtual world, you may get flamed. In both cases, you will learn, but the learning curve will be shorter if you remember to take into account the feelings of others. Let people know about your books in a polite and tasteful way, and your good manners will be appreciated.

DAY 356—Now's the time to get connected in person

People like to do business with people they know. It's just human nature. You've been locked up with your book for a long time. It's time to get out and meet people.

You don't have to do it all at once. Just make a mental list of contacts you'd like to make. Get some business cards or make some yourself and print them at home. You don't need a lot of them right now, because you'll want new ones when you have cover art. Meet some bookstore owners. If your budget allows, buy some books while you're there. If you're on vacation, check out some local bookstores and meet people there. Check out local libraries to see if they have any reading groups you'd enjoy attending. Look for conferences and workshops geared toward people who read and write books like yours.

Keep the contacts light and casual. You have nothing to sell at the moment. Just make some friends who will be interested in hearing when your book *does* come out.

DAY 357—Now's the time to get connected online

In-person contact carries much more weight than online contact, but you can reach so many more people online. Now is a good time to look for discussion groups that talk about books like yours. Presumably, you read in that genre, so you can be a valuable and contributing member in such groups. Later, when you tell group members that your book is out, they'll be congratulating you as a friend, not feeling put-upon by yet another sales pitch. In the mystery world, DorothyL is one such group. LibraryThing and Goodreads are communities that discuss practically any book that might interest you. There are sites dedicated to discussing books published on the various ebook platforms, as well. I have no doubt that, if you look hard enough, you can find people talking about any arcane subgenre you can imagine.

Similarly, you can find peer support online from writers in every imaginable genre. I learn a lot about marketing mysteries from MurderMustAdvertise.com. I learn a lot about marketing ebooks from KindleBoards.com. A cursory web search will help you locate your own peers. Seek them out and share what you've learned. They'll do the same, and everyone involved can avoid re-inventing the wheel for the 87,000,000th time.

DAY 358—It's time to read it one more time

This time, you're allowed to twiddle with even the piddliest little detail. You've already edited for overarching themes. You've analyzed your characters' behaviors and motivations for consistency. You've looked for annoying repetition and authorial tics. Now I'm giving you *carte blanche* to sweat the small stuff.

If you see a paragraph that communicates your intent perfectly well, but the third sentence feels clay-footed and wrong, take the time to recast that sentence into something graceful. Or powerful. Or mysterious. It's your choice.

DAY 359—You're still reading and editing...

...and you'll probably still be reading and editing when you get to Day 365, but I'll leave you to do it in peace after today.

Listen while you read. At this stage in the editing process, I inevitably find a surprising number of "word echoes," instances where I used a word, then turned around and used it again in the next sentence or soon after. (I'm not talking about words like "the" or "and." You have to repeat those and they don't echo in the mind's ear. I'm talking about noticeable adverbs and adjectives and nouns and verbs, like maybe "definitely" and "specialty" and "rushed" that get lodged in the subconscious until you root them out.) Perhaps I am oversensitive to word echoes, because my editor Barbara calls me on them all the time.

You want your style to be your own, but you also don't want it to overpower the story you're telling. You want it to be both beautiful and unnoticeable. When a passage is technically correct, but it sounds wrong to you, rejoice. Fix it and know that you are developing your own style.

DAY 360—No education is ever wasted, redux

Many pages ago, I told you about my father's wise saying, "No education is ever wasted." I discussed this wisdom in terms of your work as an artist. The things you have learned in this life will inform everything you ever write. Where else could all those stories come from?

Well, Daddy's advice works well in the business world, too. If you are seeking publication for your work, then you are now in the publishing business. Learn all you can about your industry. Read books like this one. Meet your peers. Read their books and try to figure out what makes them work. Make it your business to find out how books like yours are priced and marketed.

How else are you going to be able to make your work stand out among the million or two competing books in the marketplace?

DAY 361—Wear your business hat when it's appropriate, and put on your artist's hat when it's time to be an artist

The artist in you is going to weep when that first bad review comes in. On those occasion, let the businessperson win. Tell yourself this: "I wanted publicity. I got some. I don't like it, but I did get it."

Conversely, the business-oriented professional in you is going to be very impatient on those occasions when you just can't get the book right. There will be times when the proper thing to do, business-wise, is to rush the book into the marketplace, whether it's ready or not. On those occasions, let the artist win. We're not making widgets. We're doing art. We're putting our own very human feelings and thoughts onto the page, hoping that our readers will recognize them, since they're humans, too. Write the book to satisfy the artist inside you... then let the business side of you sell a million of them.

DAY 362—Are you thinking about your next book?

If you're not already thinking about your next book, I must ask you this: "Why not?"

I find that my muse works in the background, when I'm not paying attention. As I wrote my first mystery, *Artifacts*, I had two consuming fears. One was that I'd never finish the thing. The other was that I *would* finish the thing, but that I would never, never, never ever have another idea substantial enough to support a book.

I asked myself who I was kidding. How could I possibly have a career if it would require me to come up with another idea, then another, then another, all of them with enough depth to become a novel? Then, as I was finishing *Artifacts*, I had an idea that eventually developed into *Relics*, but I figured it was the last. I would never, never, never ever have another idea for a novel. As I finished *Relics*, I got the idea for the book that became *Effigies*, and at this point I began to trust the process. I had spent forty-whatever years putting information and experience into the deep well that is my subconscious and I'll spend the next forty-whatever years dipping my hand into that well and seeing what comes out.

So what will you write next? All I can say to you is this: Write the book that ignites your passion.

If I wanted to do work that I enjoyed but that didn't ignite my passion, I would still be an engineer, and I'd be making a lot more money. Novel-writing is a tough business. Few of us even make a living, and fewer still strike it rich. But there are rewards that are deeper and richer than financial rewards, so grab them. Chief among them is the exhilarating feeling of creating a world of your own and sharing it with your readers.

Write the book that only you can write.

DAY 363—Time to start another book

As you gear up to send your baby out into the world, whether you are seeking the acceptance of an agent or whether you have elected to publish your own work, you will be anxiously waiting to see how it is accepted. I think it is an excellent mental health practice to begin another book *immediately.*

It is obviously a good business practice to start a new book right away. If you are planning on a career as a writer, then you need to approach your work as if it is a real job, because it is. But I am serious when I say that moving on to a new book quickly is also a good mental health practice. If you have drafted a sizeable chunk of another book that you think is solid and well-written, any rejection you might receive will sting so much less.

Pinning all your hopes to one book is as risky as putting all your eggs in one basket. (I will allow myself a digression when I point out the other significant time in my life when this cliché sprang to mind. It was the first day my oldest child pulled out of the driveway with both my other children in the car with him. The spasm of fear was accompanied by an unoriginal but apt observation: "There go all my eggs, and they're all in a single basket.")

Your next book is going to be even better than the one you just wrote, anyway. I promise.

DAY 364—Reach out...

My goal when I teach is to tell aspiring writers the things I wish someone had told me. Some of these things aren't easy to hear. "You need to do some revisions before you start submitting this thing to publishers and agents," is chief among them, but the advice is always delivered with love and with the belief that hard work can get people where they want to go. Fortunately, some of the advice I have to give is very pleasant to put into practice.

> Writing is a solitary activity. Balance yourself by reaching out to other writers.

Did I do this when I was an aspiring writer? Heck, no. During all the years I was learning my craft, I was very, very busy. How busy?

Well, I took my first serious writing class in graduate school when I was 21. I wasn't really supposed to be taking that class, being as how I was pursuing a master's degree in chemical engineering as fast as humanly possible, but I needed something in my life besides coursework in fluidized bed heat transfer and advanced transport phenomena. I wrote in spare scraps of time during the year I was taking classes, then I took a job teaching community college math and physics during my last semester, as I finished my thesis.

A year later, I had my first child, dropped back to teaching part-time, and wrote when he was napping. Just over a year later, I had my second child, moved to Florida, and wrote whenever I could get them both to nap. Just over a year later, I divorced, took a full-time job as an engineer, and wrote when my kids were asleep at night.

What is conspicuously absent here? Um...publication. And contact with other writers.

A couple of years later, I remarried and found some time to attend occasional meetings of local writers' groups, but publication still eluded me. A couple more years later, I was on bedrest for most of my third pregnancy, so I split my time between continuing my work as an environmental consultant and writing an environmental thriller. Because I'd never written anything book-length before and I wasn't sure I could, I took a correspondence course in novel-writing, and it's one of the best decisions I ever made. I couldn't leave my house to get companionship from other writers, per medical orders, but I could do it by mail. (And yes, in 1995, I took that course by snail mail. If you take a similar course, it will be online and your life will be much easier than mine was.)

That third baby was three before I finished the environmental thriller, but I did finish it, and it got me my agent, Anne Hawkins. Having had Anne's literary companionship for 13 years and counting has made my writing life a lot less lonely and a lot less scary. She not only believed that my work was good, but she was willing to risk her valuable time on it, because she thought that it would one day make her some money. How cool is that?

Anne and I were together for years before we sold *Artifacts*, but the sale brought me more literary companionship—an editor, a publisher, and the folks at the publishing house who make things happen. The need to publicize the books took me to writers' conferences and readers' conferences and bookstores and libraries, where I met the people who read my books, as well as other writers who were hoping to publish theirs. Wonder of wonders, I also met anthology editors who have since published my short stories and essays.

Now, listen closely. I learned that my agent Anne and my editor Barbara attend writers' conferences, looking for new talent. I learned that they had both been at conferences that I could have attended but didn't because...well, look back a few paragraphs and tell me when I would have had time. Still, if I'd gone, my work might have seen print years earlier than it did...if I'd had time to write it while I was going to conferences. Yes, I know that lack of time is a vicious cycle. All we can do is the best we can.

Reach out to other writers, in person if you can and online if you can't, because you can learn from them. Reach out to them because they might soon be reporters who can cover your work or editors who can get your words out into the world. Reach out to them because it will feed your soul.

You'll be glad you did.

DAY 365—Reach out to me...

Here we are at the end of our marathon journey. I trust that some of you have completed books, and that the rest of you have written great chunks of books that you *will* eventually finish. Thank you for taking this journey with me!

Does this mean that our time together is at an end? No. It doesn't have to be. This is why God gave us the internet.

So what writing wisdom am I going to leave with you on this, the last day of our first year? Actually, it's a continuation of yesterday's advice, which was "Reach out."

Today, I'll be more specific. "Reach out to me."

I work like a serf. (That's one of the things about the publishing business that you probably didn't want to know.) I enjoy taking a break to visit with friends. And I love to talk about writing.

Come to my facebook fan page and help me start a conversation about the things we've done together here:

http://www.facebook.com/pages/Mary-Anna-Evans-author-of-the-Faye-Longchamp-archaeological-mysteries/8113134580

Tell me which writing tip(s) have been the most helpful to you. If there's a topic you'd like me to thrash within an inch of its life...um... let me try again. If there's a topic you'd like me to explore, let me know. If you have your own writing tips you'd like to share, have at it. Writing has always been a lonely business, but the internet has given this generation of writers a way to create community from the comfort of our desks.

Soon enough I'll be starting a new book. Soon after that, I'll have a new book published and I'll be immersed in promoting it. And after that, the process will begin again.

Don't make me do this alone...

What People are Saying About Mary Anna Evans' Fiction:

For short story "Land of the Flowers," published in *A Merry Band of Murderers*:

"... Three [stories] are particularly noteworthy: Mary Anna Evans' *Land of the Flowers*, Jeffrey Deaver's *The Fan*, and Val McDermid's *Long Black Veil.... A Merry Band of Murderers* is an admirable anthology of short stories by a skilled company of mystery authors." — *Mysterious Reviews*

For environmental thriller *Wounded Earth*:

"Its nail-biting intensity will keep you up late in your eagerness to find out how it ends." —*Big Al's Books and Pals*

For Florida Book Awards Bronze Medalist *Effigies*:

"We mystery lovers who've enjoyed *Artifacts* and thought *Relics* was even better may not believe this, but Ms. Evans has done it again, and *Effigies* is the best one yet. Again, she makes a lesson in our past a fascinating read."—**Tony Hillerman, recipient of the Mystery Writers of America's Grand Master Award, and the Navajo Tribe's Special Friend Award, among many other honors.**

For *Offerings,* **winner of Red Adept's 2010 Indie Award for best collection:**

"Very much recommended, very much impressed..."
— *Red Adept Book Reviews*

For Benjamin Franklin Award-winner *Artifacts*:

"It's always fun to discover a new Florida voice, especially one who can bring to life the rich texture—the sand, the sea, the moss-draped live oaks, the seedy fishing shacks, the salted boat culture—of the state's coast...the menace and the history are resolved in a hurricane of a finale."—*Tampa Tribune*

For IMBA Bestseller *Relics:*

"A fascinating look at contemporary archaeology but also a twisted story of greed and its effects."—*Dallas Morning News*

About the Author:

MARY ANNA EVANS is the author of the Faye Longchamp archaeological mysteries: *Artifacts, Relics, Effigies, Findings, Floodgates, Strangers,* and *Plunder.* She is also the author of environmental thriller *Wounded Earth,* and a collection of short works called *Jewel Box.* Her educational nonfiction book, *Mathematical Literacy in the Middle and High School Grades,* will be published in May 2012.

She has received recognition for her fiction that includes the Benjamin Franklin Award, the Mississippi Author Award, the Patrick D. Smith Florida Literature Award, and a Florida Book Awards bronze medal. Her books have been named Notable Books by *BookSense* and *IndieNext,* and they have received starred reviews from *Library Journal* and *Booklist.*

She's a chemical engineer by training and license, with a degree in engineering physics thrown in for spice, but she loves reading about history and writing about an archaeologist. Truth be told, she's a little jealous of Faye and her archaeological adventures.

She enjoys reading, writing, gardening, spending time with her family, cooking, and playing her 7-and-a-half-foot-long monster of a grand piano. Her cat helps her write, so she should probably put his name on her books. Learn more about Mary Anna and her work here:

Website:
http://www.maryannaevans.com

Facebook:
http://www.facebook.com/pages/Mary-Anna-Evans-author-of-the-Faye-Longchamp-archaeological-mysteries/8113134580

Twitter:
http://twitter.com/maryannaevans

www.ingramcontent.com/pod-product-compliance
Lightning Source LLC
Chambersburg PA
CBHW060237290526
45789CB00001B/83